Caste, Community and Conflict in Social Change

Caste, Community and Conflict in Social Change

Edited by
Virendra Prakash Singh

Commonwealth

Caste, Community and Conflict in Social Change

ISBN : 81-7169-240-0

Edition : 2017

Published by :
COMMONWEALTH PUBLISHERS (P) LTD.
4831/24, Govind Lane,
Ansari Road, Darya Ganj,
New Delhi - 110002
Ph. : 23272541, 23242541
e-mail : commonwealthpublishers2016@gmail.com

Distributed by :
ARJUN PUBLISHING HOUSE
4831/24, Govind Lane,
Ansari Road, Darya Ganj,
New Delhi - 110002
Ph. : 23272541, 23242541
e-mail : arjunbooks2001@gmail.com

Laser Typesetting by :
Dimple Computers
Delhi

Printed at :
Roshan Digital Printers
Delhi

"Dedicated to the people's
Who lost their lives in
The struggle against
Caste System."

PREFACE

The dynamics of the much discussed caste system in India has had profound and far-reaching effects on the very ethos and character of development efforts in the country. The division of society into four castes on inherently religious grounds is a theory of class which, on deeper insight, contains many more levels of reasoning related not only to an understood order in nature but also the mechanics of occupation, place in the hierarchy, the ordained structure of human endeavour and, not the least, the economic viability of the entire social and economic structure of nations. The caste system in relation to class structure and cultural change has over the years become the subject of a vast amount of literature, a large part of which can be termed as the Sociology of the Caste System.

The division of people into distinct classes with understood functions and place in overall society are not a phenomenon peculiar to India. The Japanese have their *bura-kumin*, the "untouchables", and ethnicity in South-East Asia has also bred many so-called sub-cultures and race distinctions. It is accepted, nonetheless, that in traditional society, particularly villages such as those in India and other Asian countries, there are even more subtle variations of the easte system. In fact, "caste" is, in other contexts, a purely social division based on such misconceptions as racial superiority, the arrogance of wealth and the much-vaunted educational advantage. But, at this point we may take a quick look at the dynamics of the caste system in India.

The ancient Hindu pattern of social organisation aimed at the value of *Dharama*, *Artha*, *Kama* and *Moksa* by the individual through his physical, psychological and social evolution. This evolution was calculated to be effected through the process of the Varna-asrama system. It was a comprehensive scheme of individual fulfilment with social purpose through concrete institutions. It has been regarded as the basic concept of Hindu culture and the pivot of Hindu social structure throughout the ages. At the same time it cannot be denied that the Varna Dharma has been equally the target of vehement attack by saints and scholars alike from time to time.

It would be necessary to look into the meaning of the Varnasrama Dharma. The protagonists of this system maintain that the Varna Dharma aimed at the classification of society into four Varnas—the Brahmin, the Ksatriya, the Vaisya and the Sudra, respectively, in the order of precedence and on the basis of the element of Sattva, Rajas and Tamas in the nature of human beings to fulfil the multitudinous needs and purposes of society at large. The Asrama Dharma my be best described as the vision of normal life for the individual in his social mileau. It refers to the main stages of life through which the normal individual is expected to pass—student, householder and hermit (in two stages) in the process of evolution and fulfilment of his personality. So far as the Asrama Dharma is concerned, it has been appreciated by all but what is regrettable is that with the passage of time it has been observed more in breach than in practice.

As far as the subject of Varna Dharma, it has been the most controversial theme since long and particularly of late, scholars, sociologists and politicians have held diverse opinions about the origin and usefulness of this institution. Its advocates maintain that the genesis of this fourfold classification of society is to be found in the 'Purus Sukta' of the Rgveda. We also find similar references in the Satapatha and the Taittiriya Brahmana. The Puranas and the Smritis in particular give an elaborate account of it. The Mahabharata and the Gita are also full of several references about this institution. The other school of scholars maintain that there is no mention of the four Varnas in the Vedic literature. The Veda speaks only of the Arya and Dasa Varna. The third school of scholars stress that the concept of Varna Dharma is not only eternal but also universal and it does and did exist in one form or the other in all climes, times and species. They say that the classification of society on the basis of Guna-Karma (nature and work) exists not only in the human or animal world but also in the world of inanimate things. A peep into the ancient history of Egypt, China, Japan, Persia, Greece and Rome shows that there did exist three or four distinctive classes of the priests, the warriors, the businessmen and the artisans and the agriculturists or the slaves resembling more or less the Brahmins, the Ksatriyas, the Vaisyas and Sudras of ancient India.

The next important question, although a very controversial one, that engages our attention is: What is the basis of this fourfold classification of Varnas? Whether it is Janmona (by birth) or Karmana (by work or occupation)? The Sanatana (orthodox) school of Hindu theologists regard Janmana as the basis of the Varna classification while the scholars of the reformist school emphasise the Karmana aspect. The late Dr. Bhagwan Das propounded the Karmana theory. His three-volume study of Indian social organisation has been regarded as a pioneering work in the field of Hindu sociology in modern times. The progressive school of Indian sociologists maintain that the fourfold classification of Varnas was merely a poetic concept of the ancient Hindu sociologists and it did never have a practical existence. They say that it can be proved from history that the theory of the Varna Dharma remained divorced from practice. The name of Sardar K.M. Panikkar may be cited as a representative scholar of this school. His book *Hindu Society at Crossroads* deserves careful study by students of Hindu sociology. He has tried to prove that the Brahmins alone may be regarded as illustrations of the theory of Varna Dharma while the same thing cannot be said about the other three Varnas, *i.e.*, the Ksatriyas, the Vaisyas and Sudras. But at the same time, Sri Panikkar states that slthough the concept of four Varnas is merely an imaginary creation of ancient Hindu sociologists, yet the Hindu social life is inspired and pervaded by this concept. Thousands of castes and sub-castes that comprise the Hindu society try to establish their origin from one or the other of the four Varnas. So we may say that the original concept of the four Varnas either did never find a practical form or if it ever existed in the practical world, that must have been only partially evolved. With the passage of time the original concept might have degenerated into the practical form of the castes and sub-castes that we see with all their glaring absurdities even in the present day Hindu society.

What are the cardinal principles underlying the Varna concept? The following three principles are regarded as the quintessence of the Varna Dharma:

1. Unchangeable inequality based on birth.
2. Classification of occupations and their disparity.
3. Prohibition of marriage outside one's own Varna.

The first and the third may be noted to be prevalent even doday while the second has never been observed in practice. From the Vedic times upto the present day works of history and literature provide several illustrations which show that persons born in lower castes took up occupations theoretically belonging to the higher castes and *vice versa*. Example of inter-Varna or inter-caste marriages are also cited from the ancient literature. A certain class of scholars maintain that Varna is changeable but not caste. The principle underlying the Varna theory, according to them, is Guna-karma while that of caste is birth. So one may change one's Varna but not caste. They cite illustrations from the old literature to prove their contention. But whatever they might believe about the practicability of the Varna concept, it has to be conceded that it played an important role in the evolution and development of Hindu social organisation.

The principal underlying the religious and secular activities of the Hindus has been spirituality. That one cardinal value is the realisation of unity in diversity. Hierarchy will exist as long as diversity remains in the world and without diversity there can be no world; but spiritual equality was regarded by the ancient seers of India as a permanent safeguard against the hierarchy breaking up into an anarchy of ego-centric individuals. Except in periods, according to an eminent thinker, when it displayed a downward curve, Indian culture has been a harmonisation of the individual and the collectivity. In the Mahabharat it is said that if an untouchable happens to be virtuous, even the Gods would recognise him as a Brahmin. This harmonisation of the individual and the collectivity has been regarded by many as a marvel of Hindu sociology, but there are others who lay their accusing finger on the intolerant and exclusive priestcraft and petrified social hierarchy, and conclude that it has disfigured Indian history and caused the general impression of a repression of the individual under a system of hidebound orthodoxy. Prof. A.R. Wadia has taken this stand in his *Contemporary Indian Philosophy*.

A certain section of scholars maintain that the concept of fourfold Varnas was really a novel and useful device of the Hindu sociological brain to maintain the purity and solidarity of the society but later on what caused the decay and disintegration of society was not the Varna classification but its gradual degeneration into innumerable castes and sub-castes. Not only that but the caste system, despite their glaring drawbacks, did play a very significant part in maintaining the purity and solidarity of Hindu society at the time of external aggressions and alien rule. According to these scholars, it was the caste system of Hindus that saved their culture from the onslaughts of Islam and Christianity and kept undefiled the original content.

Now we come to a very perplexing problem that poses itself before every student of Hindu sociology and that is; What is the future of the Varna and caste system after the promulgation of the present constitution of India which does not recognise any sort of disparity or inequality on the basis of caste, colour, creed, sex or religion. The concept of the modern welfare or socialistic state with authorised powers to inerfere in every sphere of human activity and to make or amend laws to fulfil its declared aims has also posed a challenge before the Hindu society which must be answered.

Sardar K.M. Panikkar's approach deserve consideration in this respect. He proves by his penetrating analysis that the various social institutions of the Hindus are not a part of religion and that they are based on laws, customs and traditions and hence they are secular. Thus he tries to establish and conclude that since these social institutions are based on laws and customs, it is desirable that the constitution or the constituted authority should re-interpret or amend them whenever the necessity arises to do so. This he has tried to establish on the basis of the amendments and reforms made in the various Smritis from time to time.

This view is not very far from truth and carries much weight. Varna and caste have now outlived their utility. It is time when we should recast our social structure on the basis of complete equality. History has proved that man is a highly individualistic and group-minded creature who is apt to divide and separate even where perfect unity and equality is intended. A concept or a system based on a view to divide may only aggrevate the division. Man's natural separatism should not be assisted by social separatism; it should rather be fought by social equalism, on all levels and at all fronts. Then only we can hope to acquire the minimum equality needed to harness human energies for progress, material and spiritual.

The inspiration for this collection of papers, articles and comments, from a wide variety of both published and unpublished sources, is drawn from the character that has marked the Indian peoples-always hospitable, adapting, loyal yet not blind and most willing to be swept off by the tumultuous changes that mark the present age. It is hoped that the anthology of reference and source material, some as old and precious, as six decades, will be useful for the student and scholar as well as sociologist and economist. Class and culture are relative terms and caste is inherent. All interact and effect in various ways the economic and social development efforts of the government. This too has become a part of our planning process, evident from the special component for Scheduled Castes and Scheduled Tribes. The Mandal Commission and the Reservation issue are just behind us. Atrocities on a caste basis continue to hamper growth and development. Caste is also an integral part of our political ethos. One hopes for change and change brings pain and suffering. India is on the move and in the midst of change.

In this effort at compilation, the publishers and I wish to thank all the librarians, assistant librarians, research scholars and academicians who assisted in identifying and also at times providing copies of the papers and articles. Due thanks are due to all of them.

EDITOR

CONTENTS

1

CASTE, OCCUPATION AND RELIGIOUS ETHOS

A clear understanding of what is meant by "caste," especially in regard to its relationship to "occupation", is of first importance. Several learned treatises on this subject, both by Europeans and Indians, are in existence. The Indian Census reports, however, contain most of the information needed for the purposes of this work and much of what follows has been culled therefrom. Anyone wishing to follow up the subject should obtain the Reports of the Census operations of 1901, 1911 and 1921.

The Indian word for caste, "jat" or "jati", is derived from a root meaning *birth*, *lineage*, *rank*. The expression now connotes that every Hindu is *born into* a caste and his caste determines his social position through life.

The legendary origin of caste is that the Aryans were divided from the dawn of time into four castes:

1. Brahmans or Priests,
2. Kshatriyas or warriors,
3. Vaishyas or merchants and cultivators, and

4. Sudras or menials and labourers, all of whom had a divine origin being born respectively from the mouth, the arms, the thighs and the feet of Brahma.

In the beginning, a man of any of the three higher castes, provided that his first marriage was with a woman of his own caste, could wed others of the divisions below his own. The marriage, however, of a woman of a higher caste with a man of a lower one was abhorrent and the offspring were relegated to the lowest position in society. In this manner other castes originated.

Modern opinion while it recognises that this traditional genealogy may possibly be correct so far as the formation of certain new castes goes, holds that "occupation" is the chief basis of caste, every separate occupation having produced a distinct caste, the status of which depends mainly or almost entirely on its occupation. Mr. J.C. Nesfield held the view, indeed, that the *whole* basis of the caste system is the division of occupations, and that the social gradation of castes corresponds precisely to the different periods of civilization during which their traditional occupation originated. "Thus the lowest castes are those allied to the primitive occupation of hunting, *e.g.*, Pasi, Bhar, Bahelia, because the pursuit of wild animals was the earliest stage in the development of human industry. Next above these come the fishing castes, fishing being considered somewhat superior to hunting because water is a more sacred element among the Hindus than land, and there is less apparent cruelty in the capturing of fish than in the slaughtering of animals; these are the Kahars, the Kewats, Dhimars and others. Above these come the pastoral castes—Ghasi, Gadaria, Gujar and Ahir; and above them the agricultural castes, following the order in which these occupations were adopted during the progress of civilization. At the top of the system stand the Chhatri or warrior, whose duty it is to protect all the lower castes, and the Brahman who is their priest and spiritual guide. Similarly, the artisan castes are divided into two main groups; the lower one consists of those whose occupations preceded the age of metallurgy, as the Chamars and Mochis or tanners,

Koris or weavers, the Telis or oil-pressers, Kalars or liquor distillers, Kumhars or potters, and Lunias or salt makers. The higher group includes those castes whose occupations were coeval with the age of metallurgy, that is, those who work in stone, wood and metals, and who make clothing and ornaments, as the Barhai or worker in wood, the Lohar or worker in iron, the Kasera or Thathera, workers in brass, and the Sonar or worker in precious metals, ranking precisely in this order of precedence, the Sonar being the highest. The theory is still further developed among the trading castes, who are arranged in a similar manner, beginning from the Banjara or forest trader, the Kunjra or green grocer, and the Bharbhunjia or grain parcher, up to the classes of Banias and Khatris or shopkeepers and Bankers."

Mr. Russell points out that it can hardly be supposed that the Hindus, either consciously or subconsciously arranged their gradation of society on a scientific order of precedence in the manner described, and suggests that the main divisions of social precedence, which have been correctly stated by Nesfield, arose naturally from the divisions of the principal social organization of India, the village community.

Sir Herbert Risley, on the other hand, in his "Castes and Tribes of Bengal" lays stress on the *racial basis* of caste, endeavouring to show that difference of race and difference of colour were the foundation of the Indian caste system. There seems reason to suppose, he argues, that the contact of the Aryans with the indigenous people of India was, to a large extent, responsible for the growth of the caste system, and the main racial basis may perhaps even now be recognised, though this racial basis has, in a great degree, vanished.

M. Emile Senart in his work "Les Castes dans l'Inde" approaches the subject historically and from an analysis of the Vedas. He has come to the conclusion that institution of caste as it is at present understood, did not exist among the Aryans of the Vedic period on their first entry into India. The word *varna*, literally "colour", which is afterwards used in speaking of the four castes, distinguishes in the Vedas *two* classes only: there are the Arya Varna and the Dasa Varna—the Aryan race and the race of enemies. In other passages of the Vedas the Dasyus are spoken of as black while in later literature the black race, Krishna Varna, are opposed to the Brahmans, the same word being used for the distinction between Aryas and Sudras. "Dasva" is used in the Vedas as signifying "people of foreign countries", just as the Heberws spoke of all others as "Gentiles", and the Mundas to-day refer to non-Mundas as "Diku".

Originally therefore there were two groups, one composed of the three higher castes, and the other of the Sudras or lowest. It is probable the first group was entirely Aryan, while the Sudras were the aliens amongst whom the Aryans were settling. There was for a long period no absorption, no large intermingling of the two groups. The power of religion was invoked to prevent any fusion and the idea of "untouchability" was established. A Sudra was excluded from religious ceremonies and could take no part in sacrifices, he was not even permitted to hear, much less to learn, commit to memory or recite Vedic texts, An Arya who had sexual intimacy with a Sudra women was to be banished; but a Sudra man having intimacy with a Arya woman was to be killed. One cannot but admire the precautions taken for race preservation by those cousins of our own remote ancestors, who, leaving the main body of Aryans in Central Asia trekked south into Hindustan.

As time unfelded, however, the Sudras had to be admitted to the Aryan body politic, though in the most humiliating fashion. The hostility, essentially racial, was felt and expressed on religious grounds. Later, possibly owing to the shortage of Aryan women, it became lawful for an Aryan to take to wife a Sudra woman, and the ultimate result, which we see to-day, has been an almost complete fusion between the two races in the bulk of the population over the greater part of the country. Nevertheless the status of Sudra still remains attached to the large community of the impure castes formed from the indigenous tribes who have settled in Hindu villages and entered the caste system. These are relegated to the most degrading and menial occupations and their touch is regarded as conveying defilement.

Indigenous tribes have not always been reduced to the impure status; for instance, some of the most prominent of the Rajput clans are held to have been derived from the aboriginal tribes. Risley gives as an instance of what has no doubt frequently occurred, the case of a sub-tribe of the Mundas, who are of particular interest to Assam and the Dooars. It is a tribute to the spirit of this fine people that they have not all followed the "Nagbangshi Mundas" and become Hinduized. The Mundas, as is well known, occupy the greater portion of the Chota Nagpur plateu and the families of the ruling chiefs, having acquired wealth, no doubt looked to social advancement from absorption into the Hindu polity. They were admitted as Chathris or Rajputs, and are known as "Nagbangshis", *i.e.*, the race of the Nag or Cobra. The following story is told of their origin[1]:—

Raja Janmejaya had declared war against the entire race of the serpents, one of whom, Pundarika Nag by name, managed to escape, and having assumed a human form, travelled to Benaras, and there succeeded in winning the hand of Parvati, the beautiful daughter of a Brahman. Notwithstanding his otherwise human appearance Pundarika could not get rid of the serpent's forked tongue, which roused the curiosity of his spouse. In order to divert her mind from this subject he took her on a pilgrimage to the holy temple of Jagannath at Puri. On their way back they passed through Jharkhand, as Chota Nagpur, then in the occupation of the Mundas, was called. Near the hill of Sutiambe, Parvati was seized with the pangs of child birth, and importuned lier husband to divulge the secret of his forked tongue. He disclosed to her his real identity, and disappeared in his proper form into a pool of water close by. Immediately after the birth of her child, Parvati, in great remorse at the consequences of her curiosity, committed *sati*.

Later a Brahman passed that way, carrying an idol of Surya Devata, the Sun God, and stopped to drink at the pool, placing the idol on the brink. When about to resume his journey, he found that the idol could not be moved. On looking about him, he saw to his astonishment a huge cobra protecting with its expanded hood a "little naked child." The serpent revealed himself to the Brahman as Pundarika Nag, and narrated his strange history. He prophesied that the child was destined to rule the country, and directed that he was to be named Phani Mukvta Rai, and that the country should be called Nagpur. The child was carried to a neighbouring Manki, who adopted him, and Phani Mukuta Rai in due course fulfilled his destiny.

Thus were the Mundas given the entree into the Hindu system as a race under the special protection of a deity. The Raj family rank as Rajputs and intermarry with families of chieftains in the Feudatory States of Chota Nagpur, Orissa and the Central Provinces who claim to be Rajputs on similar mythical grounds. Hinduized Mundas frequently call themselves Nagbangshis, Nagbangshi Mundas, or Nagpur Chathris.

We need not follow M. Senart in his masterly analysis of the evolution of caste, except to note the results of his investigation into the calling of agriclture. He shows how the different agricultural castes originated and how they acquired, to a great extent, the same status, though their origin is so diverse. The flocks and herds must have been in the possession of the Vaishas, and grounds of general probability, as well as the direct evidence adduced by M. Senart, make it clear that they were the herdsmen and cultivators and the Sudras the labourers. It is impossible of course, that the Aryans could have been a community of priests, rulers and traders, because such a community would not have had means of subsistence. Indeed, Max Muller derives the very name "*Arya*" from a root meaning *plough* (the same root as appears in the Latin *arare* to plough), and points out that in later Sanskrit it means *noble*, *of a good family*. We must bear this in mind later when considering the domination of the idea of agriculture as the highest occupation. The original Vaishvas have long since disappeared, the Brahmans themselves asserting that there, are no Kshatriyas or Vaishyas left. This is probably correct, but the modern "good cultivators" retain the status of the Vaishyas, as the Rajputs retain that of the Kshatriyas.

We have indicated some of the theories connected with the fascinating subject of the theory of caste, and now pass to what may be called a "working definition," *viz.*, that propounded by Sir Edward Gait in the Census Report of 1911.

Sir Edward Gait attempts a concise definition of Caste in the following terms:—"A caste may therefore be defined as an endogamous group or collection of such groups bearing a common name and having the same traditional occupation, who are so linked together by these and other ties, such as the tradition of a common origin and the possession of the same tutelary deity and tne same social status, ceremonial observances and family priests, that they regard themselves and are regarded by others, as forming a single homogeneous community."

To put it briefly and for the moment ignoring the aspect of marriage, *caste connotes occupation, and occupation connotes caste*. Indeed among the lower illiterate classes one can go further and assert that caste and occupation are synonymous. Sir Edward Gait gives examples of the acquisition of a caste status by foreigners following the some occupation, particularly the instance of the Jews of Kolaba who, following the trade of oil-pressing have been admitted to the Teli caste.

What is of more importance to the Tea Industry, however, is the fact that change of occupation not infrequently involves loss of caste, especially when the new occupation is "lower", this term to be understood as meaning that such occupation is the rightful means of subsistence of a community carrying a lower social status locally. There was an interesting example of this among the Mundas, which came under our personal observation some years ago. The Mundas are an aboriginal tribe. till recently comparatively free of caste prejudices, but who have lately become so saturated with Hindu ideas that they have acquired a caste conscience. Their occupation is agriculture, and among them live people of obscure origin, who are blacksmiths, weavers, carpenters, workers in bamboo or in brass who supply their domestic and agricultural requirements in these directions. Christian Missionary effort has been amply rewarded among these people, but the caste consciousness persists even after the adoption of Christianity, much to the distress of the Missionaries. For, despite the symbolic commensalism which is the outstanding feature of the Church services, Christian Mundas are beginning to refuse to eat with Christian Oraons in the same district, while mixed marriages remain an abhorrence. Also in the few cases where marriages have been solemnized between members of the same *kili* or Gotra in order to prevent the parties "living in sin", outcasting of the families of both parties has followed and been persisted in. The Roman Catholic Mission at Khunti, in the heart of the Munda Country and the headquarters of the Munda Country Sub-division of the Ranchi District, established a Weaving School, fitted out with hand looms for weaving *saris* and *dhotis* of the type dear to the aboriginal heart. Professional weavers had proved that it was possible to earn a matter of two rupees a day at the looms and Christian Mundas were invited to attend the school and ultimately establish the looms in their villages. The experiment was an utter failure, the Mundas refusing to take up weaving, the occupation of the despised Panrs who live among them. It is interesting to note, however, that an exception is now being made in favour of carpentry, the trade reputed to have been followed by the Founder of Christianity.

Another instance of the objection to a change of occupation is mentioned in one of the reports of the Assam Labour Board. The Deputy Commissioner of the Hazaribagh District found that emigration to Tea Gardens during the famine year 1918-19 was greatest from those areas of his district where there was the greatest local demand for colliery labour. People will migrate a hundred miles and work in a mine, but they will not take up this occupation where they are known, *i.e.*, in the vicinity of their own homes. Mr. Berthoud, then Deputy Commissioner, stated that he had met Santals walking along the Grand Trunk Road covered with coal dust and had questioned them as to where they had been. They invariably stated they had been cutting paddy in Eastern Bengal, or helping with transplantation! On nearing their homes, they bathed and washed their clothes and posed as good honest agriculturists!

Agriculture is the traditional occupation of the great majority of the Indian population, and is a very honourable calling, Chamars, Kumhars and Dhobis, Dombs, Kamars and Turis willingly exchange their despised trades for the opportunity of acquiring land and attaining the status of landholder, while the dignified Mundas, Oraons and Santals, Gonds, Savaras and Porjas may turn to ten without fear of social ostracism, when the devil, in the form of a poor monsoon or of a rack-renting landlord drives them to emigrate. This does not mean that they will not take up another occupation at some distance from their usual haunts if it is made worth their while. The Bengal Coalfields are full of Oraons from Ranchi, Santals from Dumka, and even Hos from Singhbhum; the great industrial concerns of Singhbhum import Bilaspuris, and men from the United Provinces, while it is well known that local labour is practically unprocurable for earth work in Railway extensions.

Agriclture is, in the estimation of tae Indian, the highest occupation. The Tea Industry, therefore, stands in a particularly favourable position when competing for the recruitment of labour—work on a Tea Garden being mainly agricultural. Provided that the *real* wages offered compare not unfavourably with those obtainable in other industries by a *family*, tea has not much to fear from other competition, but if there is an appreciable differcuce in the opportunities for earning money, labour is not altogether averse from change of occupation for solid gain, so long as relatives and friends know nothing about this change.

As has been indicated already, the fact that land is available in many parts of Assam for private cultivation on the Estate for which labour is required, or in its immediate neighbourhood, is an unquestionable attraction, as at least eight per cent. of the labour force drifts away to independence each year. Land may be obtained on easy terms direct from Government, and some irritation is caused by the facilities held out to new settlers by the Administration. There can, however, be no doubt that the prospect of acquiring the improved status of "raiyat", *i.e.*, a tenant holding under Government is a large factor in the emigration of the more desirable classes of labour, *viz.*, individuals who are agriculturists by tradition, but who have been squeezed out of economic existence by pressure on the soil in the native district. Very large numbers of those who leave Tea Estates to take up Government land borrow money from Kayahs to stock and develop their holdings, the money lender receiving a mortgage on the property. These mortgages tend to be called in when the holding becomes valuable, and the settler has to begin all over again. Ex—Tea Garden coolies are invariably to be found on the fringe of cultivation in Assam Districts, ever bringing under cultivation new areas, and as constantly being dispossessed and starting again on virgin soil. Legislation is undoubtedly required stipulating for the possession of a certain amount of capital before a holding may be taken up and prohibiting mortgages of such property for the first ten years of the lease. This would have the effect of encouraging labour to remain on Tea Estates for longer periods in order to save the requisite capital, and would stimulate better and more work. Employers of labour are beginning to form Co-operative Societies on their Estates and encouraging the formation of Co-operative Banks: one of the functions of such institutions might be to stimulate land settlement on economic lines, loans being granted equivalent to sums in deposit on account of an individual wishing to take up an independent holding.

The necessity for proceeding far afield to recruit labour, and the resulting competition of industry with industry, and between individual concerns makes such recruitment exceedingly expensive. The only solution to labour difficulties is to obtain a settled labour force. So far as Tea in Assam goes, the penal contract is not in favour, and the significance of the fact that the personality of the employer, his ability to attract new labour through contented sirdars, and his power to keep all newcomers on his Estate, is again forced on our notice. Large Industrial Concerns have recently been appointing specially selected "Labour Welfare Saperintendents" to assist in this direction; on a Tea Estate, this luxury cannot be afforded, and the Manager himself must assume the role of Pooh Bah, although without exercising that Celestial official's power of summary execution for minor offences! Armed with tact, however, and a knowledge of the susceptibilities of his subjects, much may be done, for the Indian labourer is the most easily disciplined person in the world. No Indian Wat Tyler figures in the pages of History, nor has there appeared in India a body of Spartacists, despite the efforts of non-co-operators.

With regared to natural phenomena primitive man adopted two principles:

1. like produces like, and
2. thinks which have once been in contact with each other often continue of act on each other at a distance after the physical contact has been severed.

He inferred from the first principle that he could produce any effect he desired merely by imitating it, and from the second that whatever he did to a material object would affect equally the person with whom the material object was once in contact, whether it formed part of his body or not. Thus arose the cult of Sympathetic Magic in its two branches, Imitative or Homeopathic Magic, and Contagious Magic.[2]

Every individual dabbled in magic in a small way, just as most people nowadays can produce at short notice some drug or other to cure small ailments, but the specialist in the form of the Magician soon appeared. "Private Magic," or the magical rites and incantations practised for the benefit or injury of individuals, led by logical stages to "Public Magic," or sorcery practised for the benefit of the whole community. Wherever ceremonies of this sort are performed for the public weal, the magician ceases to be a private practitioner, and becomes to some extent a public functionary. Frazer argues that the public magician who practises his art for the good of the whole community enjoys great influence and may rise to be a chief or a king. The profession attracted the acuter minds of the community for their own advantage, and there was a tendency at this stage of social evolution for the supreme power to fall into the hands of the most unscrupulous. Not that the sorcerer was always a knave and imposter; he was often quite sincerely convinced that he really possessed those wonderful powers which the credulity of his fellows ascribed to him. "The elevation to power of magicians tends to substitute a monarchy for that primitive democracy or rather oligarchy of old men, which is characteristic of savage society, and the rise of monarchy seems to be an essential condition of the emergence of mankind from savagery." Sir James Frazer develops this interesting proposition, showing that intellectual progress is dependent on economic progress which is often furthered by conquest and empire. The community was freed from the councils of a number of timid, elders, and came under the sway of the best intellect. "Even the whims and caprices of a tyrant may be of service in breaking the chain of custom which lies so heavy on the savage."

"So far, therefore, as the public profession of magic has been one of the roads by which the ablest men have passed to supreme power, it has contributed to emancipate mankind from the thraldom of tradition and to elevate them into a larger, freer life, with a broader outlook on the world. This is no small service rendered to humanity. And when we remember that in another direction magic has paved the way for science, we are forced to admit that if the black art has done much evil, it has also been the source of much good; that if it is the child of error. it has yet been the mother of freedom and truch."

Magic postulated the order and uniformity of nature: the magician did not doubt that the same causes would always produce the same effects, that the proper ceremonies accompanied by the appropriate spells would inevitably be attended by the desired results unless thwarted and foiled by the more potent charms of another sorcerer. The magician supplicated no higher power: he sued the favour of no fickle and wayward being: he abased himself before no awful deity; he could wield his power so long as he conformed to the rules of his art, to what may be called the laws of nature as conceived by him. His error lay not in his faith in his general assumption of a sequence of events determined by law, but in his total misconception of the nature of the particular laws which govern that sequence. This magic has been called the "bastard sister of science"; its "fundamental conception is identical with that of modern science; underlying the whole system is a faith, implicit, but real and firm, in the order and uniformity of nature."

We have still to consider how magic stands related to religion. Religion, according to Frazer, is the propitiation or conciliation of powers superior to man which are believed to control and direct the course of nature and of human life. "Thus defined" he adds, "religion consists of two elements, a theoretical and a practical, namely, a belief in powers higher than man and an attempt to propitiate or please them." Man realised in time the essential inefficacy of magic, this great discovery being a confession of human weakness and ignorance.

"Cut adrift from his ancient moorings and left to toss on a troubled sea of doubt and uncertainty, his old happy confidence in himself and his powers rudely shaken, our primitive philosopher must have been sadly perplexed and agitated till he came to rest, as in a quiet haven after a tempestuous voyage," in a new system of faith and practice, which seemed to offer a solution of his herassing doubts and a substitute, however precarious, for that sovereignty over nature which he had reluctantly abdicated. If the great world went on its way without the help of him or his fellows it must surely be because there were other beings, like himself, but far stronger, who, unseen themselves, directed its course, and brought about all the varied series of events which he had hitherto believed to be dependant on his own magic. It was they, as he now believed, and not he himself, who made the stormy wind to blow, the lightening to flash, and the thunder to roll; who had laid the foundations of the solid earth and set bounds to the restless sea that it migth not pass; who caused all the glorious lights to shine; who gave the fowls of the air their meat and the wild beasts of the desert their prey; who bade the fruitful lands to bring forth in abundance, the high hills to be clothed with forests, the bubbling springs to rise under the rocks in the valleys, and green pastures to grow by still waters; who breathed into man's nostrils and made him live, or turned him to destruction by famine and pestilence and war. To these mighty beings, whose handiwork he traced in all the gorgeous and varied pageantry of nature, man now addressed himself, humbly confessing his dependence on their invisible power, and beseeching them of their merey to furnish him with all good things, to defend him from the perils and dangers by which our mortal life is compassed about on every hand, and finally to bring his immortal spirit, freed from the burden of the body, to some happier world, beyond the reach of pain and sorrow, where he might rest with them and with the spirits of good men in joy and felicity for ever."

Thus was probably made the great transition from magic to religion, and "man has created gods in his own image" ever since. The degree of civilization attained by a people can accurately be gauged by a study of their pantheon: the terrible god of vengeance evolves into the merciful god as the race attains the higher planes of idealism, while the more primitive races still pay tribute to a horde of malignant spirits "which day and night for their destruction wait."[4]

The first gods were themselves magicians, able and willing to turn the course of nature for the benefit of their faithful worshippers, and this should be remembered especially when we are discussing the Hindu Pantheon. Our next chapter will consist of sketches of "Animism" and "Hinduism," and traces of the influence of the cult of magic will readily be recognized as we proceed. As will presently appear, the dividing line between Animism and Hinduism, as understood and practised by the class we have set ourselves to discuss, is extremely difficult to demarcate. Animism is probably nearer the original cult of Magic, and is perhaps cruder even than Magic as practised by some of the African tribes of to-day.

We have seen that the idea of a "spirit" appeared comparatively early in the mental history of Homo Sapiens, and was immediately extended to all animate nature. With the breakdown of Magic as a school of thought, the spirit was deified, the spirit which every natural object possessed. This is, briefly, Animism; Hinduism in its cruder forms has progressed beyond the idea that everything is possessed of a spirit endowed with more or less magical power and an extreme malevolence, and has evolvod a pantheon of a somewhat "higher" type.

Religion

It is now proposed briefly to sketch the principal religions found in the areas from which lobour is recrurited. One of the objects of this compilation is to enumerate and describe the principal festivals of the people we employ, and these are intimately bound up with their respective religions. When discussing subsequently in detail the various castes and tribes, reference will be made to special festivals peculiar to individual communities. Most castes, however, are Hindu by religion and broadly speaking, all aboriginals are animist; a general description of these two schools of thought may, therefore, be useful, as festivals and ceremonies common to all professing Hinduism or practising Animism can conveniently be considered.

Animism

We have indicated in a previous section how it came about that primitive people imagined all nature to be inhabited by "spirits" and have now to consider in greater detail the religion of the majority of the tribes discussed in Part II. We may, therefore, indulge in a brief recapitulation.

Primitive man, on the analogy of what is found still surviving in backward races and as a result of a study of child psychology, is supposed to have regarded all nature as being alive and conscious, as soon as he realised that he himself was alive and conscious. When he propounded to himself the idea of a "spirit" he attributed to all nature a similar spirit. When Magic as a theory of the working of Nature broke down, "spirit" was deified, and the supernatural inhabitant of each natural object was regarded as a god. People who hold these theories are termed "animists" and their religion "animism."

Generally speaking, the "spirit in the woods" is malevolent; among the Mundas and Uraons, with one exception, the deities are hositile to human beings, the one exception being the Sun God who is regarded as above such pettiness. The spirits of the departed are generally considered to be earth bound, inhabiting the houses in which they dwelt before disembodiment. These too appear to be worshipped and propitiated and we find the germs of ancestor worship in several communities. Traces of the idea of the re-birth of the spirit is also noticeable, linked up with the notion of transmigration to higher or lower forms according to the deserts of the individual. None of the Indian aboriginals, however, appears to have formulated the theory of "happy hunting fields." As might be expected form the general gloominess of their outlook, we find among these people no joyous pantheon such as the Greeks and Romans imagined, and as a consequence, religious observance consists of the performance of ceremonies to propitiate the various "godlings," these rites being linked very closely still to magical performances.

Sickness and disease are regarded as being due to the operation of some minor deity or malevolent spirit—one can hardly use the word *deity* to describe each and every member of the pantheon. This malevolent spirit *feeds* on the life of the person who is ill, and the steps generally taken to deal with the enemy are interesting as indicating the working of the primitive mind. It is imagined that the spirit—*bonga* as the Mundas call it—is unable to fosten on to the life of a human being without the assistance of a human familiar (*najom*—Mundari) and the first step, therefore, is to discover the familiar. Recourse is had to the soothsayer or witchfinder (*Sokha*) who discovers the *familiar* with the aid of grains of rice and the magic art. He also ascertains what particular sacrifice the *bonga* is willing to accept in order to loose his hold on the sick person. The *najom* or familiar is then approached by the relatives and friends of the patient and very politely requested to perform the necessary sacrifice of a black or white cock, a goat, or even a buffalo, the *najom*, of course, providing the victim. The utmost pressure is brought to bear on the unfortunate person indicated as the familiar, and refusal to comply with the demand is dangerous. For, with perfect logic, it is argued that if the *bonga* is not provided with the life of another living being by his familiar, the desired end may be attained by removing the familiar, who is frequently murdered under exceedingly cruel circumstances. In Chota Nagpur there are at least a hundred such cases of witchcraft murder each year.

The *meriah* sacrifices among the Gonds of the Madras Agency Tracts have only recently been suppressed and had a magico--religious significance. "A life for a life" seems to have been the law of the Nature-spirits, and as the crops, good hunting, good fishing and all that the primitive soul longs for and needs, were regarded as endowed with life, the sacrifice of a life to ensure fertility and abundance of food seemed essential. The more valuable the victim, the greater the merit, the more potent the power of the sacrifice. Human sacrifice to-day is a last resort and is occasionally met with in Chota Nagpur and in Central India.

Most of the minor deities wield power, however, only within the boundaries of the village where lies their habitat. It would appear that the village itself and all that appertains thereto is regarded as a living entity. Members of the family of the original settler, the pioneer who first began to reclaim the village site, are regarded with special veneration, and among the Mundas only a member of that family may sacrifice to the village deities. In Uraon villages in Chota Nagpur, we find Mundas acting as priests and even in the western districts of the Central Provinces a similar custom prevails a family of the original inhabitants being maintained to carry on the worship of the indigenous deities. Among the Mundas themselves only members of the family of the original settler may be buried within the confines of the village and the right is jealousy guarded. It is used as a test of membership of the family.

When jungle is cleared for-cultivation, a small grove is invariably left for the housing of the spirits, called by the Mundas and Uraons the *Surna*. It is here the principal ceremonies of public worship are performed.

A very common sight in travelling through the areas inhabited by primitive people is the collection of rubbish dumped on the road just outside the village boundary. The rubbish is collected from each house and placed where the local deities are powerless, rubbish being supposed, very properly, to be one of the media used by malevolent spirits for the spread of disease.

As is to be expected, there is considerable variety in the way the different peoples explain the existence of this world of ours. We give a brief account of the Santal story of creation which is typical of all others:

> In the beginning Singh Bonga—the great sun-god, brooded over the waters which covered the face of nature and finally created two birds, male and female, which glided continuously over the waste of seas. At last they complained to Singh Bonga that they could get no rest and he created a tree on which they perched. In due course, and in compliance with their insistent demands, land appeared and grass and food grains. As a result perhaps of proper nourishment, the lady bird laid an egg from which were hatched our first ancestors, Pilchu Haram and Pilehu Budhi, man and woman. They were innocent, and perhaps as happy, as Adam and Eve in Eden, till Singh Bonga, *not* in the guise of a serpent, brewed rice beer for them, and while in a state os intoxication, the woman conceived and ultimately bore a son. They liked rice beer and, in due course, twelve sons and twelve daughters were born. Despite the example of their own case, Pilchu Haram and Pilchu Budhi had already apparently acquired certain glimmerings of the principles of exogamy, for they did not instruct their off-spring in the use of rice beer. The twelve young men drifted away to the chase, hunting and subsisting on the game which by this peopled the forests and they wandered about together for some years.

In order to see their quarry from a distance, it was the practice to climb a tall tree, and on a certain occasion one of our young men descended rapidly, from his perch, exclaiming that he had seen a wonderful sight. The brothers all mounted trees and saw in the distance a row of huts and cultivated fields in a forest clearing. They had forgotten their parentage and sisters till this moment, and on presenting themselves at the settlement, were made very welcome. The maidens, unable to follow and secure or slay animals for food had taken to the cultivation of rice.

Pilchu Haram and Pilchu Budhi consulted Singh Bonga on

the subject of rice beer, and on his advice, a great feast was arranged. Masses of rice and venison were prepared and many jars of beer. Man and maid drifted together in the friendliness of intoxication and knowledge duly came to each pair, who, in the course of time, founded families which are now represented by the twelve principal septs or *Killis*. The drinking of rice beer is exalted to the status of a ritual, and finds a place in every ceremony. In the Provinces of Bengal and Bihar and Orissa, aboriginals are permitted to brew rice beer without let or hindrance from the Exciseman, and it is interesting to note that a "Pussyfoot" resolution was recently turned down in the Bihar and Orissa Legislative Assembly on the grounds of the sacrosanct character of rice beer among aboriginals.

Festivals among Animists usually have some agricultural bearing and we enumerate below the principal public feasts:

1. *Spring Festival* (Phagooa—Mundari):—Celebrated at the time of the Full Moon of the month (January—Febrnary). The harvest is in and grain and liquor are to be had in abundance. The household and village deities are venerated and propitiated.
2. *The Summer Festival* (Sarhul—Mundari):—This festival symbolises the marriage of Mother Earth with the Sun God. Frequently a ceremony of marriage between the village priet and his wife is publicly performed, and all weddings in the village are postponed until its completion. New fruits, flowers or vegetables may not be gathered for a month previously, nor is any agricultural operation permitted. At the festival itself the utmost license is allowed, which some writers think is a magical performance to ensure the fecundity of Mother Earth.
3. *Monsoon Festival* celebrated in Asarh (June):—Just before transplantation is commenced, with sacrifices of fowls and magical rites to ensure a plenteous rainfall and a full crop of rice.

(a) The *Karam* festival has evidently been borrowed from the Hindus and takes place in Bhado (August —September). The object seems to be to ensure thc fertility of the growing rice, branches of the Karam tree being planted in each field.

4. *The Harvest Festival* in Kartik (October—November):-- Cattle are venerated, decorated and fed on boiled rice. Fowls are sacrificed and much beer is drunk and the newly harvested rice is ceremonially eaten. This festival is probably a thanks-giving service, with a "lively sense of favours to come."

At all these festivals dances are held and the dances are supposed to have a magical significance. At the Spring festival among the Mundas and Uraons, for instance, the operations of sowing are *imitated* by the women dancers; at the Harvest festival, the gestures proper to reaping are given prominence, the girls punctuating their singing with "Hiss-Hiss," in imitation of the sigh of the laden corn yielding to the stroke of the sickle. Mundas, Urabns, Savaras and Korkus, Gonds, Kharias and Bhumij dance at all seasons and though it may be that in origin the dance had some mystical meaning, all who have watched these delightful people at their gambols will agree that their dancing is now an expression of the sheer physical joy of living.

It is hardly possible to generalise regarding festivals obligatory on individuals, as the ceremonies may vary widely, and will be described when particular tribes are under consideration. It will suffice to mention here that at childbirth and at death certain rites-must be performed. There is usually a public acceptance by a father of the new born infant, and a purificatory ceremony when a member of the family deceases. Traces of the *Couvade* are found in India as in Europe, the husband going to bed and behaving as though he himself were in the pangs of childbirth when his wife is in labour. Among some people this is now restricted to the prohibition of all work to the husband on the day his child is born. This also has probably a magical significance, being intended to alleviate the pangs of the mother.

We may conclude this section on Animism by describing an interesting recent development among the Uraons which has not been without effect on Tea Estates in North India; it has certainly adversely affected recruiting in Chota Nagpur. This is *Tana Bhagat* movement, and it has several interesting aspects. It preceded non-co-operation by ten years, but was exploited by the followers of Gandhi to advance his theories. The expression means "Compulsory Purity' and its votaries become vegetarians and give up drink. While maintaining a belief in the existence of the spirits which inhabit trees and stones, their *attitude* towards these changed entirely. Instead of propitiation, it was considered possible by fasting and personal chastity to drive them away from their villages where alone they were potent. In the year 1915, a cordon extending from North to South of the Uraon country in the Ranchi District was formed and each village was responsible for driving the spirits away to the East. A description of an occurence which needed the attention of the Police may be of interest. The whol: village turned out for the spirit drive and armed themselves with twigs or branches, of the tamarind tree. They advanced from West to East, being lined up North and South along the western boundary. Each man—women took no part but remained *behind* the party—swept the ground in front of him with his tamarind twig, sweeping also each stone and the base of each bush and tree, uttering *mantras.* The *mantras* were curious and seemed to be an invocation of every known powerful agent heard of, such us "*bom-gola madad de*" (may bombs help us), *Tar madad de* (telegraph), *Injan madad de* (Railway engine), *German Raj madad de* and so on. As the line advanced one or other of the men would become "possessed" and crying that the spirit had entered into him, would dance and gambol while his neighbours uttered *mantras* and brushed him with the tamarind branches. One individual was intoxicated and the *bonga* frequently took possession of him. The line had passed the *basti*, when our drunken friend once more claimed to be "possessed." On this occasion, however, he was rupidly brought to his senses by blows from a somewhat stout tamarind branch. He broke line and ran back to the *basti* pursued by the whole crowd yelling that the *bonga* had run back. The man fled to his house where he was cornered and in his terror, when the "brushings" began again, stated that the spirit had now left him and had entered into his wife and an old woman then standing in the courtyard. The crowd turned on her and beat her to death, a dreadful orgie ensuing.

The old beliefs are being weakened under the ever advancing influence of Christianity and Hinduism and this idea of driving out the minor gods altogether marks a great mental advance. Other gods of a less repulsive character will, no doubt, be substituted.

Hinduism

It is impossible in a compilation of this nature to give an adequate idea of the meaning of the term Hinduism with reference to religion, as it embraces no definite creed and the beliefs of recognised Hindus, often differ more widely than those of Christians and Muhammedans.

As has been shown in the preceding section, Hindu religious beliefs are not, in many respects, very far removed from the original Animistic cults of pre-Aryan days. The Census Report of 1911 gives a very good idea of the elasticity of the term "Hinduism" as applied to religion in which it is stated that the term includes "A complex congeries of creeds and doctrines. It sheters within its portals, monotheists, polytheists, and pantheists; worshippers of the great gods Siva and Vishnu or of ther female counterparts, as well as worshippers of the divine mothers, of the spirits of trees, rocks and streams and of the tutelary village deities; persons who propitiate their deity by all number of bloody sacrifices and persons who will not only not kill any living creature, but who must not even use the word 'cut"; those whose ritual consists mainly of prayers and hymns and those who indulge in unspeakable orgies in the name of religions; and a host of more or less heterodox sectariés, many of whem deny the supremacy of the Brahmans, or at least have non-Brahmanical religions leaders."

The extensiveness of "Hinduism" was also commented upon by Mr. Mclver when reporting for the Madras Census of 1881 and the variety of the religious beliefs covered by the cloak of Hinduism is clearly demonstrated where he says that "as a religious classification it lumps the purest surviving forms of Vedic belief with the demon worshippers of Tinnevelly and South Canara."

It will, therefore, be seen that Hinduism gives no sign whereby it would be possible to consider the term in relation to a definite creed. The Hindu word "dharma" is the nearest equivalent to "religion" but this term connotes conduct rather than religion. Religion in this country does not play the important part in the classification of society that it does in the West. Indians are judged more by their social status than by their religious denomination and the average person in far more interested in knowing whether or not he may associate with and take water from his neighbour than in his neighbour's religious views.

Prior to the Aryan invasion there were in existence a great number of small communities, each having a religion and tribal priests of their own who administered to their spiritual needs. Their beliefs were, for the greater part, of the amorphous. Animistic type similar to those held by various primitive races in other parts of the world The primitive Aryans were devout worshippers of the great forces of nature, but in the course of time the gradual intermixing with indigenous aborigines led to the adoption of many of the local deities now found in the Hindu pantheon.

With the steady growth of social organisation and the evolution of the caste system, the differences in religious thought were gradually forced into the background and had to give place to the more important factors of caste and class distinction. The agricultural castes in particular are and have always been extremely tolerant of their neighbours' religious beliefs; the fact of having many deities of their own, invoked fear of criticism of their neighbours' gods which were not perhaps in their own particular pantheon, as undoubtedly these unknown gods were vested with powers of the supernatural and if angered, their wrath might be visited upon the offenders indiscriminately.

Religion has not played a very important part in the development of the caste and social system that has been handed down from the past, and the only time when religious influence has made itself felt to any extent has been when some new cult has been expounded, having a very strong social backing or has been joined to some political agitation that has made itself felt in the community. A case in point is given in the Census Report of 1911 where Buddhists were strong enough to break away and repudiate the supremacy of the Brahmans; also when the converts to Jainism were powerful enough to deny the authority of the Vedas and thirdly, where Sikhism as preached by Guru Gobind who openly aimed at the establishment of a political ascendancy, repudiated many of the ordinary Hindu scruples.

As already stated, (Hinduism covers a multitude of indigenous beliefs but the only religions other than that generally recognised as "Hinduism" of sufficient importance to warrant special attention are Buddhism, Jainism, Sikhism, Muhammadanism and the Animistic beliefs of the aboriginal tribes). The last mentioned have already been considered and a brief outline of the others will follow. Many minor cults, such as the Satnamis and Panchpiriyas are in existence and are quite as diverse from the generally recognised Hindu doctrine as those cited above, but are comparatively unimportant and for this reason need not be considered as separate religions.

Mention has already been made of the small advance made in theology since the time of the Aryans, (and the origin of the present Hindu beliefs must be looked for in the distant past when the Aryans invaded Hindustan and settled on the banks of the Indus and Sarasvati. The Rig Veda—an illuminating anthology of hymns composed about the year 1400 B.C. and handed down verbally by the early Aryan settlers until about the year 300 B.C. when it was written—affords a valuable religious history of these early people.) From this Veda has been gathered the fact that the gods of the Aryans were of the cheerful type, very different from the demons who tormented the aboriginal tribes they found in India. These people seemed to have placed their faith in a spirit which controlled the whole of their world and was also responsible for the solar system. In the course of time, they came to recognise the great forces of nature as seperate deities and worshipped them as their needs arose. In this manner all the known forces of nature were ultimately found to require worship or propitiation to ensure, preservation of life and property. Major C.H. Buck, I.A., of the Punjab Commission in his extremely interesting book on the "*Faiths, Fairs and Festivals of India*" his drawn a striking comparison between certain of the gods of the Indo-Aryans and the deties invoked by the Greeks and Romans. He shows how Dyas, the "sky" or "Heavenly father" was the Zeus of Greece, the Jupiter of Rome and the old god Tiu of our Tusday.

It is impossible to trace in the space at our disposal, the various phases through which Hinduism has passed from the time of the composition of the Rig Veda to the present day and for the purposes of this work, it is not necessary.

So far, Hinduism has been considered only as a term relating to religion, but when deciding whether or not a man is a Hindu, factors other than religion have to be taken into consideration. Many efforts have been made to arrive at a clear definition of the term, but opinion is still so widely divergent that a generally accepted definition is hard to find.

Sir Alfred Lyall has made the following attempt which certainly covers all the admitted theories on the point. He says:—(Hinduism is not exclusively a religious denomination, but denotes also a country and, to a certain extent, a race... When a man tells me he is a Hindu, I know that he means all three things taken together: religion, parentage and country. Hinduism is a matter of birthright and inheritance—it means a civil community quite as much as reltgious association. A man does not become a Hindu, but is born into Hinduism.") Gait, commenting on this definition in the Ceasus Report of 1911, stipulates that in view of the important part the caste system plays in Hindu life, social organisation should also be added to the three factors mentioned, for it is obvious that a man who is not a member of a recognised caste, cannot be a Hindu.

Efforts hcve been made from time to time to determine the criteria by which a man may be considered to be a genuine Hindu in the popular acceptance of the term but opinion has been so diverse, that it has been impossible to arrive at any definite conclusions. The view is held by certain authorities that Hinduism is exclusively a matter of religious belief and that social organisation is a thing apart. As stated previously, Hinduism embraces no definite creed and the religious beliefs of recognised Hindus are often widely divergent. Barth in his "Religions of India" says:—"The sectarian or neo-Brahmanic religions which we embrace under the general designation of Hinduism, constitute a fluctuating mass of beliefs, opinions, usages, observances, religious and social ideas, in which we recognise a certain ground-principle and a very decided family likeness indeed, but from which it would be very difficult to educe any accurate definition. At the present time, it is next to impossible to say exactly what Hinduism is, where it begins and where it ends. Diversity is its very essence and its proper manifestation is "sect," sect in constant mobility and reduced to such a state of division that nothing similar to it was ever seen in any other religious system."

Others again, hold the theory that Hinduism is a matter of race and that the term is synonymous with "Arya," connoting the Indo-Iranic people. All modern castes are alleged to have descended from the four traditional castes mentioned on page 6 and if this idea is maintained, all members of recognised castes must, accordingly, be Hindus irrespective of their religious beliefs. We have already seen, however, that the descendants of certain aboriginal tribes who now embrace Hinduism, have no claim whatever to "Aryan" origin. As mentioned on page 10 a section of the Mundas—an aboriginal tribe of non-Aryan descent—have now become Hinduised and are recognised as such. Further arguments could be brought to disprove this theory in view of the contemptuous references made in Hindu law books and epics against "non-Aryan aborigines" but this attitude, as has been suggested, was probably adopted with a view to race preservation. In the passage from the "Religions of India" cited above, the author has laid stress on the religious aspect of the case, but recognition of the "caste" theory has also been given in another place. "In sectarian India at present, and since the appearance of foreign proselytising religions, caste is the express badge of Hinduism. The man who is a member of a caste is a Hindu; he who is not, is not a Hindu. And caste is not merely the symbol of Hinduism; but, according to the testimony of all who have studied it on the spot, it is its stronghold. It is this, much more than their creeds which attaches the masses to these vague religions and gives them such astonishing vitality."

Those theorists who propound the idea of race contend that all inhabitants of India other than Christians and Muhammedans are Hindus—the suggestion being that the term was applied by the early Muhammedan invaders to the people living to the east of the Iudus. When considering this point of view, it must, however, be remembered, that there were in existence, but far removed from the Indus, tribes of totally different origin and customs from those conquered by the Muhammedans and in fact, of whose existence, the invaders were totally unaware.

From the foregoing, it will be seen that the term Hindu can

be interpreted as denoting social organisation, race, religion or country; a man might be classified as a Hindu in the light of his eligibility from one or two points of view, yet be disqualified by reason of his inability to conform to the remaining requirements.

At the moment we are chiefly concerned with the religious aspect of the case. For all general purposes, a "Hindu" may be classified as such if he conforms to the following:

(a) Acknowledges the supremacy of the Brahmans.

(b) Recognises the authorily of the Vedas.

(c) Is admitted to the interior of the Hindu Temples.

(d) Worships the great Hindu Gods.

(e) Reverences the cow and does not eat beef.

(f) Will receive the "mantra" from a Brahman or other recognised "guru."

(g) Is susceptible to pollution by touch or within a certain distance of "defiled castes."

(h) Will be served by Brahmans as family priests.

These were some of the tests of Hinduism which the Provincial Superintendents were asked to apply at the time of the Census of 1911. The results varied very considerably in different parts of the country and no satisfactory conclusions could be arrived at. In the Central Provinces and Berar, a quarted of the people classified as Hindus deny the supremacy of the Brahmans and the authority of the Vedas and more than a half do not receive the "mantra" from a recognised "guru." Again, in Bengal and Orissa, Mr. O'Malley reported that there are 59 castes including seven with a strength of a quarter of a million and upwards, who do not conform to some of the tests. He also points out that whilst the "untouchables" are not admitted to the interior of the temples, they are recognised as part of the Hindu Polity and they are served also by Brahman priests. From the reports received from Southern India it appeared that the supremacy of the Brahman is denied by the Lingayats—an important sectarian group—and also by certain artisan castes who themselves claim to be Brahmans.

It has been shown in the previous section how the early Aryan settlers in this country appeared to have believed originally in one power or spirit which ruled supreme and controlled all things both in heaven and earth, but in course of time, their ideas of God underwent a change and in the place of one divine being was substituted a number of deities representing separately the great forces of nature.

Idol worship does not appear to have been a vogue until after the Aryans had intermixed and settled with the indigenous aborigines and it was only with the development of Hinduism that attempts were made to introduce idolatrous manifestations of the various gods.

REFERENCES

1. From S.C. Roy's "The Mundas and their Country."
2. From the *Golden Bough.*
3. *Ibid.*
4. *Ibid.*

2

CASTE CONFLICT: HISTORICAL BACKGROUND

The history of mankind is as old as the history of human conflict. Truly, human race has since ever been struggling hard for its existence. Every age has been the age of struggle, conflict and crisis. May that age be the age of human civilization or agricultural, primitive or modern, in every age and at every point of time, a direct correlation between man and conflict has been explicitly observed. In all ages of human civilization, it is universally factual and widely acceptable that conflict and human evolution have always gone parallel to each other. Today, the whole cosmos of mankind seems to be burning in rampant fire of conflict. The trinity of the clash of interests between individuals or groups, the rampant desire of gaining power, and the extreme want to lead a prestigious social position, have severely dashed every individual from other individuals distant, creating a deeper gulf which is a matter of great curiosity, anxiety and serious thought.

To understand conflict from sociological point of view, the rerearcher has picked up Indian caste system. It is here desired to see conflict inherent in somewhat less or more degree in Indian caste system through ages. India's caste system is the defective or twisted from of its varna system, we view the fundamentals of conflict seeded in its very root. Here, it is contextual to find out the prevailing elements of conflict present in inter-personal relationship of the structural components of Varna order. These components are Brahman, Kshatriya, Vaishya and Shudra.

F. Max Muller has described the gravity of Brahmans in a systematic manner in his world fame book entitled *The Sacred Books of the East* which can be mentioned as under:

> Man is said to be purer above the novel than below, therefore, the self-existent (Swayambhu) has declared it as His purest organ (face).[1]

Since, Brahman has originated from the mouth of Brahma, and since he is elder and authority of Vedas, and therefore, he is master of whole creation.[2] Because, self-existent, after the total subsistence, created him from his mouth, so that the sacrificial things might be conveyed to Gods, and worldly men and world as a whole might be given protection.[3] Who can dare to avoid him through whole mouth, the Gods themselves continuously consume the sacrificial things, and tell the things offered to dead bodies as the feast of forefathers.[4] The birth of Brahman is, then, as external incarnation of holy law to provide protection to the property of God, and he disappears alongwith the disappearance of Brahma.[5] When a Brahman comes into existence, he takes birth upon the earth as a superhuman and highest and as a master of all the creatures.[6] Whatever exists in the universe, that is all the property of Brahman being supermost since birth. Of course, Brahman is the authority of all these things.[7] A Brahman, whether he is idle or learned, is a master of a great excellence just like fire.[8]

The provision of punishment for Brahman in Varna system was as follows:

> To ensure ceremony is most appropriate for Brahmans in the place of capital punishment. But other Varnas shall have to accept capital punishment.[9] No Brahman should be

killed in any condition irrespective of his numerous crime commitments. Such Brahman criminal should be exiled and his whole property should be allowed to be with him and his body should not be tortured.[10] No more severe crime is known on the earth than to kill a Brahman. So, a king should not and may not even think mentally to kill a Brahman.[11]

The Birth for Shudras for Enslavement

But a Shudra, whether purchased or not, can be forcibly pressed to work as a slave, because self-existent has himself created a Shudra to be slave of Brahmans. A Shudra, even after getting rid of his master, cannot get rid of slavery. Because, slavery is associated with his birth. Who can allow him to be free from that? A Brahmin, after being assured, may capture the property of his slave (Shudra), because a Shudra (slave) has no right to possess property. His master may have right over his existence.

To serve Brahmans is the only means of livelihood declared for Shudras, because whatever a Shudra shall do other than service to Brahmans, this shall all be fruitless.[12] Shudras, even after being capable to accumulate the wealth, should never do so. Because the prosperous or wealthy Shudra aggrieves the Brahmans.[13]

The Award of Slavery

They should certainly provide the Shudras enough for their livelihood and for the livelihood of his family and this should be done, for which he is bound, only after a careful examination and consideration of his capacity, labour and number.[14] He must be given food defiled by eating and also old cloths, the remains of grains etc.

Penal System for Shudras

If a Shudra uses abusive languages to assault a dwij (Brahman), his tongue shall be cut and shall be separated from body;

because he belongs to low family. If he class the name of a dwij or mentions his caste with disrespect, a burning iron nail whose length is equivalent to breadth of ten fingers (ten anguls long) would be poured into his mouth.[15]

If he preaches the Brahmans of their duties, the king would arrange hot oil to pour into his mouth and ears. If the low varna person, whether why not by any organ of his body, tortures the higher varnas, his that organ shall be cut.[16] This is the preaching of Manu. He who uses his hand or stick for this purpose, his hand shall be damaged; he who aggressively kicks out by his leg, his leg shall be cut. If a low varna person tries to substitute himself at the place of a Brahman his hip shall be branded by hot iron and he shall be exiled, or the king shall make an arrangement to make a deeper wound at his hip. If he spits at a person superior to him due to pride, the king shall make an arrangement to cut his both the lips. If he makes water at him, his penis; if he discharged polluted air before him, his 'guda' shall be cut. If he snatches the hairs of a higher varna, the king ought to cut his hand without hitch. Similarly, if he touches the Brahman's feet with scribbling, then his beard, neck or 'andkos.[17]

The prescribed standard of behaviour for some Varnas:[18]

The residence of Chandals and Shwapakis shall be out of village. They shall be disabled and dogs and mules shall be the only wealth of theirs. Their cloths shall be cadavour-like dress. They shall eat in broken dish. The black iron shall be their ornaments, and they shall necessarily move from one place to another.[19]

A Shudra shall not commit such a crime less his race should go to extinction. He shall not enjoy holy religious texts. He has no right to follow the rules of rituals, even then, he is not prohibited to follow some parts of Aryan cult. Therefore, a Shudra should not be given an advice. Neither he should be given the remains of food-stuff, nor the offerings to God (Prasad), nor religious explanation before him, nor provision of penance. He who puts the explanation of religious rules before a Shudra shall also drown in hell known as Asamvrit.[20]

> The provision of penance in case a person kills a Shudra:[21] Any person who kills a Shudra may practice penance of his sin by killing a cat, a mongoose, a magpie, a frog, a dog, a lizard, an owl, or a crow.[22]

Through the analysis of the facts mentioned above, it reveals that the social status of Brahmans in India's varna system was hightest and that of Shudras, the lowest. Warriors or Kings (Kshatriyas) were working under the direction of Brahmans. In this way, Brahmans worked as pressure group. In Varna system, where, on one hand, one finds division of labour and as a consequence the emergence of group of experts (specialists), on the other hand, the tendency of exploitation rooted in the system is found. In this reference, Davis's work may be cited who mentioned that inequality exists in a society due to unequal distribution' of power, prestige and rewards.[23] To deprive the Shudras of social, economic, political and cultural provisions is certainly in-human. This is undoubtedly true that in such a system, the Shudras might have been frustrated and held felt a sense of social insecurity and injustice. But, why did they not fight against Brahmans in past can best be explained and argued in ways said below. It is and it may be that Shudras had no education and, therefore, had no consciousness and hence, they were uncapable of raising their voices of deprivation of values against Brahmans. Secondly, there was the provision of severe penal system for Shudras and therefore on Shudra dared to react against any Brahman or Kshatriya. Thirdly, even Kshatriyas (King) were controlled, directed, regulated and conducted by Brahmans. The Brahman Varna as a whole because of his intelligence and spiritual power and command over all sorts of knowledge related to every aspect of human race was easily able to exercise his power over all other varnas. The analysis of all these facts does not contain in itself the denial of non-existence of elements of revenge and conflict in the system. They were of course seeded in the system-ground but were not in the process of evolution. The seeds of conflict were depressed; oppressed and suppressed by the heavy and polluted storm of established codes of conduct. It is true that evolution has a direct link with environment. A seed can never grow in absence of proper environment. A particular human behaviour is directed proportional to time and space. As the time and space very, human behaviour also varies. Underground seed if unevolved becomes rotten. Similarly, the seed of conflict which could never emerge in classical India is diffusing today due to numerous of changes brought by legal legislations enacted by Government of India. Today, India Government is committed to establish democratic values based on equality, faternity, and justice before law. Today, political institutions have come into existence to fight against injustice made towards any individual, caste, verna, creed or tribe.

Due to spread of education and provision of eradication of mass illiteracy through adult education scheme; economic growth of lower castes and lower classes; industrialization; urbanization; occupational mobility; the special provision of reservation of seats to backwards and scheduled castes including scheduled tribes, social security measures; and untouchability removed act have made the untouchables and lower caste people to form organization. Now, they have awaken to fight against injustice. They darely put forth their problems. They now do not fear from higner castes. Today, the whole India's scene is surrounded by factionalism, casteism, caste conflict and class conflict within caste system.

Brahmans since tradition have been religiously trust worthy and only because of their such prejudiced religious staunchness, the conflict on large scale between Brahmanism and revolutionary movements like Buddhism and Jainism was obviously seen in medieval India, and Buddhism was defeated for ever. In this period, after the establishment of Moghul imperialism, where on one hand the Indian Hindus were undergoing conversion in Islamic religion, on the other hand, unadaptive

Hindu religious staunchness was firmly standing forth. Numerous of religious social reformers tried their best to reduce the width and breadth of the gulf between the two conflicting religious groups through the process of negotiation, but India's low castes used to undergo Islamic conversion only so as to be free from grievances caused by higher castes. This is the reason why Buddhism had been people's religion and it remained, maintained and continued for thousands of years. Likely, in Moghul period, the Indian people began to adopt Istalmic style of religion through conversion only because Islam provided them social equality and opportunities to enhance their social status in the world. But being alert from this dangerous siren, some social reformers tried to bring out change in social structure of Hindus. The first attempt of this reform was 'Vir Shiva movement' which aimed at ending the caste system and removing other social restraints.[24] The pioneer of this movement was a Brahman named Basava, as a consequence of whose efforts the people broke the barriers of caste rules and established marriage relations between Brahmans and Chandals. Basava widely propagated the gravity and essentiality of hard work. In his leadership. Lingayat sect came into existence who fought against priests to end the importance of tamples and statueworship.

Some words of Basava seem to be full of modern revolutionary emotions which are as under:

> What is the use of listening to Shastras and Puranas? Of what use is it to us if we read the Vedas and Vettantas? May I admit the greatness of the Shastras? It enforces Karma. May I regard the Vedas as important? They advise slaughter of animals.

> The Adipurana tells only of Asuras; the Veda Purana resorts to the slaughter of goats; Ramayan speaks only of demons (Rakshasas); the Mahabharata relates family feuds. All these Puranas preach Karma first; but your Purana is matchless, O Lord Kudala Sangama.[25]

Furthermore:

> Those who are well versed in the Veda, Shastra, Purana, Agama etc. are not great. A rope-dancer is a master of sixty four lores. Is he then inferior? This is not the right criterion. It is quite different. All these are bread earning lores; therefore he is great who has realized vurtya, knowledge and religious conduct and purity...[26]

A Brahmin is not born to read the Veda and the Shastra:

> A Kshatriya is not meant to kill and be merry,
>
> Trading is not the monopoly of Vaishya;
>
> Our god Kama Bhima does not consent without
>
> Examining the merits and demerits of a former.

Basava preached the men to lead their lives through labour and hard work. His preachings were propagated at large scale among the traders and peasants of Karnatak. Today, Lingayats have got their separate social identity as a caste. They have got their own style of life. Their priests are just like Brahmans of staunch Hindu society.

Another reform-oriented movement also started from south and diffused in whole India which is universally known as 'Vaishnava movement'. The followers of this movement believe in salvation through Bhakti. The movement refused the significance of caste barriers and raised its voice against inequality between males and females. The pioneers of this movement in north India were Rama Nand and Kabir who was the son of a Muslim weaver. Besides these, the names of Dadu, Nanak and Nam Deo are also associated with this movement. Ultimately comes Chaitanya Deo of Bengal. The movement propounded by Chaitanya Deo was accelerated and pushed forth as a reform-oriented movement by Nitya Nand and hir son Vir Chand. This movement, in social aspect of human life, was competitor of Islam. Afterwards, a group emergen as a consequence of the movement which was called as 'Jati Vaishnava'.

Even today, any person belonging to any caste may become the member of this group after taking the prescribed education and initiation. This group (Jati-Vaishnava) has disrupted the caste-discrimination. Still today, it is an orphanage for those who are socially depressed and boycotted.[27]

Although, the objectives of these reform-oriented movements were to end caste discriminations but their social consequences were that the different movements formed their separate castes. Some of them claimed themselves to be Brahman, for example, Nath-sect. Later on, all these sects separately became endogamous social groups and they all became the victim of Brahmanic cult. Of course, after time-interval, the Brahman cult again became so dominant that without accepting the Brahmanic rules and ways it was impossible to achieve social prestige.

In modern India even, numerous of reform-oriented movements have been started in Hindu society and surprising changes have taken place in many aspects of India's social life. An example of M.K. Gandhi, the father of Indian nation, may be cited in this regard, who started 'Harijan movement' in order to chance the socio-economic conditions of untouchables, but unfortunately this movement too became a caste organization. Consequently, backward castes also got their own caste organizations as well as the organization of amalgamation of analogous castes.

From these facts, we may pass a concluding remark that caste-patriotism and casteism in India are more prevalent than nationalism and this reality is a threat and challenge to Indian national integration.

Caste in British India

Before the introduction of Britishers in India, it was clearly observed that the jurisdictions of the states were scattered, evety region (Ilaka) of a Chief or King remained separate from each other. Generally, there was emperor himself or his subedar above such chief and below them remained sardars. The jurisdictions or limits of regions of chiefs were always changing. This change in jurisdiction depended upon the armed force of chiefs or king and also upon the fact as to how firmly did emperor control over chiefs. Although, these jurisdictions used to change in time range, they created cleavages between the people of different states under the control of individual chiefs or kings. Hence, naturally such type of political system firmly checked the horizontal extension of caste-relations. In short, it can be stated that the political limits were determinant of some effective social extension, if not more, of every caste residing in the same region.[28] In a particular situation, these limits used to change. The meaning of this fact is that the cultural ties were frequently breaking across the existing political limits of that time.

The natural consequence of such political system which checked the tendency of horizontal extension of castes was that numerous of castes living in a particular region were intuited to cooperate each other. The occupational specialization of different castes also bound them to be inter-dependent as every caste depended upon other caste for its livelihood. Further, all the members of every caste were desirous of availing services, facilities, and advantages rendered by other castes; and it is clearly meant that there was antagonism in social relationship among members of a caste. This tendency of economic ties which cut across the caste barriers was supported by political and economic barriers. After the establishment of british imperialism, the castes became free from those bounds.

Due to construction of roads in whole India, introduction of communication such as Railway, Post and Telegraphs, cheap papers and printing press specially in local or regional languages, there emerged many caste organizations which were never so in past. The news of meetings (baithak) of caste-organization were communicated to the castemen spread at distant places through a post-card and when they felt necessity they assembled at a place from distant villages by train. Due to publication and easy availability of cheap newspapers, it was very simple and easy take to maintain, write, publish and send 'caste-journals'. The main objective of these journals was to encourage the interests of own castes. Generally, it is narrated that Railways and factories have weakened the food restrictions and rules of social intercourse but this argument is biased and exparte. Availability of papers on cheap rates counted much in writing caste disputes due to which rules, laws, and constitution, and old matters got permanent shape, which, in past, depended only upon the memory of old persons and which could be challenged at any time in case the same was forgotten by some persons. Many castes of Gujarat province have got their caste-constitutions published.

The impact of English empires on Indian caste system has been intellectually interpreted by eminent Professor Dr. Govind Sadashiva Ghuaye in the light of which the disruption in caste system in modern India, anomie, and tension may be clearly viewed and understood. Most of the people suppose that the major portion of authorities and powers which were conferred to caste Panchayats before the implementation of civil and penal codes by British Raj in Indian peninsula, became inherent in these codes. British authorities maintained a distinction between secular and religious matters.[30] In former, British principles of equal opportunity and equality before law were to be applied. Religious matters were to be left to traditional authorities. The principles of equality before law irrespective of caste were enjoyed by some peasants through judiciary but it does not mean that village/caste panchayat have lost their importance in rural India. Really, these two institutions have significant role in the solution of rural problems today also. It is true that British Raj have established and developed economic forces in the country, and consequently the traditional caste hierarchy has certainly been observed disrupted, but it is never meant that casteism has weakened. Surely, lower caste people have got opportunities to change their traditional occupations and earn more money but when they tried to claim their social status higher than other traditionally superior castes, they were opposed. Furthermore, when such claim of lower castes was accepted by higher or other castes, the intensity of opposition did not reduce. Instead of urging for an end of existing caste system, the lower caste new bourgeoisie always made frequent efforts that they might attain higher social status and people might recognize and welcome them.

There was the provision of mentioning caste of all individuals in 'Ten-Year Census' by the English, which encou aged social mobility. As a consequence the lower castes rich as well as poor persons began to address themselves by new and highly Sanskritized names.' Therefore, the 'Ten-Year Census' propounded by the British Raj may be viewed as a part of movement in the direction of 'higher-status-achievement' by lower caste people. The British Raj, from time to time, tried its best to provide financial assistance to the poor castes, but its benefit generally went to higher caste persons. Setting some defiled and degraded occupations aside, in almost all sectors of economic action, the higher caste persons were benefited. The Western education gave them ample opportunity to enter these sectors and the higher castes such as Brahmans, Vaishyas and Kayasthas were benefited of these opportunities upto maximum. Those castes whose socio-economic position was pre-dominant became doctors, engineers teachers, officers, laweyers and clerks. The Vaishyas availed the maximum commercial facilities provided by the British. In the then period, a new class of intellectuals comprising of these three castes emerged whlch took the complete responsibility of Indian National Movement on their shoulders. The higher caste persons were full of sentiments of nationalism, but they were also quite familiar with this fact that they were Hindus first. Specially Brahmans were more cautious and conscious towards this fact as they were highly privileged in traditional caste-hierarchy, and were enjoying special authority.

Where, on one hand, the matter of providing priority to

lower caste people by the British was humanitarian, on the other hand, its social impact was that the lower castes began to attract and orient towards the Britishers and cleavage between higher and lower castes was observed, which was specially manifest in Indian sub-peninsula.

Prof. Ghurye has written that Brahmans and Rajputs were mainly the model castes with highest frequency in Bengal defence before Indian Revolt of 1857 and they specially played pioneering role in the creation of revolt. Immediately after this, the idea in England was more emphasized that the high-caste personnel should be expelled out of defence. A commission was established under the headship of Lord Peal to reorganize India's defence in which statements were generated from high rank holding English authorities. After the collection of information, it was proposed to appoint the soldiers of different castes in inland Indian defence. It was also proposed that the different caste soldiers might generally be kept commingled, in each and every regiment. Just after it, the number of higher caste persons began to lower down gradually. Ghurye mentions that by this revolt, the English administrators began to realize the fact that it is essential to divide Indian people on the basis of caste in order to persist and maintain the smooth functioning of British Raj. The fact that Indian society was divided in many groups due to casteism was also known to the British administrators which was the main barrier in the development of national sentiments.[31]

The efforts of non-acceptance of superiority of Brahmans have always been witnessed by history of India but non-Brahmin movement of this century is different from previous movements not only from extension and influence point of view but also from principle point of view. The lectures that the leaders of non-Brahmin movement delivered at Madras during 1920-1929 seemed to be influenced by European liberal and reformative ideas.[32] Non-Brahmin leaders laid emphasis upon the fact that they were equally superior as Brahmins were, and they wanted that British administrators might give them primary treatment so that they might be universally recognized as superior rank-holders.

Non-Brahmin movement was a response of depressed class of Hindu society to the challenges of castes of Indian peninsulas in new contexts of British regime and Western liberal reformatism. One of the founders of this movement was Jyoti Rao Phule (1827-1889) of Poona, by caste Mali who established 'Satya Shodhak Samaj' (the Society for the Search of Truth) in 1873 which aimed at propounding the significant importance of human being and humanity without considering caste factor. He urged non-Brahmins not to call Brahmins for ritual acts. In 1848, he, recognizing the necessity of educational expansion of non-Brahmins, founded a branch to educate non-Brahmin boys and girls. In 1851, he opened next branch at Poona to educate untouchables. He put his demand forth for the representation of all castes in services and local institutions.

There was dominance of Brahmins in administrative and simple services in whole Indian continent except Kerala state till the beginning of first world war. It was objected that Brahmins were favoured and non-Brahmins were discriminated and when non-Brahmins emerged as dominant, they harassed the Brahmans who worked under them. Prof. Ghurye[33] has quoted a memorandum sent by Bombay government to the Indian Statutory Commission in 1928, by which it was learnt that in those schools of district board where non-Brahmans were in majority, they tried to expel Brahmin teachers without considering their academic efficiency.

Caste in Independent India

In no small measure due to the emergence of Western-style corporate caste bodies in both north and south India, the function of caste in Hindu society has radically altered in the last century, as many writers have endeavoured to show.[34] The Indian political arena today provides the setting for the most effective assertion of the interests of particular castes. It is also likely that caste interests and loyalties are the most influential factors in current Indian political life.[35] One half century ago, however, most caste groups were directing their primary attention to improvements in their social and economic status; indeed, political questions were barred from consideration by the important caste conferences and sabhas. Many of the caste associations which were initially organized for non-political purposes later assumed political importance, while retaining their earlier interests in social and economic advancement. In independent India, the rate of intensity and activity of caste loyalty and casteism grew in the same proportion in which the Indian people began to get the political power and authority from India government. The transfer of power started from British period and ended till constitution of Indian republic, in which every adult was given the voting power in every five year election.

Bihar Congress displayed rampant caste based competition in 1951 election. There were three main castes—Rajput (which was led by the then finance and food minister Shri A.N. Singh), Bhumihar (which was led by the then Chief Minister Dr. Shri Krishna (Singh), and Kayastha (under the leadership of Shri K.B. Sahay, the then Revenue and Customs Minister). It was learnt through Times of India (3rd January, 1952) that many congressmen were supporting many Nir-Dal contestants and frustrated congress leaders against authorised candidates. In short, Rajputs were supporting Rajputs, Bhumihars were supporting Bhumihars, and sometimes, denying the party-prestige and rules, Kayastha caste was divided into two factions out of which one faction was giving support to Shri A.N. Singh. Congressmen took the advantage of theory of casteism.

Some reformative steps taken for depressed castes in 1951 were reported in a newspaper[36] which aimed at improving socio-economic conditions of low castes through establishing an organization entitled 'Shosit Sangh' in Uttar Pradesh. This is an indication of the fact that caste consciousness in increasing in U.P. It is possibly predicted that competition grows more between Rajputs and Chamars for winning political power. Rajputs lived in rural areas in separate groups till recently, but now, they seem to be more curious in awarding the status of Rajput to other aspirant groups in order to strengthen themselves so that they may mobilize their political aim. Not only this, today every caste has become conscious of its caste-interests. Political leaders encourage casteism for their political victory and goal-satisfaction. The competition to avail socio-economic facilities in based on caste. Many educational institutions are established in the name of castes where the students of particular castes are admitted and given facilities. There are some other non-educational institutions where members of a particular caste are appointed. This results in frustration among other castes and caste-bitterness comes into being. There are many such temples which are established in the name of some particular caste members, they are run and represented by their managerial organization.

In 1947, when India realized independence, it was thought of abolishing Zamindari system in order to improve farmer's condition. Gradually, this idea came into force in whole country. Ultimately, Zamindari system was abolished in whole U.P. on 10th January, 1951 through an act. As a consequence of this step taken, some cases of robbery came into being in some parts of Uttar Pradesh, robbers were recruited from Thakur, Mallah and Gujar castes. Similarly, those Thakurs, Rajputs, and Gujars who were badly affected by Zamindari Abolition and Land Reforms Act of Uttar Pradesh began to rob in Middle India.[37] In 1952, these robbers frequently looted, fired and murdered untouchables of some villages of district Bhind and Muraina of Middle India. The editor of times of India described that the movement started by ex-landlords against untouchable was a 'class-conflict.'[38]

In modern India, casteism and caste-tension are rooted in different steps and measures taken and used by India government. The policy of providing educational, economic, political and social privileges to the members of a particular caste may be equalitarianism, but latently, they have created cleavages and gulfs between higher and lower castes. Today, every one thinks that privileges should be given by government not on caste base but on economic base. Even privileged caste members internally agree with this view. A pilot survey of post-graduate students of a Post-graduate College at Akbarpur of Faizabad district was conducted and the conclusion drawn threw light on the fact that even scheduled caste privileged students expressed their opinion that government might give economic advantages to all those who deserve on the basis of their poor economic background.

Social inequality is curse for human society. Steps are being taken in this regard. Glen and Johnson[39] have quoted from unpublished thesis of Lelah Dushkin (1957), *The Policy of the Indian National Congress Towards the Depressed Classes—An Historical Study*, the different Indian Government progrommes for the welfare of Scheduled Castes and Scheduled Tribes—"probably nowhere in the world is so large a lower class minority granted so much favourable special treatment by the government as are the depressed class of India." The favourable treatment begins with the Constitution of India adopted in 1950. The Constitution abolished untouchability and forbids its practices in any form (Article 17). Article 15 (2) further provides that:

> No citizen shall, on grounds only of religion, race, caste, sex, place of birth or any of them, be subject to any disability, liability, restriction or condition with regard to:
>
> (a) access to shops, public restaurants, hotels and places of public entertainments; or
>
> (b) the use of wells, tanks, bathing ghats, roads, and places of public resort maintained wholly or partly out of State funds or dedicated to the use of the general public.

In the Directive Principles of State Policy, a unique section stating the intentions of the policy but un-enforceable in the Court, the Constitution imposes upon the Government of India the positive obligation to assist the social educational and economic interests of backward classes (Article 46). The Constitution also contains several specific stipulations designed to aid the scheduled castes. Article 330 reserves 77 of the 521 seats in the Lok Sabha for scheduled caste persons.[40] Article 332 reserves seats in the State Legislative Assemblies for scheduled caste persons in proportion to their population in each state. Article 339 establishes the office of the Commissioner for Scheduled Castes and Scheduled Tribes with responsibility for over-seeing the progress of these social groups.

Parliament is specifically directed by the Constitution to implement Article 17 by making laws prercribing punishment for the enforcement of any disability arising out of 'untouchability'. In discharge of this directive, the Untouchability (Offences) Act of 1955 was adopted.

The Constitution provides provision of reservation of posts to appoint scheduled castes and scheduled tribes in Central and State Services. Under Article 35, having maintained the administrative capacity, the claims ot members of scheduled castes and scheduled tribes are kept in mind at the time of appointments in central and state services. 12.6 per cent of seats are reserved for them even in open competitions held for filling up the posts in Central and All India Services. In recruitments other than above cited competitive recruitment, the reservation is raised upto 16.5 per cent. Instead, some states have shown best efforts to enhance betterment in economic, educational and social conditions of scheduled castes and scheduled tribes. Some states have passed bill to provide special reservation to scheduled castes.[41] The bill involves different degree colleges and universities where some definite seats are reserved for them for admission in medical and engineering courses.

It is uncontroversial that caste system is most disturbing element.in establishment of equality-based society, but by acceptance of some particular castes as backwards, the existing caste discrimination may remain continued, and it may also be that this discrimiation shall prevail permanently. The strong and prejudiced sentiments of casteism today exhibit a naked dance in almost all spheres of human life. Today, untouchables realize a sensc of legal security in its fullest sense and law and constitution are with them. They immediately react when a high caste person tries to depress or assault them. Sometimes, it is observed that they try to threat higher castes behind the curtain of law, and in doing so, they succeed even. Whenever dispute on a reason or issue takes place between untouchable and higher caste members, the member of untouchable caste immediately burns his hut and rushes towards nearest Police Station to lodge F.I.R. against higher castes. These cases are frequently obvious in rural areas of Uttar Pradesh.

Because of the certain legislative measures, provisions of social security to the untouchables, and grace shown by Gandhi towards them, they have shown a tendency of caste awakening, awareness and consciousness. They have also got their organized councils to meet, discuss and solve their grievances. A detail discussion has been mentioned by Atal,[42] while studying the viliage Khiria which is located in the Sagar district of Madhya Pradesh. The district is an extension of Malwa Plateau. In the region of Khiria, the leather worker castes known by the generic term Chamar arranged a Sabha (meeting) in Ron village in the year 1955. The pamphlet issued at that time is reproduced here. It began with a couplet.

"Jisko Na Nij Gaurav Tatha Nij Jati Ka Abhiman Hai Vah Nar Nahin, Hai Pashu Nira Aur Mritak Saman Hai."

(One who is not proud of his honour and of his caste, is not a man; he is mere beast and like dead).

A translation of the pamphlet is given below:

Dear Charmkar (Raidas) Brethren,

By the grace of respected Bapu we are free, but social inequality still persists. This we have to eradicate by our good deeds so that we can progress and help the nation.

Today many problems face us. Our agriculturist breathren in the village do not accord us human treatment. We have difficulties in regard to cattle, labour, wells, tanks, etc.

The law made by the Government for our convenience is misused by the cultivators for their selfish interests. As a result, we poor labourers suffer in every way. If we make any kind of complaint, the responsible persons of the village prove it baseless and do not allow it to go further. Where there is a bidi industry, the cultivators close it down to compel us to work at reduced rates. If the poorer labourer does not go to his master without being called, he is troubled in many ways and as a result he takes refuge in the city and settles down there. Therefore, we request the village cultivators, clean caste Hindus (Savarnas), and the state government that, looking to our difficulties, they should treat us with kindness and sympathy as they did before and save the growing bitterness in the country and the deterioration of agriculture.

Our economic condition, the future of our children, should be directed towards the progress of our nation. If we were to obey the sermon of Gandhiji telling us to go back to the villages, we should be given facilities and opportunity to live in the villages. May our request not be seen with envy and may our interests be safeguarded in good faith. Our protectors (Rakshak) do not be our devourers (Bhakshak).

Raidas brethren are requested to contribute between Rs. 5 and Rs. 25 plus grain for the meeting that is to be held in Ron (Kumari) to make it a success and to fulfil their duties. This pamphlet was issued by the District Raidas Committee and signed by 21 persons.

On another occasion in February, 1959, (when Shri Jagjiwan Ram, then Railway Minister in the Central Cabinet, visited Sagar) a backward classes Conference (Dalit Varg Sammelan) was organised. Pamphlets announcing the conference were distributed in all the villages. In this pamphlet the Railway Minister was referred to as Chaudhri, a designation used for the Chamar.

In the political area, and in socio-economic life, the lower castes have shown a tendency towards reinforcing solidarity. In other castes the trend has been in the opposite direction; the sphere and degree of control of caste councils, for example, have diminished considerably. There are instances where caste decisions have been flouted and recourse taken to courts of law. For example, a caste known as Kachhi Kudariya in Khiriya village took a decision against an individual who was keeping a woman who was already married to another man. This decision was not accepted by him, so the other party had to go to a court of law. Another caste Dangi of a neighbouring village started bidi-making, which was objected to by the caste members from other villages. The former, however, ignored the decision and continued bidi-making. Now there is no objection to their making of bidis.

There are many social factors that are responsible for bringing about changes in the various frontiers of caste.[43] One of the most important factors is migration, particularly to urban centres, with a view to permanently settling down there. Migration from one village to another within the same region, either temporary or permanent, is generally governed by:

(i) family reasons or by,
(ii) the purchase and/or sale of commodities etc.

Moving permanently to a city is contemplated with a view to enhancing status by:

(i) change of occupation, and

(ii) educational achievement.

Frequent visits to urban centres are greatly facilitated by the introduction of modern means of transportation. Visits to the migrated families bring new ideas of some slices of the urban pattern of living to the village. The families who have left show a change in dress and in occupation, and do not appear particular about the observance of traditional commensal restrictions. In urban setting and during travel the villager finds his position much less strictly defined than in the village; consequently, he finds himself relatively free from the norms that govern his behaviour in the village. Also a frequent visitor to the cities and towns gradually begins to adopt urban norms and to aspire for a life of urban amenities. Such people act as carriers of new ideas and innovations which penetrate into the village life. Such people are prone to occupational shifts.

A different factor, namely, the favourable and sympathetic attitude of the government in regard to the weaker sections—the untouchable castes—also deserves notice and mention. This factor has not only succeeded in abolishing untouchability but has rather had the opposite effect of motivating some revivalistic trends among these sections. It has helped strengthen the ties of caste. Caste consciousness has increased in the past few years. Srinivas aptly remarks in a newspaper article. "The tendency to continue to think in terms of backward and forward castes is producing new tensions and difficulties which may become more intractable in the near future, Actually many powerful castes have a vested interest in backwardness, and they will resist any attempt to remove them from the backward category." The higher castes resent or show anger towards the move of backward groups. In this context, it may be mentioned that the efforts at strengthening caste are being exerted at the level of caste clusters. The fact of a common name or the fact of backwardness is exploited in the formation of a caste cluster based organisation. Such organisations are politically-oriented interest groups and do not, generally, aim at impinging on the endogamous frontiers. its sub-divisions. Where they do so, smaller sub-groups are merged to form a bigger unit with endogamous character and caste-consciousness.

A case of caste-prejudice, caste-consciousness, casteism, caste-tension, caste-conflict and cnste-war has been highlighted in a newspaper *Northern India Patrika* which reflects a high intensity and severity of caste-conflict between two backward castes Dhanuks and Yadavas in Piparia village of Bihar.[44] Caste-prejudices, so strong among the people of this area, have permented almost all facets of public life. The social fabric of the villages is woven around caste distinctions, and its economic structure demarcated by class divisions. Casteism is centuries old institution and governs traditional morality as well as an instrument of oppression. The big landlords of this area stroke the fires of economic and social discontent and prompt divisions in the ranks of the backward castes. The dynamics of inequality are inherent in this institution and the economic disparities have led to a polarisation in the caste structure conferring considerable social and political power of the landlords who use them to consolidate their advantages. They tend to monopolize government services and institutions and use them to consolidate their advantages. They tend to monopolize government services and institutions and use to exploit the poor.

The village economy here is dominated by the Bhumiyars who own most of the land. But land is useless without labour. The Yadavas and Dhanuks, which from a substantial portion of the population, are mostly engaged in the fields belonging to Bhumiyar community as agricultural labourers and share-croppers. A small segment of this section are marginal farmers forming the middle caste peasantry.

The landlord's influence and the power he wields extend the parametres of the village. With the wealth, he succeeds in buying the favour of the police, the judges and politicians.

His gains are greater if the men in the administrative set-up are those sharing his caste sympathies. Perhaps nothing is as strong in the rural polity as caste solidarity.

It is in this backdrop that the series of killings that have taken place in Piparia and its neighbouring areas have to be viewed. The incidents are no isolated exhibitions of chivalry or bravado. Neither are they expressions of sudden emotional outbursts. The unending spate of killings is the consequence of decades of exploitations of the landless and middle peasantry. Frustrations are an offshoot of social staticism and progress is retarted by the scourge of caste politics. Agrarian reforms meet stiff resistance. Where class oppositions obvious—as between the labourers and land-owning caste—other social ties slice through them. The average village is far more conscious of caste and tribe than he is of his economic class. The institutions of the law prevent equality before the law. The Yadavas of this reason earned the wrath of the power-wielding Bhumiyars with their entrance into the political process. This entry was facilitated by the breakdown of feudal relations in the rural economy. The top peasantry found themselves in a tight corner in which the middle castes had gained some economical strength following certain land-reform measures and the abolition of the Zamindari system. With economic power they started gaining political power. A rise in their strength evoked bitterness among the landlord castes. Antagonism between the two castes began to grow and the battle lines were firmly drawn.

Cultivable land in this belt is scarce as the region is made up mostly or diara territory whose soul is not conducive for any agriculture and is covered with wild shrubs and Khas grass. About one-fifth of the area is annually submerged by the waters of Ganges and cultivation on such land is at best seasonal. Land hunger in this area, which has a population of about 10,000, had reached acute proportions in recent decades. The Ganges here is capricious and each year eats away large chunks of land, leaving their owners homeless and destitute.

In other places they recede leaving silt banks of new fertile lands known as chars. Nearly a third of the Piparia region is char land which becomes the object of bitter and violent struggles for profession, invariably won by the richer castes, who can bring along the biggest contingent of armed relatives, supporters and thugs.

Many of the clashes between the Bhumiyars, Yadavas and Dhanuks in this region have revolved around the dispute of such char lands. There are strong indications that the recent kidnappings were a result of enmity between the Dhanuks and Yadavas over about 1500 acres of cuitivable land.

In Piparia and its surrounding areas, there is no organisation of the poor and landless peasants who are hard put to reap the profits that may accure from any agrarian reform. An attempt at building such an organisation had cost a 60 year old villager his life a few months ago. The poverty among lower castes is the greatest threat to their solidarity. Clashes frequently occur between the Dhanuks and Yadavas, which leave several dead on either camp. Such clashes are a result of competition with each other for the benefits—job or share crop land—that the rich increasingly control.

The administration is hard pressed to control the increasing crime in the region. The apparent failure of the police to arrest the criminals—only 20 per cent of the recent killings investigations yielded any arrests—had led to the loss of faith in the law enforcing agencies by the public. The local police strength is woefully inadequate and the ratio of the number of policemen to the population is perhaps the smallest in this region compared to the other areas of the state.

In modern rural India, due to advanced technology, mechanisation of agriculture, introduction of new scientific varieties of seeds, and use of chemicals in huger amount, lower caste persons have now begun to realize a sense of their economic advancement. Urbanization and industrialization have led them to tend to migrate towards urban and industrial centres. They are freely giving up their traditional occupations and trying to enjoy new and advantageous occupations. Some of them are being socialized through moder Western-oriented education and showing a change-oriented trend. Numerous of untouchables and low caste individuals in the country are becoming doctor, engineer, teacher, lawyer and clerk. Chitambar[45] has rightly pointed out that, "with the advanced technology, mechanization of agriculture, industrialization, and modern communication, disruption of the system and increasing conflict in traditional roles have occurred. Caste occupations and consequent roles are replaced by remuerative occupations, perhaps in nearby factories."

Chitambar further writes that "...the traditional caste system in India has in effect been disorganized through legislation, and while action on the basis of caste affiliation is illegal, the system is very much a part of the structure of rural society and the feelings of rural people."[46]

Social stratification may "set the stage" for inter-stratum rivalry and conflict.[47] Sich conflict may take various forms but in general results from an upthrust from lower strata to share equal rights with the upper strata and down thrust from upper strata to keep lower strata in their place. Such conflict frequently occurs when stratification systems are weakening, or in the process of disintegration being subjected to a variety of influential forces within society such as new ideologies, pressure groups, collective frustration of lower strata, and/or political and other interest groups. Examples of this phenomenon in operation are in the caste system in India, and in racial conflict in the U.S.A., South Africa, and countries newly independent or immediately prior to achievement of independence from colonialism.

I see, almost all villages of Akbarpur Tehsil of Faizabad district are disputed in one form or another. The population of all such villages is divided either in factions or in castes. Every faction or caste claims to be dominant. Similarly, every caste discooperates and looks down each other. Credit and obligation go to M.L.As. and M.Ps. in organizing lower castes against higher castes. These leaders encourage and provoke their castemen to pose their superiority and dominance thereby creating an environment favourable to recognize their influence at least within their own caste-communities. Sometimes, leaders from backward castes organize the whole backward castes against higher castes as a whole. This is also true in case of high caste leaders. It is reported that in situation of any problem, all castes utilize their leader's advice.

Numerous of examples of class conflict within caste system is contribution of modern era. There were mainly two issues involved in a conflict between Brahmans of Panjupur (Newada) and Bhars of Ashraf Patti (Newada) of Akbarpur Block. The first issue was related to the unnecessary dominance of Brahmans over Bhars and harassment; the second was related to the payment of lowest wage to the Bhars. Different sorts of harassments and assaults converted into physical coercion between the two. As a consequence, a Brahman was severely beaten and ultimately he was found to break his last. Likewise, in a village known as Rabipur Bahauddinpur, the main issue of conflict between Bhar and Kurmi castes was the village election of 1982, The election was fought by contestants on the basis of their castes. Due to casteism one of the contestants belonging to Bhar caste (Gaya Prasad by caste Bhar) was declared elected because of having largest size of voters within his own caste community. The other issues are described in detail in fifth chapter.

The economic independence of and occupational mobility among lower caste persons have created a cleavage between higher and lower castes. This cleavage has resulted in caste tension. I remember an instance in this regard. Somewhat educated Chamar of Hariharpur village in Varansi district of Uttar Pradesh used to respect the Brahmans when living in the village, but as he left the village for Bombay and got an appointment on a lower post in a hospital at Bombay and when he turned back to his village to pass some leave and holidays, this time a major change in his behaviour was observed and was found not doing 'pranam' to the Brahmans.

Although untouchability still persists in modern India as surveyed by All India Harijan Sevak Sangh[48] scheduled caste students experience frequent discrimination in University and College campuses, nevertheless, they have realized themselves as more protected and more secured. For example, in rural areas of Akbarpur in Faizabad district, Chamars experience themselves as more protected. In a village Hazipur Marui, there is tension between Chamar and Kurmi castes. The Kurmis of this area form a dominant group having more numerical strength, higher land holding, prosperous economic status ann politically active. They do not have prestigious attitude towards higher castes. They are closely organized and form a close knit net. During Janata regime (1977-80) they emerged as power group and did every act right or wrong wilfully without any hesitation because their caste representatives were holding power position at state and national level. Although Janta regime went to extinction in 1980 and Cong. (I) came in power in the same year, but the mentality of backward castemen remained as usual. In Hazipur Marui, there is inter-caste tension between Kurmis and Chamars over land issue. The land is under the possession of Chamars where they tie their cattles but Kurmis claim of their own. Against the super-imposition of superiority on the part of Kurmis, the Chamars face all the situation holding under the guidance of an young educated Chamar casteman who for all sorts of legal proceedings helps, supports and guides his men. The Chamars of this village do not afraid of any other caste as they consider themselves legally secured. They say, "Law is in our favour." By this it can be inferred that legal provision propounded by India government plays significant role in bringing confidence, boldness, enthusiasm and a sense of socio-economic and political security among the people of Chamar caste.

A somewhat similar situation is observable in village

Dhir Ka Pura (Sijhauliya) of Akbarpur Tehsil where down-trodden community does not respect Brahmans. Due to educational enhancement among the members of such community, they openly oppose the deeds of Brahmans. They do not like to tolerate misconduct, misbehaviour and assaults done by Brahmins towards Harijans (Chamars). Tension is seen more actute when higher caste persons fail to pay the justified wage to working Chamars.

A case of social tension between Chamar and Brahman castes is also tangible in villages of Akbarpur known as Govindpur and Ganeshpur respectively. The most surprising phenomenon which has occurred in these villages is the awakening of Chamars under the direction and leadership of a Brahmin named as Shri Mahadeo Tewari. There is also intra-Brahmin conflict in these villages and the whole Brahmin community is divided into three groups each trying to dominate others through the exhibitions of possessions like wealth and agricultural facilities as teachers etc. No speaking term continues among them or it continuously in a last magnitude. Shri Mahadeo Tewari is also a leader of a group consisting of depressed cases like Rajbhar, Ahir, Chamar (some families), Mallah (Kewat) (30%) and carpenters. The issues of tension between Brahmins and Chamars is given below:

(a) Refusal by Brahmans to lay land left for scheduled caste people;

(b) To capture the same land by Brahmins in the name of religion, to construct temples or to use the land as play-ground and to prevent the Chamars to use the same.

From the facts cited above it is obvious that the Chamars face deprivation and frustration as their needs remained blocked by Brahmins.

India's stratificatory system which was based on cooperation of its constituent units in past seem to be marked by cleavages among different strata at present. Against the predominance of higher caste members, there has emerged revenging attitude among those who fall on bottom. The higher caste persons who had enjoyed a prestigious life, still want to enjoy the same by ruling over lower castes without caring the changed circumstances in modern age. In modern age, untouchables and backward castes are more organized than the higher one. In such changed situation, Brahmans and Rajbhars of village Panjupur and Ashraf Patti (Newada) of Akbarpur Tehsil have met conflicting situation over the prestige points and wage issues.

REFERENCES

1. F. Max Muller, *The Sacred Books of the East* (ed.) quoted in N. Prasad, Jati, Vyavastha, Raj Kamal Prakshan, Delhi, 1965, p. 19.
2. *Loc. cit.*
3. *Loc. cit.*
4. *Loc. cit.*
5. *Loc. cit.*
6. *Loc. cit.*
7. *Loc. cit,*
8. *Loc. cit.*
9. *Loc. cit.*
10. *Ibid.*; pp. 19-20.
11. *Ibid.*; p. 20.
12. *Loc. cit.*
13. *Ibid.*, p. 21,
14. *Loc. cit.*
15. *Loc. cit.*
16. *Ibid.*, p. 22.
17. *Loc. cit.*
18. *Loc. cit.*

19. *Ibid.*, p. 22.
20. *Loc. cit.*
21. *Loc. cit.*
22. *Loc. cit.*
23. Kingsley Davis, *Human Society*, The Macmillan Company, New York, 1969, pp. 373-74.
24. S.K. Ayyanagar, *Some Contributions of South India to Indian Culture* in N. Prasad, *Jati Vyvastha*, 1965, p. 49.
25. S.M. Hunashal, *The Lingayat Movement*, Karnatak Sahitya Mandir, Dharwar, 1947, p. 99.
26. *Ibid.*, p. 96.
27. B.N. Dutta, *Studies in Indian Social Policy*, Quoted in N. Prasad, *op. cit.*, p. 48.
28. E.J. Miller, *Village Structure in North Kerala*, (ed) in M.N. Srivastava, *India's Villages*, Asia Publishing House, Bombay, 1960, p. 46.
29. G.S. Ghurye, *Caste and Class in India*, Popular Prakshan, Bombay, 1952.
30. For detailed study, please see the article of M. Glen and Sipra Bose Johnson on "Social Mobility among Untouchables" in Giri Raj Gupta, *Cohesion and Conflect in Modern India*, Vikas Publishing House Pvt Ltd., New Delhi, 1978, pp. 60-95.
31. G.S. Ghurye, *op. cit.*, pp. 175-176.
32. See the proceedings of the first provincial congress of the league of Non-Brahman Youth (Central) Madras and the administrative report of the league of Non-Brahman Youth, Madras, 1926-27.
33. G.S. Ghurye, *op. cit.*, pp. 175, 183.
34. *e.g.* M.N. Srinivas, "Caste in Modern India", *Journal of Asian Studies*, XVI, in which the author shows that strengthening of caste ties and the new functions, which castes perform are the result of British rule, in particular the expansion of communications and the development of a representative political system. See also F.G. Bailey, *Caste and the Economic Frontier*.
35. The new political importance of caste, operating within the limits of linguistically defined regions, has been unquestionably established in Selig Harrison's *India: The Most Dangerous Decades*. Harrison's conclusion night be tempered if read in conjunction with the ideas presented by Lloyd I, and Susan H. Rudolph in

"The Political Role of India's Caste Associations", *Pacific Affairs*, XXXIII, I, esp. p. 9: "The Caste Associaton brings political democracy to Indian villages through the familiar and accepted institution of caste. In the process, it is changing of caste. By creating conditions in which a caste's significance and power is (sic) biginning to depend on its numbers, rather than its ritual and social status, and by encouraging egalitarian aspirations among its members, the caste association is exerting a liberating influence... its successful assertions of privilege and rights are in many ways comparable to the extension of corporate feudal liberties which characterize the develepment of English liberalism. They are perhaps more truly indigenous gssertions of liberties than the liberalism of the northern Indian middle classes."

36. *The Times of India*, November 14, 1951.
37. *Ibid.*, November 14, 1951.
38. *The Times of India*, January 26, 1953.
39. M. Glen and Sipra Bose Johnson, *op. cit.*, pp. 69-71.
40. This provision was originally to last for ten years. It has been thrice extended for ten year periods and is now due to expire in 1990.
41. Report of Seminar on "Casteism and removal of untouchability", 1955, pp. 98-100.
42. Yogesh Atal, *The Changing Frontiers of Caste, op. cit.*, pp. 235-237.
43. *Ibid.*, p. 243.
44. *Northern India Patrika*, 1984, Monday, January, 23, p. 3.
45. J.B. Chitambar: *Introductory Rural Sociology*, John Wiley and Sons, New Yotk, 1973, p. 83.
46. *Ibid.*, p. 117.
47. *Ibid.*, p. 233.
48. *The Times of India*, 1983, Tuesday, March 29, p. 1.

3

A STUDY OF CLASS RELATIONS IN BENGAL VILLAGES

Class relations in society have their basis in one or more to the three great urges in human beings that make them thing and act. The urges are of self-preservation, of sex and of the ego. The order is noted in the Chanakya sloka "Save thyself first, they the wife and next wealth", for wealth offers prestige in civilised a ciety. In times of war, the urge in the soldier, and now in civil in as well, to save oneself is uppermost as the threat to life is urgen. In times of peace, among people secure in the ways of life, set plays an important role, and less than that, the ego. These two urges are however interrelated, as failure in the life of sex has far-reaching effect on the ego feeling. Apart from these urges in individuals, it may be noted that the belief based on actual imagined facts, that certain persons can promote, or destory well being of group leads to their higher ranking in society. If such beliefs come to be associated with a group which is hereditary the nature or to which access of outsiders is difficult, the group man be termed a class, generally a closed or semi-open class.

Ranking is not however essential to a closed or semi-open class. Among primitive Australians, there was a belief that of men had magical powers and thereby they could help or hand individuals. Hence old men were respected in such society and they ruled it. It was not a closed class as ageing and acquiring wisdom is not restricted. In this gerontocracy, the old men has the power to override the urges of sex of young men by appropriating as polygynous wives most of the mature young women of the society, tempering such practice by the rule of lending wives to young folk by customs like the piraurru in many tribes. Among our nomadic Birhors (now much less so) the question of food was important. The Lays or priest who blessed the nets to catch game at cqmmunity hunting had a higher rank among them. In the Middle Ages in England, France and Italy, the barons who had wives organised soldiers under them, compelled the commont peasan to accept them as overlords. For they could protect or despossible them. Another set of people, the bishops and obbots, and priests in general who held out hopes of a future world with a better life were also honoured. With these preachers of religion were also associated the belief in magic taken over from their earlier submerged culture.

Although our villages for many centuries have not gone through a feudal stage in the strict sense, nevertheless class divisons had been on somewhat similar lines. The local ruler or zamindar had more or less absolute sway in almost all matters. The central ruler, until in the modern age, cared nothing if the local baron with his armed men saw to the killing of a recalcitrant person who may not have deserved death. Very aften it were men of the Brahman and Rajput castes and in Bengal, the Kayastha caste who were such overlords. In addition, the Brahmans were needed for all ceremonies, of birth, of marriage and at funerals for welfare of the individual, of the family to which he belonged and in the society in which he lived. Even where pure caste Brahmans were not available, the people in the lower castc levels got their priests, sometimes an impoverished Brahman who had married among them, to serve their needs in these matters and termed them their Varna Brahmans. The secular power and the trem endous power of a hope and a belief in a better life after the poor way of living among the common people, led the latter to look up to and respect the rights of the class above them—above them in wealth and in secular and religious power.

With contacts from outside, not in conformity with the older sittitudes and practices, certain changes occurred. When the caste system first developed in India, the inhcrent inequalities in it must have led to conflicts. Mixed artisan groups and some slightly mixed elements of the earlier folk who benefited through cultural and acial contact with the new-comers of higher culture and organisation no doubt accepted the system willingly even as tribal folk a India in modern times accepted as benefactors and learnt to aspect the missionaries who started schools and hospitals among them and taught them new crafts and the technique of occupations to raise their standard of living. The bulk of the people, tribal character, could not in ancient times count on such large benefit and remained discontented. This happened more so in Bengal and especially Eastern Bengal where cultural conditioning to the caste pattern siarted a thousand years later then in Uttar Pradesh. As noted before, there were conflicts due to the inequalities, seed and economic in the caste system, and these found expressions social behaviour. These had to be suppressed and submerge. Socially, there was the accepted mythology that the Brahman to Ksatriya, the Rajput and Kayastha were the rightful upper classes of society. The suppressed tendency to oppose and overthrow to system is revealed in folk cults and folk literature of the lower groups. They extol the virtue of semi-tribal groups, of lowly position, and when the Moslems came to conquer and overthrow to upper classes, they equated the invaders to their own deities with thus avenged their wrongs. The conversion of the less culturals conditioned among these groups to Islam was a very easy stepts such circumstances. The mythology had been created that the deity and the saints and deity of Islam were similar. The large at practical reduction in social inequality resulting from convensions accelerated the change-over to the new society where the confidence was thus resolve In South India, Islam never held such sweet in most areas and there were militant groups who often ended after limited rule. But with the coming of Christianity and a more powerful and pre-vasive political rule, the same change-over to the conflict in the socially repressed semi-tribal folk occurred in certan areas where the inequalities in wealth and economic power were greatest.

I have noted these details about factors that lead to ranking and class formation in India and elsewhere and the changes the have occurred here in the past as they throw light on what is on curring at present.

Even in the last century our villages had their own lock authority based on their carlier practices. Such bodies were presied over by a Morol in Bengal, and a Prodhan in Orissa. Unlike the ryotwari villages in Central Provinces, for example, they were not however vested with any statutory authority later. One result of it was that their power decayed. An example may be quoted from among the Santals. Traditional leadership in Santal society vested in the village headman who with his assistants formed the More-Hor or panchayet who judged village cases. A group of villages were bunched together under the authority of a superior headman, the Parganait, who had his deputies, termed Des-Manjhi in some areas and Sakha-Parganait in Jhargram. The selection of persons:

(a) not of the traditional families as headman and Parganait by the Government of Bengal (before partition),

(b) the lack of secular authority among them, and

(c) the case with which social boycott may be evaded by running to mining areas, railway colonies and tea gardens led to the decay of the Governmental attempt to revive local leadership among Santals.[1]

There is no doubt that tribals are aware of the importance of pleasing Government officials in their own interest and they have become somewhat sceptical of their belief in their own deities. But both sets of beliefs coexist. The same may be said to be true of our own village folk. The older fears of magic and of curses, of the fear of offending deities persist and to this extent there is awe of the Brahman caste, except where something derogatory is known against a particular individual. But social and economic life in our villages have never been so simple or democratic as in a Santal or Korku village. The class division has been there for a very large number of generations. In a paper on methodology to study social change I have shown how changes in economic condition tends to alter social rules in a simple tribal society, it bring into existence in increased frequency, forms of ritual more in conformity with economic change. But in a saciety with class divisions, the prestige of following a practice in conformity with the higher strata so as to be more like them may lead to changes the do not fit in with altered economic conditions.[2]

An attempt will be made against these background details to discuss a limited amount of data regarding village customs which throw some light on present class relations therein. Emphasis will be laid only on Hindu caste groups.

Some fifty years ago and even earlier, from published modern records, it is apparent that a Brahman of acknowledged puris of descent occupied the highest position in village society in Bengal. There were other Brahmans of lower status, from some of which water was not even accepted by high caste Brahmans. Below the topranking Brahmans came the Vaidyas and Kayasthas of pure descent. Somewhat below them came craftsmen like blacksmiths potters, the spice merchants, sweetmeat makers and weaver. Brahmans accepted from them water, and food cooked in butty from them but not cooked rice. Below this middle level to the termed B came another group from whom water was not accepted by Brahmans;

among some of these castes, the touch also pollute. These will be referred to as the C group. At the earlier perimentioned it was the practice in a village to invite at marriages of festivals not only kinsfolk and castemen but also important may from all castes in the hamlet, of a large village or of the who village if of small size, provided means permitted it. It was usual to feed Brahmans and pure castemen on the same day (or evening but in separate rooms or areas. But both groups would be fed in the floor of an enclosed space with raised plinth where the house holder and his family usually took their food. But men of group C would be fed in the open courtyard. In the matter of seating on social calls, a Brahman, Vaidya and Kayastha would allot a seat to pure castes on the basis of caste precedence and prestige in the village, but generally a seat of an inferior kind. Men of group C were offered no seats but were expected to squat on the ground. As noted before the high castes of Brahman, Vaidya and Kayastha generally were much better off earlier than men of group C. In 1944, a survey was conducted by the present writer of about 500 villages selected on a random sample basis, in forty Sub-divisions of undivided Bengal, studying 18,000 family units. The structure of the family and holding of land (owned and share cropped) were among the details noted. An attempt was made to study in 1956-58 as many as 150 of these villages which fall in West Bengal south of the Ganges and Padma rivers *i.e.*, excluding the northern districts. Due to lack of funds only 24 of these could however de surveyed. These are distributed in thirteen subdivisions in eight districts of the area mentioned. Questions were asked about offering of seats at social calls, of feeding at marriage ceremonies, and also about economic holding and family structure.

It is evident from Table 3.1 and Table 3.2 that the High Castes and Pure Castes were much better placed than Impure Castes in 1939. As a holding of 5 acres and more spells comfort, we not that 13.3 per cent of the former were in that position as agains 1.1 per cent among Impure castes. In the later period also 21.3 per cent of the higher group were in this

TABLE 3.1

Distribution of Land by Acres for High and Pure Castes by Number and Percentage of Families

Period	*0-2 acres*		*2 to 5 acres*		*5 and above acres*		*Total families*
	No.	*Per cent*	*No.*	*Per cent*	*No.*	*Per cent*	
1939	319	66.5	97	20.2	64	13.3	480
1956-58	225	49.9	129	28.6	97	21.5	451

TABLE 3.2

Distribution of Land by Acres for Impure Castes by Number and Percentage of Families

Period	*0-2 acres*		*2 to 5 acres*		*5 and above acres*		*Total families*
	No.	*Per cent*	*No.*	*Per cent*	*No.*	*Per cent*	
1939	255	93.1	16	5.8	3	1.1	274
1956-58	234	86.7	26	9.6	10	3.7	270

TABLE 3.3

Owed and Share Corpped Land

Community	*Period*	*Cultivation mainly*	*Share cropping mainly*
Pure and High Castes	1939	214	60
	1956-58	292	40
Impure Castes	1939	52	32
	1956-58	32	51

position as against 3.1 per cent of the lower group. In counting acreage of land, the amount share cropped has been reduced to 50 per cent of the actual, although a little less than 30 per cent is spent on cost to cultivation. Hence the reduction should have been to a thing. Actually share croppers are in a worse position than the acreage shows. Among High and Pure Castes share cropping has been reduced to two-thirds of the earlier period, but among Impure Castes it has increased by fifty per cent. So their position is really would than the figures for land holding indicate.

Owing to the decrease in the rerlier religious feeling, presting of Brahmans has decreased. But the better economic position of the higher castes has led to greater influence of that group in view of the prestige of economic values at present. In the case of the higher group of castes, below Brahmans and the other two castes of nearly the same status, the decrease in prestige of Brahmans is apparent in certain social rules. On a tabulation of caste social relation data it was found that generally the social levels noted to A, B, C were generally accepted in the 24 villages, with some changes in a few areas. In the matter of ordinary social visits, the pure castes of stratum B were offered equal seats by the low group and they in their turn offered similar seats to the important. Bagdi caste where the latter were numerically strong. Brahmans, and also Rajputs in the few villages where the latter are found did not however offer equal seats to men of stratum C. Further Brahmans usually offered slightly inferior seats to men of stratum B and the latter expressed the view that if a Brahman came to their house, the visitor would get a better seat. It may be noted here that the field investigators were of the Vaidya and Kayastha castes, so there is no predilection on their part to favour Brahmans.

About feeding at marriage ceremonies, it was found that in some villages the Bagdis and people of their status (group C) were fed in raised verandahs like the people of group B but at a different time. Where however the Bagdis were numerically weak and the pure castes predominated and were well off they did not enjoy this privilege. Thus in five villages out of the twenty-four studied, the Bagdis and others of stratum C had to take their food in the courtyard and not in the verandah like pure castes. Castes even ranking lower than Bagdis, if invited, usually eat in the courtyard, if they come. In six villages the pure castes did not invite the castes of status C including Bagdis at marriages. Presumably this occurred in part due to the demand of the Bagdis to feed on the verandah like pure castes and opposition of the latter to concede to such a demand. In one area the Telis (traders) were important; there were no Brahmans or Kayasthas. The Telis refused to invite impure castemen at marriage. In another area Telis fed pure castemen in rooms but asked Bagdis to feed in the courtyard. Here there were Brahmans; but they did not invite Bagdis at marriage. It seems that in the village where the Telis are the dominant caste group, they behaved like Brahmans. In some villages in Howrah where there were industrial labourers and workers the usual pattern was followed. But in one suburban village in Howrah where there were Service men and also labourers in industry, some of the effects found in an urban area were found. Brahmans and other pure castes fed together in the same room, although the impure castes were fed separately. A survey of such social practices on evenly spaced sample blocks of a hundred Bengali Hindu families totalling eight hundred in Calcutta, ranging from Shambazar to Subodh Mallik Square and again in Bhawnipur shows that in feeding at marriage kinsfolk, friends and neighbours invited normally sit thgether without any separete arrangement, although some of the informants stated that it would be different in their village homes. In two villages where to Mahisyas had attained Group B status, they were fed in verande in Brahman houses though the Brahmans themselves were fed in rooms. This last practice of feeding Brahmans in rooms separate was followed by pure castes in all villages except the suburbe village mentioned above. It is clear that caste ranking is a strong in villages on ceremonial occasions, except where urban contact has modified it. Also some of the pure castes and partial raised impure castes are attempting to follow in the steps of the earlier Brahman orthodoxy. This was observed for example to Dharma worship by the present writer in a village in Ghati Subdivision. The Bagdis had there, as a result of local liberty influence, secured the right from Sadgopes and others to more the raised plinth of the floor where the Dharma deity will enthroned. But the Bagdis in their turn flatly refused to allow the Muchis to step on it. They had to remain outside the barring enclosing this level.

In former times the acceptance of social inequality, although there was suppressed resentment that found expression at difference suitable periods, had been more or less enforced by generations to cultural conditioning and lack of knowledge to permit deviation. At present primary education, though spreading slowly, is progresing much faster than under British rule. Further, prospere peasants and village traders seek to send their sons to secondary schools and colleges. With reservation of stipends and set for backward communities, and the changed conditions under in dependence, the other castes in villages are slowly breaking awe from the awe and respect towards Brahmans. The impure casts have felt the impact as they know that under the Indian Constitution, untouchability and disabilities due to it are unlawful. The feeling of equality supported by the low of the land has brought into the open the carlier suppressed resentment. It is finding expression in voting on caste lines for the State Assembly and Lok Sabha and this fissiparous tendency has been deliberately accelerated by the political parties including the Congress.[3] Within the village caste rivalries and the desire of impure castes to have equal rights with the pure castes have disrupted the unity that, on the surface, prevailed earlier in village festivals.

A new kind of integration on an economic level tended to grow up with the rise of peasant movements for better rights on land. Although some of the demands have been conceded by the State in independent India, there are big lacunae through which the land reforms are evaded by wealthy landowners.

Further, the constructive phase in villages, which was observed by the present writer during his tour of villages in 1944 to help relief and rehabilitation on behalf of a Relief Committee with a democratic base among the people, seem to have largely turned out to be a somewhat temporary phase based on the then acute conditions. There has not been much of a steady regular follow-up. Enquiries in some of the Community Development Project areas suggest this conclusion. There is an undue dependance on State help and less of self-selp, although it is alleged in some cases that self-help, criticism, and self-reliance is not much encouraged. Actually the weakness of Congress propaganda prior to independence and of Leftist propaganda after independence has been that there has always been more of demanding various rights and less of building up of something constructive. The present write who was an office-bearer in the Congress from 1923 to 1948 found it extremely difficult to make professional Congress workers to continue steadily to devote themselves to a civic or educational job not directly connected with politics. The same remark applies also to many Leftist workers, even though they can do a particular temporary job quite thoroughly. This type of example has a bad effect the work in villages as important political leaders tend to be up on a pedestal as a local leader in general, and their mod followed the working lives. It discourages steady unexciting route work, not immediately bringing recognition.

Actually there is a definite attempt on the part of a economically better off classes in villages to appropriate the leadership that had remained earlier on social, religious and economic grounds in the hands of the important landowners, mostly of a three highest castes Brahman, Rajput-cum-Kayastha and Vaide with an occasional spirnkling of some other pure caste ground Trade and commerce was not a favourite with this top group earlier times, and there seems to be a change in leadership villages to people that follow these latter avocations with success. There is unfortunately no detailed statistics on this point in the limited survey.

REFERENCES

1. Report on Santals by K.P. Chattopadhyay, Calcutta University—1946. Criticism has been levelled by a Government Department against reasons (a) and (b). It is alleged that evidence of success when traditional families are selected have not been noted in my Report. As no such selection was made in Bengal, no example could be quoted for that State. But the success in social matters in Mayurbhanj (Orissa) and the Damin-in-Koh where such selection was made is well known. The claim that Government officials gave support to their Parganaits is fantastic. The examples I have noted in my report show that officials gave judgements in blatant disregard of Santal customs. This was stated to be usual by a number of spokesmen at a conference I attended at Silda of headmen and Parganaits. In another note published in Jnan Vijnan I have mentioned how in a Garo area of matrilineal inheritance in the Garo foothills in Susong Zamindari, the Government official decided in favour of inheritance by a son, disregarding a daughter's righful claim as extremely foolish. These are examples of alleged Governmental support to tribal customs in 1945.

2. Some Approaches to Study of Social Change by K.P. Chattopadhaya, R. Kala Memorial Lecture, Gokhale Institute of Politics and Economics, Poona, 9.

3. M.N. Srinivas—Presidential Address "Caste in Modern India" in Section of Anthropology, Indian Science Congress, 1957. Ghurye has also noted such details and these are mentioned by Srinivas. The present writer saw caste voting in operation in West Bengal Assembly election in Midnapore in 1952 and 1957.

4

EVOLUTIONARY STATUS OF CASTE IN PEASANT INDIA

In "Caste as Social Process" (1967:354) I wrote that "speculations and inferences about the origins and development of caste systems in India and elsewhere are apparently immune to empirical verification, but the origins of particular castes, the conditions attending their origins, and the consequences of the occurrence of caste systems are not."

This paper contradicts the implications of that statement in that it addresses the place of caste in India in social-political evolutionary sequence. I will not document its origins but I will try to historically situate it, discussing its probable development and the implications thereof for peasant society in India.

I suggest here that caste (*jati*) originated as an intermediate stage between the pre-state, kin-based inequality of bands, tribes and chiefdoms (cf. Sahlins, 1968), and the non-kin class stratification characteristic of state societies (cf. Fried, 1960, 1967; Service, 1971, 1975). I emphasize the peculiar historical circumstances of the South Asian subcontinent wherein a great number and wide variety of pre-state ethnic groups or tribes evidently came under the control of early state-organized, stratified, conquering peoples of Indo-Aryan origin around 5000 years ago, in addition to earlier, less intense contact with the Indus civilization. Thereafter the indigenous small-scale ethnic/tribal groups were absorbed into the emerging larger and differentials in control over productive resources take procedence in rank assignment.

Gould suggests that occupationalization of work was the basis for emergence of stratification in the Middle East, and "...ethnic, political and military considerations more than technological elaborations..." (Gould, 1971:9) were its basis in sub-Saharan Africa. In India, it seems to me, it was quite clearly a combination of the two.

As essential feature of that combination, and one which makes caste (*jati*) comprehensible in evolutionary terms, is the fact that castes are kin groups; maximal and putative kin groups to be sure, but kin groups none the less in the very real sense that they are composed of people who are regarded as actual or classificatory affinal and consanguineal relatives. Castes are often said to constitute marriage networks and even have been *defined* as ranked marriage networks. The caste, of course, is made up of smaller kin groupings: extended joint families comprising one or more households and including several nuclear units and more than one generation in many cases; these in turn are organized into lineages, the lineages into sibs (or clans), the sibs often into phratries (*gotra*). The local village segments of these entities may be organized for many purposes including ritual ones in such a manner as to combine principles of lineality and locality in what Murdock has termed "compromise kin groups" (Murdock, 1949:66; Berreman, 1962). This makes of each caste a maximal kin group of considerable internal complexity not unlike that to be found in many tribes and chiefdoms. Included in such complexity is a kind of kin-based role ranking and "conical clan" ranking (cf. Sahlins, 1968:20-27 *within* my castes, similar to that found in unstratified societies, and which no doubt existed in these entities before they became the kin-strata—the micro-strata composed of putative kinsmen—which we call castes. But such internal ranking is not stratification as is the ranking of castes relative to one another. It has an entirely different character precisely because it is a ranking of kinsmen, with all of the matuality that implies, rather than a ranking of unrelated entities with the conflict of interest and lack of mutuality inherent therein.

While caste is like other pre-state social aggregates in that it is a kin-based group and inequality within it is organized and expressed in terms of kinship, there is this crucial difference: unlike the ranked conical clans found in the chiefdoms described by Sahlins, and unlike the ranked kin roles of bands and tribes (Fried, 1960, 1967), castes are in radical disjunction one from another. The members of one caste are not and cannot be at all related to those of another, and castes as social entities are not even putatively related to one another (except in the remote, metaphorical sense that the four or five major caste categories—the *varnas*—are said scripturally to have originated from different parts of a primordial body). They are ranked as disjunctive entities, not as kinsmen: caste ranking is the ranking *among* castes and is independent of whatever ranking occurs *within* them among individuals or roles.

In social evolution (according to Sahlins, Fried, Service and others) until emergence of the state, kinship and rank of hierarchy were inextricable: hierarchy *was* a ranking among kinsmen. With the emergence of caste in the process of state formation in South Asia these elements, kinship and hierarchy, were retained but were separated entirely. The hierarchy became a ranking among unrelated aggregates of kinsmen, and unrelatable ones at that because they were endogamous. In place of such principles as primogeniture and lineality to determine rank among kinsmen were substituted tribal or ethnic identity, as Karve insists, and occupations, as Gould insists, and a variety of other economic relations including most importantly control over land and other productive resources, access to productivity, income and wealth, accumulation of wealth, control over the labour of others, etc., as I here insist. In short, kin ranking was replaced by stratification, *i.e.*, the ranking of categories of people (in this case, categories regarded as being bound by kin ties); role ranking was replaced by class ranking. The result was the appearance of *kin-classes*, which is what castes in fact are, as they are also stratification emergent.

As I have suggested above, relying in part on Karve, the Indo-Aryans evidently brought ranked occupation—hence early class stratification—to India where it was assimilated to or imposed upon extant culturally distinct, largely endogamous groupings with perhaps a degree of economic specialization and interdependence within regions. The Indo-Aryans placed themselves and those they could not disposses of their land, at the top of the hierarchy, appropriating to themselves the land and labour of those they dispossessed. From this emerged caste: occupationalized, ranked, birth-ascribed, culturally distinct groups of putative kinsmen—the maximal kin group and the maximal extent of potentially egalitarian social relations (cf. Berreman, 1968)—with little choice but to do their assigned tasks and contribute the corvee labour, clientship, rents and taxes imposed upon them in the peasant economy of the emerging states.

Thus, the emergence of caste combined traditional principles of kin organization and ranking with new principles of the ranking of social aggregates according to economic as well as cultural (ethnic) criteria. It is for these reasons that I refer to castes as "kin-classes," or "kin-strata"—a stage in the development of stratification in South Asia's peasant society. This is a stage in which the ranked groupings and the rank system were regionally, even locally, specific and delimited rather than continental in scope; a stage in which the ranked, occupationalized, kin-based groups were perforce self-contained, local micro-strata.

The kin component of caste in India is expressed and

reinforced in every istitutionalized sphere of life. *Economically* it is to be seen in the sharing of occupation within family and caste, in the organization of work which therefore takes place within and among kin groups; it is seen in the "*jajmani* system," (cf. Kolenda, 1963), whereby inter-caste ritual and economic relations are carried out to a major extent through a system of patron-client relations determined not only by caste, but by family, and are generally passed down from generation to generation within the family. In the *political* realm, the kin basis for caste is expressed in the caste *panchayats* or governing councils: institutions which are made up of heads of families or lineages comprising the local caste segment, and it is usually the panchayat or combined panchayats of the economically and politically dominant high caste or allied dominant high castes (cf. Srinivas, 1959), which govern the village or locality, resolve disputes and punish offenders. In the *religious* sphere the pre-state-like kin basis for caste is manifest in the very nature of Hinduism wherein genealogy is endorsed by, and closely identified with, religious ideology. This is a religion which is oriented to the individual, the kin group and the caste as closely interrelated foci of supernatural belief and activity rather than to society, the state or humanity at large. There is no sacerdotal hierarchy or ultimate authority. The paramount priest for most Hndus is the family priest (*purohit*) who oversees the well-being of the family, family worship and life-cycle rites of family members; among the most important deities are household, family, lineage, sib (clan) and caste deities (often in that order), whose relevance to the individual is passed down within the family or more extensive kin group, or is acquired from affines who have come to live with members of those groups. Ancestors and the recently deceased are important foci of supernatural concern for family and kin; it is members of kin groups: family, lineage, sib (clan), phratry, case—in that order—whose members participate together in, and contribute to, life-cycle observances and other ritual events. (For case material on kin and caste in religion, see: Berreman 1972:95-98, 110, 126-133).

Gould has suggested that it was the Brahmin religious elite who, through processes he declines to speculate upon, had become powerful and influential in early India and '...invented and propagated a religion that sacralized the occupational order and occupationalized the sacred order" (Gould, 1971:10), thereby contributing in an essential way to the unique nature of the Hindu caste system. Hindu religion plays a clearly definable role in Indian society as religion does in other complex societies, rationalizing, justifying and obfuscating social, economic and political relations within the society (a role, incidentally, which can be and has been, played also by social science: see critique in Berreman, 1971). Gould attends to this role of religion (1971:10-12), but since I have come to it independently and from a somewhat different perspective over the years, I will briefly present my own discussion as follows.

Hinduism claims to justify the caste system by reference to a powerful and nicely articulated set of concepts: *dharma*, whereby one's religious/moral duty is to fulfil to the best of one's ability the obligation inherent in the status to which one has been born—especially caste (and sex) status. One should not strive for another status even if one were to be successful in fulfilling it. *Karma* refers to the process whereby one reaps the consequences of one's actions as just desserts in the form of reward for performing dharma and punishment for violating it. The concept of *purity and pollution* includes both acquired pollution (whose removal brings relative purity), and inborn, inherent degrees of purity-pollution. The latter accounts for differences in the intrinsic worth among castes by which they are said to be ranked. The degree of birth-ascribed purity-pollution is tied directly to occupation, diet, ritual behaviour, religious and secular prerogatives, life-syle and other aspects of caste dharma. It forms a perfect circle: inborn purity or pollution requires specified behaviours which have inevitable consequences including degree of inborn purity or pollution in the next life. Purity-pollution is the rationale for caste rank, hence for most of caste members' social, economic, political and religious experiences and opportunities. In this way, those who are perpetrators and beneficiaries of the purity-pollution hierarchy, and those who are its victims are each enjoined to behave as they do and are rewarded and punished accordingly: in this life for being born pure or impure, respectively, and in the next life for the extent to which one has fulfilled (or acquiesced in) one's *dharma*. Under this concept it is specifically decreed that high castes (who own most of the land) must not till the soil nor work with their hands, while it is the low (and landless) who are allowed to, and therefore must do so. The fundamental division of India's agricultural, peasant society into land owners and land workers is thus enjoined and reinforced by ideology and divine sanction. Deviation is, of course, as common in this as in other commandments from on high.

Reincarnation, to which reference has been made immediately above, is a basic tenet of Hinduism which defines the nature and locus of one's *karma*—of the just desserts that follow from the way in which one's *dharma*—has been fulfilled or unfulfilled. In the next life, one is rewarded or punished, in effect, by rebirth in a higher or lower, happier or more miserable caste, life-form or situation. *Maya*, commonly translated as "cosmic illusion," is the basic Hindu idea that the suffering and rewards of daily life and earthly existence are in any case illusory and do not be made matters of significant concern. Earthly desires, comforts, possessions, pleasures and even survival are irrelevant and unworthy goals in an ultimate sense. Release from this mortal coil of birth, striving, and rebirth, is all that really matters. The many, of course, suffer in the painful illusions of life, while the very few reveal in the delightful illusions accessible to and reversed for them at the expense of the rest. It is worth noting that it is the few, the elites—not the masses—who enunciate and most ardently advocate this credo, a credo akin to the Christian "the meek shall inherit the earth" (in Hinduism, the meek shall advance on the path to release *from* the earth). Those advocates are in a position to wield the power to enforce the credo, which clearly is not designed to foment or condone revolution or even social mobility.

In short, Hinduism decrees that whatever one's lot in life, it is earned, deserved, irreversible and ultimately irrelevant. What is relevant is that one fulfils one's *dharma* so as to move toward person salvation, the highest goal. Birth is the basis for caste membership and therefore for caste *dharma*. Birth, in turn, is defined by parentage: people of ritually equivalent parentage are themselves ritually and socially equivalent, *i.e.*, of the same caste. For these reasons kin relations are central to the religious-ideological rationale for caste stratification as well as to its more pragmatic aspects. That rationale is advocated primarily by the high-caste beneficiaries of the system. Those whose exploitation it is designed to justify consistently see their status as the result of historical circumstances rather than divine will (Berreman, 1971; cf. Berreman, 1972:209, 253-256). Power is the mechanism by which the system is enforced—the ideology realized—for power and privilege are congruent in caste as in other forms of social stratification.

Summary and Significance

The relevance of this discussion for an understanding of caste in the evolution of peasant society in India may now be summarized, enumerating some points which have been made explicitly or implicitly above:

1. The caste system in India originated and persisted as a from of institutionalized inequality in which ethnically distinct social entities were absorbed into a status and economic hierarchy as ranked, endogamous, birth-ascribed, kin-based, occupational groups—kin strata, in effect—in order to provide land, labour, rent and taxes for the surplus agricultural production organized by and for the benefit of those who acquired their land through the exercise of military, administrative and economic power.

2. The kin-based caste system benefited the elites by effectively fractionating the rest of the society, preventing or inhibiting the development of class consciousness and class mobilization by the membership exclusiveness and the mutually exclusive vested interests (status interests resulting in status competition) of the castes as localized, kin-based, ranked groups. Caste endogamy prevented the formation of caste alliance through marriage. The kin- and caste-based nature of economic relations, political relations and supernaturally and ideologically endorsed relations of all sorts, reinforced this fractionation, mutual suspicion, competition and hence the vulnerability of the landless and labouring castes to those who controlled land and labour. It thereby minimized the likelihood of multi-caste organization for change.

3. Narrow occupationalization and minimal security of livelihood served this function as well. Non elite castes held little significant control over productive resources including land and occupation, and therefore was unable to make a living except through the exchange of their labour for elite-controlled goods, at rates determined almost entirely by the elites. There was no prodoction for use sufficient to support the landless castes, who were inevitably clients dependent upon the patronage of the landed castes.

4. The congruity on kin, caste, occupation and ethnicity prevented both individual upward mobility and horizontal (occupational and geographic) mobility. In the case of the latter, there was little open social space of occupational space into which mobile persons or groups could move because kin- and caste-based patron-client relations (the *jajmani* system) assured that in any locality there were already established occupational role occupants with firm ties by family and caste to patron families and castes. In the case of vertical mobility, the congruity of caste and occupation

> in social ranking, together with birth-ascription of both, prohibited mobility. Where horizontal mobility did occur, it was usually at the behest of the elites who simply replaced a client group (often for recalcitrance). When vertical mobility did occur, it was a result of changed circumstances which enabled a caste to make good the claim which every low caste makes that in fact it is a high caste unjustly maligned or misidentified as to its ancestrally determined identity—circumstances such as a new-found occupational monopoly on an essential service; universal adult franchise among a numerically large, low-status group; access to legal or legislative power or to powerful allies; new sources of livelihood independent of traditional caste controls; etc. In the case of either kind of mobility, power is the mechanism for change; ideology is marshalled to justify the change, *i.e.*, a caste does not move up, its "true" indentity is simply discovered and acted upon.

In sum, the Indian caste system comprises a unique congruity among kin, status, rank, occupation, class, ethnicity (culture), and power, creating a powerful, involute and total system of stratification—a system well suited to agricultural production under early state organization with a sharp distinction between owners and non-owners of major productive resources. But it is *not* well suited to complex, technologically rapidly changing, urban, industrial organization. As a result of the emergence of the latter kind of society, we see changes in Indian caste toward, on the one hand a familial and narrowly ritual phenomenon, and on the other a more broadly defined vehicle for political and economic mobilization in new occupations, technologies, bureaucracies and politics. As urban migration offers new arenas for mobilization in pursuit of shared interests, traditional localized caste status-striving tends to get left behind in the village (where, let it not be forgotten, 80 per cent of the population still lives). But the analysis of changing caste in contemporary India is another topic, which is beyond the scope of the present discussion.

Let me close with the observation that India is perhaps unique among peasant societies in the degree and consistency with which even the humblest of its peasant agriculturists—those with even the slightest interest in (*i.e.*, control over) land—have at their command an underclass of lower castes who perform agricultural labour and service occupations in support of the agriculturists. To a very major extent, owner and worker, exploiter and exploited, identify their economic interests with their caste interests, and their caste interests with family interests. If family was the first form of class consciousness in Europe, as Rayna Rapp has suggested (Rapp, 1978), than I would suggest that caste was the form that consciousness was molded into early in the history and development of peasant India. Like family, partly because it is in fact an extension of family, caste has been a persistent and portentous form of social organization and consciousness in the evolution of India's peasant and emerging post-peasant society.

Post-Script

I have suggested here that caste in India is an archaic form of social stratification. It also seems to many observers to be becoming an increasingly anachronistic one with the emergence of industrialization, capitalism, democratic self-government, mass communications, secularism in many spheres, and the striving by some castes, allied castes and caste-categories to metamorphose themselves into activist class groupings.

In the world at large during the past 30 years we have witnessed increasing disparities between rich and poor both among nations and, within nations, among social strata and among communal entities (ethnic groups, races, castes, language groups, religions, etc). Monumental confrontations and reactive repressions have resulted, arising from the economic, political and social competition and conflicts of interest inherent in such disparities. Increasingly these conflicts have been carried out through the mobilization of social aggregates on the basis of shared "primordial sentiments" (cf. Shils, 1957). These aggregates are communal groups of various sorts which, by their very definition and recruitment are pre-formed, self-aware, bounded, interests and action groups. The consciousness of common interests on the part of their members, unlike that of the members of class categories, need to be created or raised in order to mobilize them because such consciousness is the essence of their existence. That is, conflicts that are basically economic and political—conflicts of class interest—are assimilated to, and expressed as, conflicts that are cultural, *i.e.*, communal. The conflicts are perceived by individuals through the lens of sentiments shared by their membership group(s) and therefore are responded to in terms of group self-interest rather than in terms of the interests of class or other analytic categories. Such conflicts seem to be increasing rather than diminishing in frequency, intensity and devastation, although the preponderance of economic and military power in the hands of the privileged, so long as it remains or is believed by most of the population to remain, makes remote the likelihood of widespread mobilization for change toward diminution of the inequality that generates the conflict. The locus and definition of such power can and does change, however, when it is too widely and oppressively exercised, as several recent regimes have discovered to their dismay.

In this context caste in India, like a number of other characteristics sometimes described as symptoms of the backwardness of that troubled nation, may in fact anticipate the future of an increasingly fractionated and inegalitarian world, and of other inereasingly divided nations in that world. In short, the trends we see today in Indian caste and its relationship to class, may represent our future more accurately even that we have supposed it might represent a contemporary (and temporary) survival of our pre-feudal and feudal past. As castes redefine their roles and rationales, as they mobilize, compete and conflict in pursuit of their interests in an increasingly industrialized state fully involved in the world economy, we perhaps see a foreshadowing of the form competing interest-group processes will take within and among nations on a worldwide scale. If so, it is a sobering prospect, deserving careful attention and analysis.

REFERENCES

Berreman, Gerald D. 1960 Caste in India and the United States. *The American Journal of Sociology* 66:120-027.

——1962 Sib and Clan among the Pahari of North India. *Ethnology* 1:574-528.

——1967 Caste as Social Process. *Southwestern Journal of Anthropology* 23: 351-370.

——1968 Caste—The Concept. In *International Encyclopedia of the Social Science* (D. Sills, ed.). New York: Macmillan and Free Press. Vol. 2, pp. 338-339.

——1971 The Brahmanical View of Caste. *Contributions to Indian Sociology* (New Series) No. V: 18-25.

——1972 *Hindus of the Himalayas, Ethnography and Change* (Second edition). Berkeley: University of California Press. (Also: First Edition, 1963)

——1978 Scale and Social Relations. *Current Anthropology* 19:225-245.

Fried, Morton 1960 On the Evolution of Social Stratification and the State. In *Culture in History: Essays in Honor of Paul Radin* (S. Diamond, ed.). New York: Columbia University Press, pp. 713-731.

——1967 *The Evolution of Political Society*. New York: Random House.

Ghurye, G.S. 1952 *Caste and Class in India*. New York: Philosophical Library.

Gould, Harold 1971 *Caste and Class: A Comparative View*. Reading, Mass.: Addison-Wesley Modular Publications.

Isaacs, Harold R. 1975 *Idols of the Tribe*. New York: Happer and Row.

Karve, Irawati 1961 *Hindu Society—An Interpretation*. Poona: Deccan College.

Kolenda, Pauline M. 1963 Toward a Model of the Hindu Jajmani System. *Human Organization*: 22: 11-31.

Murdock, George P. 1949 *Social Structure*, New York: Macmillan.

Rapp, Rayna 1978 Peasants into Proletarians from the Household Out. Paper prepared for session on "Social Anthropology of Peasantry," Post-Plenary Session of the Xth International Congress of Anthropological and Ethnological Sciences. Lucknow, December 19-21, 1978.

Sahlins, Marshall 1968 *Tribesmen*. Englewood Cliffs, New Jersey: Prentice-Hall.

Service, Elman R. 1971 *Primitive Social Organization* (Second edition). New York: Random House.

1975 *Origins of the State and Civilization*. New York: W.W. Norton.

Shills, Edward A. 1957 Primordial, Personal, Sacred and Civil Ties. *The British Journal of Sociology* 8; 130-145.

Srinivas, M.N. 1959 The Dominant Caste in Rampura. *American Anthropologist* 61: 1-16.

5

WOMAN, CASTE AND SOCIETY

The Hindu religion commands;

"Women must be honored and adorned by their fathers, brothern, husbands, and brothers-in-law, who desire their own welfare."

"Where women are honored, there the gods are pleased; but where they are not honored, no sacred rite yields rewards."

"Where the female relations live in grief, the family soon wholly perishes; but that family where they are not unhappy ever prospers."

"The houses on which female relations, not being duly honored, pronounce a curse, completely, as if destroyed by magic."

"Hence men who seek their own welfare, should always honor women on holidays and festivals with (gifts of) ornaments, clothes and dainty food."

"In that family where the husband is pleased with his wife, and the wife her husband, happiness will assuredly be lasting."

"For if the wife is not radiant with beauty, she will not

attract her husband; but if she has no attractions for him, no children will be born."

"If the wife is radiant with beauty, the whole house is bright; but if she is destitute of beauty, all will appear dismal."—*Manu*, iii., 55-62

These commandments are very significant. Our Aryan Hindus did, and still do honor woman to a certain extent. The honor bestowed upon the *mother* is without parallel in any other country. Although the woman is looked upon as an inferior being, the mother is nevertheless the chief person and worthy to receive all honor from the son. One of the great commandments of the Hindu Scriptures. is, "Let thy mother be to thee like unto a god."*

*My readers would perhaps be interested to see these commandments; they are as follows: "After having taught the Veda, the teacher instructs the pupil:

Say what is true.

Do thy duty.

Do not neglect the study of the Veda.

After having brought to thy teacher his proper reward, do not cut off the line of children! (*i.e.* Do not remain unmarried).

Do not swerve from the truth.

Do not swerve frem duty.

Do not neglect what is useful.

Do not neglect the learning and teaching of the Veda.

Do not neglect the sacrificial works due to the gods and fathers.

Let thy mother be to thee like unto a god.

Let thy father be to thee like unto a god.

Let thy teacher be to thee like unto a god,

Let thy guests be to thee like unto a god.

Whatever actions are blameless those should be regard, not others.

Whatever good works have been performed by us should be observed by thee, not others."—***Taittiriya Upanishad***, Valli, i. An. xi, I,

The mother is the queen of the son's household. She wields great power there, and is generally obeyed as the head of the family by her sons and by her daughters-in-law.

But there is a reverse side to the shield that should not be left unobserved. This is best studied in the laws of Manu, as all Hindus, with a few exceptions believe implicitly what that law-giver says about women:

> "It is the nature of women to seduce men in this world; for that reason the wise are never unguarded in the company of females."
>
> "For women are able to lead astray in this world not only a food, but even a learned man, and to make him a slave of desire and anger."—*Manu*, ii., 213-214.
>
> "Women do not care for beauty, nor is their attention fixed on age; thinking 'it is enough that he is a man,' they give themselves to the handsome and to the ugly."
>
> "Through their passion for men, through their mutable temper, through their natural heartlessness, they become disloyal towards their husbands, however carefully they may be guarded in this world."
>
> "Knowing their disposition, which the Lord of creatures laid in them at the creation, to be such, every man should most strenuously exert himself to guard them."
>
> "When creating them, Manu allotted to women a love of their bed, of their seat and of ornament, impure desires, wrath, dishonesty, malice and bad conduct."
>
> "For women no sacramental rite is performed with sacred texts, thus the law is settled; women who are destitute of strength and destitute of the knowledge of Vedic texts, are as impure as falsehood itself, that is a fixed rule."—*Manu* ix., 14-18.

Such is the opinion of Manu concerning all women; and all men with more or less faith in the law regard women, even though they be their own mothers, "as impure as falsehood itself."

"And to this effect many sacred texts are chanted also in the Vedas, in ord r to make fully known the true disposition of women; hear now those texts which refer to the expiation of their sins."

"It my mother, going astray and unfaithful, conceived illicit desires, may my father keep that seed from me,' that is the scriptural text."—*Manu* ix., 19, 20.

Such distrust and such low estimate of woman's nature and character in general, is at the root of the custom of seclusion of women in India. This mischievous custom has greatly increased and has become intensely tyrannical since the Mahomedan invasion; but that it existed from about the sixth century, B.C., cannot be denied. All made relatives are commanded by the law to deprive the women of the household of all their freedom:

"Day and night women must be kept in dependence by he males of their families, and if they attach themselves to sensual enjoyments, they must be kept under one's control."

"Her father protects her in childhood, her husbond protects her in youth, and her sons protect her in old age; a women is never fit for independence."—*Manu* ix., 2, 3.

"Women must particularly be guarded against evil inclinations, however trifling they may appear; for if they are not guarded; they will bring sorrow on twc families."

"Considering that the highest duty of all castes, even weak husbands must strive to guard their wives."—*Manu* ix., 5, 6.

"No man can completely guard women by force; but they can be guarded by the employment of the following expedients:"

"Let the husband employ his wife in the collection and expenditure of his wealth, in keeping everything clean, in the fulfilnent of religious duties, in the prepaıation of his food, and in looking after the household utensils."—*Manu* ix., 10, 11.

Those who diligently and impartially read Sanscrit literature in the original, cannot fail to recognize the law-giver Manu as one of those hundreds who have done their best to make woman a hateful being in the world's eye. To employ her in housekeeping and kindred occupations is though to be the only means of keeping her of mischief, the blessed enjoyment of literary culture being denied her. She is forbidden to read the sacred scriptures, she has no right to pronounce a single syllable out of them. To appease her uncultivated, low kind of desire by giving her ornaments to adorn her person, and by giving her dainty food together with an occasional bow which costs nothing, are the highest honours to which a Hindu woman is entitled. She, the loving mother of the nation, the devoted wife, the tender sister and affectionate daughter is never fit for independence, and is "as impure as falsehood itself." She is never to be trusted; matters of importance are never to be committed to her.

I can say honestly and truthfully, that I have never read any sacred book in Sanscrit literature without meeting this kind of hateful sentiment about women. True, they contain here and there a kind word about them, but such words seem to me a heartless mockery after having charged them, as a class, with crime and evil deeds.

Profance literature is by no means less severe or more respectful towards women. I quote from the ethical teachings, parts of a catechism and also a few proverbs:

Q. What is cruel?

A. The heart of a viper.

Q. What is more cruel than that?

A. The heart of a woman.

Q. What is the cruelest of all?

A. The heart of a sonless, penniless widow.

A catechism on moral subjects written by a Hindu gentleman, of high literary reputation says:

Q. What is the chief gete to hell?

A. A woman.

Q. What bewitches like wine?

A. A woman.

Q. Who is the wisest of the wise?

A. He who has not been deceived by women who may be compared to malignant fiends.

Q. What are fetters to men?

A. Women.

Q. What is that which cannot be trusted?

A. Women.

Q. What poison is that which appears like nectar?

A. Women.

Proverbs

"Never put your trust in women."

"Women's counsel leads to destruction."

"Woman is a great whirlpool of suspicion, a dwellingplace of vices, full of deceise a hindrance in the way of heaven, the gate of hell."

Having fairly illustrated the popular belief about woman's nature, I now proceed to state woman's religion. Virtues such as truthfulness, forbearance, fortitude, purity of heart and uprightness, are common to men and women, but religion, as the word is commonly understood, has two distinct natures in the Hindu law; the masculine and the feminine. The masculine religion has its own peculiar duties, privileges and honours. The feminine religion also has its peculiarities.

The sum and substance of the latter may be given in a few words:—To look upon her husband as a god, to hope for salvation only through him, to be obedient to him in all things, never to covet independence, never to do anything but that which is approved by law and custom.

"Hear now the duties of women," says the law-giver, Manu:

> "By a girl, by a young woman, or even by an aged one, nothing must be done independently, even in her own house."
>
> "In childhood, a female must be subject to her father, in youth, to her husband, when her lord is dead, to her sons; a woman must never be independent."
>
> "She must not seek to separate herself from her father, husband, or sons; by leaving them she would make both her own and her husband's families contemptible."
>
> "She must always be cheerful, clever in the management of her household affairs, careful in cleaning her utensils, and economical in expenditure."
>
> "Him to whom her father may give her, or her brother with the father's permission, she shall obey as long as he lives, and when he is dead, she must not insult his memory."
>
> "For the sake of procuring good fortune to brides, the recitation a benedictory texts, and the sacrifice of the Lord of creatures are used at weddings; but the betrothal by the father or guardian is the cause of the husband's dominion over his wife."
>
> "The husband who wedded her with sacred texts, always gives happiness to his wife, both in season and out of season, in this world and in the next."
>
> "Though destitute of virtue, or seeking elsewhere, or devoid of good qualities, yet a husband must be constantly worshipped as a god by a faithful wife."
>
> "No sacrifice, no vow, no fast must be performed by women

apart from their husbands; if a wife obeys her husband, she will for that reason alone, be exalted in heaven."

"A faithful wife, who desires to dwell after death with her husband, must never do anything that might displease him who took her hand whether he be alive or dead."—*Manu* v., 147-156.

"By violating her duty towards her husband, a wife is disgraced in this world, after death she enters the womb of a jackal, and is tormented by diseases, the punishment of her sin."

"She who, controlling her thoughts, words and deeds, never slights her lord, resides after death with her husband in heaven, and is called a virtuous wife."

"In reward of such conduct, a female who controls her thoughts, speech and actions, gains in this life highest renown, and in the next world a place near her husband." —*Manu* v., 164-166.

Marital Rights

"He only is a perfect man who consists of three persons united, his wife himself and his offspring; thus says the Veda, and learned Brahmanas propound this maxim likewise, 'The husband is declared to be one with the wife." —*Manu* ix., 45.

The wife is declared to be the "marital property" of her husband, and is classed with "cows, mares, female, camels, slave-girls, buffalo-cows, she-goats and ewes."—(See Manu ix., 48-51.)

The wife is punishable for treating her husband with aversion:—

"For one year let a husband bear with a wife who hates him; but after a lapse of a year, let him deprive her of her property and cease to live with her."

"She who shows disrespect to a husband who is addicted to some evil passion, is a drunkard, or diseased, shall be deserted for three months, and be deprived of her ornaments and furniture."—*Manu* ix., 77, 78.

"She who drinks spirituous liquor, is of bad conduct, rebellious, diseased, mischievous or wasteful, may at any time be superseded by another wife."

"A barren wife may be superseded in the eighth year, she whose children all die in the tenth, she who bears only daughters in the eleventh, but she who is quarrelsome without delay."—*Manu* ix., 80, 81.

"A wife who, being superseded, in anger departs from her husband's house, must either be instantly confined or cast off in the presence of the family."—*Manu* ix., 83.

"Though a man may have accepted a damsel in due form, he may abandon her if she be blemished or diseased, and if she have been given with fraud."—*Manu* ix., 72.

But no such provision is made for the woman; on the contrary, she must remain with and revere her husband as a god, even though he be "destitute of virtue, and seek pleasure elsewhere, or be devoid of good qualities, addicted to evil passion, fond of spirituous liquors or diseased." and what not!

How much impartial justice is shown in the treatment of womankind by Hindu law, can be fairly understood after reading the above quotations. In olden times these laws were enforced by the community; a husband had absolute power over his wife; she could do nothing but submit to his will without uttering a word of protest. Now, under the so-called Christain British rule, the woman is in no better condition than of old. True, the husband cannot as in the golden age, take her wherever she may be found, and drag her to his house, but his absolute power over her person has not suffered in the least. He is now bound to bring suit against her in the courts of justice to claim his "marital property," if she he unwilling to submit to him by any other means.

A near relative of mine had been given in her childhood in marriage to a boy whose parents agreed to let him stay and be educated with her in her own home. No sooner however, had the marriage ceremony been concluded than they forgot their agreement; the boy was taken to the home of his parents where he remained to grow up to be a worthless dunce, while his wife through the kindness and advanced views of her father, developed into a bright young woman and well accomplished.

Thirteen years later, the young man came to claim his wife, but the parents had no heart to send their darling daughter with a beggar who possessed neither the power nor the sense to make an honest living, and was unable to support and protect his wife. The wife too, had no wish to go with him since he was a stranger to her; under the circumstances she could neither love nor respect him. A number of orthodox people in the community who saw no reason why a wife should not follow her husband even though he be a worthless man, collected funds to enable him to sue her and her parents in the British Court of Justice. The case was examined with due ceremony and the verdict, was given in the man's favour, according to Hindu law,* The wife was doomed to go with him. Fortunately she was soon released from this sorrowful world by cholera. Whatever may be said of the epidemics that yearly assail our country, they are not unwelcome among the unfortunate women who are thus persecuted by social, religious and State laws. Many women put an end to their earthly sufferings by committing suicide. Suits at law between husband and wife are remarkable for their rarity in the British Courts in India, owing to the ever submissive conduct of women who suffer silently, knowing that the gods and justice always favour the men.

*In all cases except those directly connected with life and death, the British Government is bound according to the treaties concluded with the inhabitants of India, not to interfere with their social and religious customs and laws; judicial decisions are given accordingly.

The case of Rakhmabai, that has lately profoundly agitated Hindu society, is only one of thousands of the same class. The remarkable thing about her is that she is a well-educated lady, who was brought up under the loving care of her father, and had learned from him how to defend herself against the assaults of social and religious bigotries. But as soon as her father died the man who claimed to be her husband, brought suit against her in the court of Bombay. The young woman bravely defended herself, declining to go to live with the man on the ground that the marriage that was concluded without her consent could not be legally considered as such. Mr. Justice Pinhey, who tried the case in the first instance, had a sufficient sense of justice to refuse to force the lady to live with her husband against her will. Upon hearing this decision, the conservative party all over India rose as one man and grided their loins to denounce the helpless woman and her handful of friends. The encouraged the alleged husband to stand his ground firmly, threatening the British government with public displeasure if it failed to keep its agreement to force the woman to go to live with the husband according to Hindu law. Large sums were collected for the benefit of this man, Dadajee, to enable him to appeal against the decision to the full bench, whereupon, to the horror of all right-thinking people, the chief-justice sent back the case to the lower court for re-trial on its merits, as judged by the Hindu laws. The painful termination of this trial, I have in a letter written by my dear friend Rakhmabai herself, bearing date Bombay, March 18th, 1887. I quote from her latter:

> "The learned and civilized judges of the full bench are determined to enforce, in this enlightened age, the inhuman laws enacted in barbaric times, four thousand years ago. They have not only commanded me to go to live with the man, but also have obliged me to pay the costs of the dispute. Just think of this extraordinary decision! Are we not living under the impartial British government, which boasts of giving equal justice to all, and are we not ruled by the Queen-Empress Victoria, herself a woman? My dear

friend, I shall have been cast into the State prison when this letter reaches you; this is because I do not, and cannot obey the order of Mr. Justice Farran.

"There is no hope for women in India, whether they be under Hindu rule or British rule; some are of the opinion that my case so curelly decided, may bring about a better condition for woman by turning public opinion in her favour, but I fear it will be otherwise. The hard-hearted mothers-in-law will now be greatly strengthened, and will induce their sons, who have for some reason or other, been slow to enforce the conjugal rights to sue their wives in the British Courts, since they are now fully assured that under no circumstances can the British government act adversely to the Hindu law."

Taught by the experience of the past, we are not at all surprised at this decision of the Bombay court. Our only wonder is that a defenseless woman like Rakhmabai dared to raise her voice in the face of the powerful Hindu law, the mighty British government, the one hundred and twenty-nine million men and the three hundred and thirty million gods of the Hindus, all these having conspired together to crush her into nothingness. We cannot blame the English government for not defending a helpless woman; it is only fulfilling its agreement made with the male population of India. How very true are the words of the Saviour, "Ye cannot serve God and Mammon." Should England serve God by protecting a helpless woman against the powers and principalities of ancient institutions, Mammon would surely be displeased, and British profit and rule in India might be endangered thereby. Let us wish it success, no matter if that success be achieved at the sacrifice of the rights and the comfort of over one hundred million women.

Meanwhile, we shall patiently await the advent of the kingdom of righteousness, wherein the weak, the lowly and the helpless shall be made happy because the great Judge Himself "shall wipe away all tears from their eyes."

CONDITION OF WOMEN AND SOCIETY

Those who have done their best to keep women in a state of complete dependence and ignorance, vehemently deny that this has anything to with the present degradation of the Hindu nation. I pass over the hundreds of nonsenses which are brought forward as the strongest reasons for keeping women in ignorance ond dependence. They have already been forced out into the broad day-light of a generous civilization, and have been put to the fiery proof of science and found wanting. Above all, the noble example of thousands of women in many countries have burned the so-called reasons to ashes. But their ghosts are still hovering over the land of the Hindus and are frightening the timid and the ignorant to death. Let us hope that in God's good time, all these devils shall be forever cast out of India's body; meanwhile it is our duty to take the matter into serious consideration, and to put forth our best endeavours to hasten the glad day for India's daughters, aye, and for her her sons also; because in spite of the proud assertions of our brethren that they have not suffered from the degradation of women, their own condition betrays but too plainly the contray.

Since men and women are indissolubly united by Providence as members of the same body of human society, each must suffer when their fellow-members suffer, whether they will confess it or not. In the animal as well as in the vegetable kingdom, nature demands that all living beings shall freely comply with its conditions of growth or they cannot become that which they were orginally designed to be. Why should any exception to this law be made for the purdah women? Closely confined to the four walls of their house, deprived throughout their lives of the opportunity to breathe healthy fresh air, or to drink in the wholesome sunshine, they become weaker and weaker from generation to generation, their physical statures dwarfed, their spirts crushed under the weight of social prejudices and superstitions, and their minds starved from absolute lack of literary food and of opportunity to observe the world. Thus fettered, in ninety cases out of a hundred, at the least calculation, they grow to be selfish slaves to their petty individual interests, indifferent to the welfare of their own immediate neighbours, much more to their nation's well-being. How could these imprisoned mothers be expected to bring forth children better than themselves, for as the tree and soil are, so shall the fruit be. Consequently we see all around us in India a generation of men least deserving that exalted appellation.

The doctrine of "pre-natal influence" can nowhere be more satisfactorily proved than in India. The mother's spirits being depressed, and mind as well as body weakened by the monotony and inactivity of her life, the unborn child cannot escape the evil consequences. The men of Hindustan do not when babes, suck from the mother's breast, true patriotism, and in their boyhood, the mother, poor woman, is unable to develope that divine faculty in them owing to her utter ignorance of the past and present condition of her native land. Fault-finding with neighbours, bitter feelings towards tyrant relatives expressed in words and actions, selfish interest in personal and family affairs, these are the chief lessons that children learn at the mother's knee, from babyhood up to the seventh or eighth year of age.

Again, how does it come to pass that each succeeding generation grows weaker than the one preceding it, if not because the progenitors of each generation lack the mental and physical strength which children are destined to inherit? The father may have been free and healthy in mind, as well as in body, but the mother was not; she undoubtedly has bequeathed the fatal legacy of weakness and dullness to her children. The complete submission of women under the Hindu law has in the lapse of milleniums of years converted them into slavery-loving creatures. They are glad to lean upon any one and be altogether dependent, and thus it has come to pass that their sons as a race, desire to depend upon some other nation, and not upon themselves. The seclusion, complete dependence and the absolute ignorance forced upon the mothers of our nation have been gradually and fatally telling upon the mental and physical health of the men, and in these last times they have borne the poisonous fruit that will compel the Hindu nation to die a miserable and prolonged death if a timely remedy is not taken to them.

Moreover the Hindu woman's ignorance prevents liberal-minded and progressive men from making necessary and important changes in the manners and habits of the household; bigoted women also prevent their husbands and sons from such important enterprises as crossing the ocean in the pursuit of useful knowledge, or for purposes of trade.

To add to all the disabilities of the Hindu mother in the discharge of her sacred maternal duties, she is as a rule, wholly ignorant of the commonest hygienic laws. It must be remembered that she is herself a girl scarcely out of her babyhood, when she becomes a mother. At about fourteen, fifteen or sixteen years of age she cannot be expected to know all that is necessary in order to take good care of her child. The first and second of the children of this young mother usually die, and if they survive, they are apt to grow up to be weak and unhealthy adults. Until they are seven or eight years of age, the children of the household are left to themselves without any one to take care of them, and no influence is exerted mould their character at this most interesting and important period of life. Who but an intelligent and loving mother can do this all-important work for her children at that age?

Having thus far endeavoured to bring to the notice of Western women the condition of a class of their oriental sisters, I now desire to direct their attention definitely to our chief needs. After many years of careful observation and thought, I have come to the conclusion that the chief needs of high-caste Hindu women are:

1. 1st, Self-Reliance;

2. 2nd, Education;

3. 3rd, Native Women Teachers.

I. Self-Reliance—The state of complete dependence in which men are required by the law-giver to keep women from birth to the end of their lives makes it impossible for them to have self-reliance, without which a human being becomes a pitiful parasite. Women of the working classes are better off than their sisters of high castes in India, for in many cases they are obliged to depend upon themselves, and an opportunity for cultivating self-reliance is thus afforded them by which they largely profit. But high-caste women, unless their families are actually destitute of means to keep them, are shut up within the four walls of their house. In after time, if they are left without a protector, *i.e.*, a male relative to support and care for them, they literally do not know what to do with themselves. They have been so cruelly cropped in their early days that self-reliance and energy are dead within them; helpless victims of indolence and false timidity they are easily frightened out of their wits and have little or no strength to withstand the trials and difficulties which must be encountered by a person on her way toward progress. But it is idle to hope that the condition of my country-women will ever improve without individual self-reliance; therefore; is it not the duty of our Western sisters to teach them how they may become self-reliant?

II. Education—The lack of education among the women of India can be fairly realized by scanning the report of the Educational Commission for 1883, and the census returns of 1880-81. Of the ninety-nine million seven hundred thousand women and girls directly under British rule, ninety-nine and one-half millions are returned as unable to read and write; the remaining two hundred thousand who are able either to read or write, cannot all be reckoned as educated, for the school-going period of a girl is generally between seven and nine years of age; within that short time she acquires little more than ability to read the second or the third vernacular reading-book, and a little knowledge of arithmetic which usually comprehends no more than the four simple rules. It should be remembered that the two hundred thousand women able to read or write are the "*alumna*" of the government schools, mission schools, private schools conducted by the inhabitants of India indspendently, private societies and Zenana mission agencies all reckoned together. It is surprising how even this small number of women can have acquired the limited knowledge indicated, when we consider the powers and principalities that are incessantly fighting against female education in India. Girls of nine and ten when recently out of school and given in marriage are wholly cut off from reading or writing, because it is a young woman or girl to hold a paper or book in her hand, or to read in the presence of others in her husband's house. It is a popular belief among high-caste women that their husbands will die if they should read or should hold a pen in their fingers. The fear of becoming a widow overcomes their hunger and thirst for knowledge. Moreover the little wives can get but scanty time to devote to self-culture; any one fortunate enough to possess the desire and able to command the time is in constant fear of being seen by her husband's relatives. Her employment cannot long be kept secret where every one is on the lookout, and when discovered she is ridiculed, laughed at and even commanded by the elders to leave off this nonsense. Her literary pursuits are now at an end unless the proceedings of the elders be interfered with by her progressive husband; but alas, such husbands are extremely rare. Our schools, too, are not very attractive to children; the teachers of primary schools, (and it is to these schools that girls are usually sent), are but nominally educated, and do not know how to make to lessons interesting for children. Consequently a great many of the giris who have been educated up to the second or third standard (grade) in these primary schools make it their business quickly ta forget their lessons as soon as they find an opportunity. Shut in fram the world and destitute of the ability to engage in newspaper and useful book-reading, they have little or no knowledge of common things around them, and of the most important events that are daily occurring in their own or foreign lands. Ignorant, unpatriotic, selfish and uncultivated, they drag the men down with them into the dark abyss where they dwell together without hope, without ambition to be something or to something in the world.

III. Native Women Teachers—American and English women as Zenana missionaries are doing all they can to elevate and enlighten India's daughters. These good people deserve respect and praise from all, and the heart-felt thanks of those for whose elevation they toil, but the disabilities of an unfriendly climate, and of an unknown tongue make it exceedingly difficult for them to enter upon their work for some time after reaching India: and then, "what are these among so many." They are literally lost among the nearly one hundred millions of women under British rule to whom must be added several millians more under Hindu and Mahommedan rule. In America and in England we hear encouraging reports from mission fields, which state that a few thousand Hindu and Mahommedan women and girls are being instructed in schools or in their own homes, but these seem as nothing, compared to the vast multitude of the female population of Hindustan. In a country where castes and the seclusion of women are regarded as essential tenets of the national creed, we can scarcely hope for a general spread of useful knowledge among women, through either men of their own race or through foreign women. All experience in the past history of mankind has shown that efforts for the elevation of a nation must come from within and work outward to be effectual.

The one thing needful, therefore, for the general diffusion of ***education among women in India is a body of persons from among*** *themselves who shall make it their life-work to teach by precept and exaniple their followcorn rywomen.*

6

CASTE AND CLASS AMONG BUDDHISTS

The Buddhists in India today even decades after the first great Diksha ceremony at Nagpur (October 14, 1956) where Dr. B. R. Ambedkar, the great Mahar leader, publicly proclaimed himself a Buddhist, are yet to be free from "caste".[1] The conversion during the last two decades of over three million untouchables to Buddhism may be described as a rejection of and attempt to escape from the caste system. Caste to the outcaste has meant centuries of economic, social, political and religious oppression, a denial of their humanity, legitimised by religion in the concepts of pollution and purity. Buddhism was seen by Ambedkar as a religion that was Indian but anti-caste; he taught that in ancient Buddhist India there had been equality, and that the misery of the untochables has come from Hinduism and the Brahmins who used it for oppression. The causes of the injustice lie not in the position of the untouchables in the system but in the system itself.[2] This dream of escaping caste by a return to the "original" Buddhism still possesses the followers of Dr. Ambedkar but they are usually realistic in the appraisal of their actual situation.

Asked what has happened in the last two decades for them, they might well say, "not much".[3] This paper will present chiefly the opinions of the Buddhists themselves and of some of their critics (interviewed chiefly in Maharashtra, 1966-67) on their own situation as Buddhists *vis-a-vis* the caste system of India. 'Caste' as internal to themselves will not be discussed here. The points to be made are:

1. The constitutional and legal attempt to eliminate untouchability has done a little, but very little, to remedy the situation;
2. Buddhism is actually a handicap in regard to these legal rights of untouchables;
3. The rejection of caste in Buddhism has had less exterior effect—economic, social, educational—than interior, a psychological breaking free, which is its chief strength.

The Buddhist conversions, it should be said, have been chiefly in Maharashtra and Agra, and there almost exclusively among the Mahars and the Jatavs. Other untouchable castes have not followed them in appreciable numbers. However, in almost all parts of India—the Punjab, U.P., Bengal, Madras, Mysore,—there are some to be found.[4]

The problem of 'untouchability and the law', especially the anti-disabilities legislation since Independence, has been well analysed by Marc Galanter.[5] The laws may be all on the side of the untouchables but the law's enforcers are not. As under the British Raj so now in the few cases brought by untouchables, usually under pressure from social workers or reformers, the decisions are too often against them. They are aware of the law but still more aware of its dangers for them and of the very mild penalty that, even should they win the case, their adversary would suffer—a fine of a few rupees at best. The complainments themselves and their witnesses are extremely vulnerable to intimidation and reprisals such as boycott, eviction, denial of grazing rights—not to mention physical assault, houseburnings and the like.[7] In 1967 I had been invited to a wedding in a village about 30 miles from

Poona but was warned not to go. The bridegroom's party were all government employees and drove to the village, fortunately for them, in a governmen-towned bus. In the village they and the bride's party were attacked and badly beaten; they escaped a wore fate only because the villagers hesitated to burn the government bus. For weeks after in Poona they were afraid even to mention what had happened; the thought of making a charge against their assailants never occurred to them—they felt that they and the bride's family in the village would have been further endangered. The untouchables therefore continue to suffer under restrictions that weigh heavily upon them—not merely the usual disabilities—exclusion form hotels, restaurants, use of utensils, wells, and water-service by barbers washermen—but above all a widespread harassment and discrimination that keeps many of them living in squalid destitution and prevents even the educated and more wealthy urban dwellers from any real acceptance in society.[8]

However the legislation includes not only the ineffective anti-disabilities laws but also other programmes for guaranteed seats in legislatures, government jobs, educational grants, financial aid for housing and the like. This is the most constructive side of the government approach to untouchability and has undoubtedly resulted in a vast increase in educational opportunities—but these advantages are restricted to 'Hindu' Scheduled Castes; Buddhists are excluded. This is in spite of the fact that untouchables have never been accepted as 'Hindus', and were excluded from temple entry and any but fringe participation in village religious activities. Many, therefore, in order to share this "protected discrimination", at least until their education is complete do not admit to being Buddhist legally, though they claim to be Buddhist at heart. Christians, incidentally, are also excluded from government aid as they do not fit into the "classes and sections of Hindus". "... an untouchable who converts openly to Christianity, Buddhism or Islam ceases thereby to be untouchable (and therefore a member of a Scheduled Caste) even though the majority continues to discriminate against him as before".[11]

How then does Buddhism affect caste among the untouchables? As far as the law is concerned, it does so negatively. Buddhists are legally not 'Scheduled Caste' yet in practice are discriminated against as much as if they were. However there are certain postive values received by them from their new religion. Such, at least, was the conclusion drawn from interviews, chiefly in Maharashtra, 1966-67. (The quoted statements are identified by the type of the person interviewed, *i.e.*, Buddhist, Brahman, *etc.*).

Economic Betterment

The economic situation of the untouchables has been desperate for centuries—90 per cent have lived in villages as landless workers. Their specialised skills were 'unclean' occupations and poorly paid. They have been and are the 'poorest segment of the landless class'; poverty and squalor is their lot--whether in their little village slum or in the great horror slums of Bombay and Calcutta. This is due to their situation as outcaste, as unclean and polluting.[11] The hereditary work of the Mahars, for example was to remove dead cattle from the village, sweep the streets, run errands for the village officers, watch the village property. They were given a small piece of land (*imam*) but never cultivated it themselves. Today they work in textile and sugar mills and ammunition factories.[12]

There is little evidence that conversion to Buddhism directly improves the untouchable's economic condition. That the Mahars no longer work' as village peons but are hired by village development workers and paid for their work, is not due to their new religion. In the Poona area and probably elsewhere, they are hired for field work but not for domestic work, except in "some advanced Brahmin families that are westernised and don't mind."[13] (Buddhist) Principal Wankhede of Milind College, Aurangabad, pointed out the "definite attraction of cities for the new Buddhists. In a factory, no one asks about one's religion, etc. It is a long process. Education and industry alone will change caste." It is said that because they no longer do the village services or share the village festivals that therefore they do not belong to any society at all. "They are now in the clutches of another system. The Buddhist organisation]. Enormous sums are collected from each house, but there is no check on the collectors and no accounting for what they do with the funds." This statement from a Brahmin intellectual is clearly exaggerated. He believed that the untouchables' "lot was economically better before 1937 and before Independence, though they now have more education." Another said: "It is impossible to make generalisations. In some areas the Buddhists are now well off but elsewhere, as in Konkan, they are very poor."

There is however, one way in which Buddhists point out that their religion has helped economically. It has eliminated the payments to Brahmin priests for ritual, divination (horoscopes) and above all by cutting down on marriage expenses. Weddings formerly put the family in debt for life. "It is no longer a five-day celebration with animal slaughter" in Hadapsar village. Modest extravagances may reappear in weddings, but the gifts provide for many bridegrooms their one chance to get a new suit and a new pair of shoes, and for the bride, a sari. This ritual change may seem minor, but in fact it has a very beneficial financial result for those whose income is the lowest in India.

Social and Moral Betterment

The Buddhists link social betterment with Buddhism and morality it teaches. "Our concern is more social than religious. We are now free from Hindu ideas and are much happier. So we will never change from Buddhism. We were never real Hindus before." And at the same time, they will add, "Religion is therefore a needed thing. Only when morality is there, then only your life will be happy; otherwise, you live like an animal." "Why is the 'public', (*i.e.*, the untouchables) attracted to Buddhism?" "The suppression we suffered before is now ended. We could not run a hotel before. We were untouchables. We are not now, since Buddha taught us equality." (Buddhist). "Quarrels between families have stopped; we are closer and have good relations with others. We forget differences because of education; also they (the upper castes) fear legal consequences." (Chikkilwadi Village). Now Buddhists can enter "hotels", shops, use wells. There is "no trouble from the people in the last five or six years, it just came about by itself." (Lolikand Village). When asked if their conditions were better, they said that they can use the village well (though they actually do not as they have their own), can join in functions together, at weddings sit down together, and even eat together. Whether or not these claims are excessive, some few can truly say: "Now we are free on every level; we can live in Brahmin society and become friends, very good friends." (Buddhist lawyer). The term "Brahmin Society", however, needs qualification here— "the society of *some* Brahmins," especially in a town like Wai, to which the speaker was referring.

It is doubtful, in fact, the Buddhism itself betters the social position. "Educated persons like us can't get accommodations even in cities. We must live in the outskirts. Even though we feel different, there is no change in others. We are getting more fearless. We all come together and have strength behind us. But until village structure is changed, decentralised, *i.e.*, Panchayat Raj, we will not be better off." (Buddhist College Teacher). "The change is now because of Buddhism and because of the laws. But villages have not changed much. We can't buy a house in the Brahmin quarter in Poona. Some are renting, not buying. May be after some years, we can. My apartment here is small but it is better than the ordinary people get in Poona, a very Brahmin city, because it is a government project." (Buddhist lawyer). The social position is, in fact, not much changed. They are still a persecuted minority. Indian 'tolerance' is indifference, *i.e.*, your religion doesn't matter as long as you keep your caste station. (Brahmin)

In some areas, as in Ahmednagar, the Buddhist propaganda is almost entirely economic and social. "You will get this and that." (Social worker). This always includes behavioural changes, however. "They used to drink, to gamble, to eat meat; now all deny this and dress properly, and try to be clean." (Brahmin sociologist). Mr. Katti, a Buddhist politician, speaking of Mysore conditions, said:

> At present there is a radical change from the Hindu way of life in belief. We accept no gods.
>
> To give up 33 scores of gods is some change, not a small thing. And a number don't drink, not that before they were drinkers. And Ahimsa doesen't mean not eating meat but not killing. There is no change in dress but we would like to show a difference. The cleanliness is due to financial well-being as well as to Buddhism.

"Before we had no standard of living, now there is cleanliness, order, etc., a swift and remarkable change. Some too have stopped drinking; some have started again." (Buddhist lawyer). "We have changed houses, dress, customs. . . " (Budhhist civil servant). "We can go anywhere now, hotels, etc. We don't *want* to go to the temples." (Buddhist peon). In Sanskrit University, Varanasi, in the Department of Buddhist Studies there are untouchables. "We take wanter and food from them. This in unusal in any university." (Brahmin professor). "Life as Buddhists is better than as Hindus. There is no untouchability, we are free from it, and are treated better now because we are Buddhists." (Agra Buddhist group). "Things are better due to Buddhism more than to laws. We were formerly culturally and morally backward, would steal, cheat, etc. We have discarded these and are confident there is progress due to Panchsheel (the five precepts) and the three refugees. We can go through their [Barhmin] localities, are accepted by society, not cut off any more. The whole level of society is going up, but we go faster due to Buddhism." (Buddhist in Mahad). It is notable that they never speak of the former unfortunate position of their women who were not infrequently prostitutes, nor of their former reputation as sorcerers—both are repudiated by silence.

One critic distinguished between people and leaders. "My impression is that the masses are trying to live by the Punch-sheel seriously. The leaders are not. They indulge in drinking parties after the diksha ceremony, which confuses people." (This source is a person who has had much conflict with the leaders). "In villages, only the older people still drink. They used to have feasts for drinking only and always celebrated on the wrong day so they had to celebrate it twice." (Educated Buddhist). Some of the lay leaders pride themselves on eating no meat or fish, and on never drinking. In fact, their vegetarianism goes boyond the requirements of Buddhism. On the other hand, the claims of villagers to have given up carrion-eating and alcoholic drinks are not always true, though they express an ideal. In Ahmednagar, a policeman begged a missionary to stop them cutting meat from a carcase, for the sake of their self-respect. In a village near Poona, the claim to abstinence was denied loudly by one of the group, who then departed, to return quite drunk in a relatively short time.

In Jullunder and Jammu areas, the "social problem", according to Mr. Bellay, a Buddhist leader and writer there, takes a different colour, due to a long religious tradition predating Buddhism. The Punjab Sufit saints and Sikh gurus, he claimed, had long taught social equality. In Jammu many people are followers of the Scheduled Caste Saint, Ravidas; only the Batwals (converted recently in Bashnar) have no such leader and so are "adopting Buddhism". In the South, where the Buddhist movement predates Ambedkar, social conditions seem little changed. In a Tamil poem dedicated to Pandit Ayodhidas, an early untouchable Buddhist encouraged by Colonel Olcott and the Theosophists, the author, V. V. Murugesar, expresses the relation of sociol emancipation to Buddhist teaching:

To Ayodhyadasar

He lived when barbers

Refused to shave,
When men were tied to the
Stake and whipped,
When people were scared to tread
Where the buffalo roamed,
A time when the dhobhy refused
to wash,
When no one went to the temple.
At such a time
Came Ayodhyadasar—
He thundered!

H set the law to Tamils
To the worked, the old and the new
He was a Pandit, a lamp to
The Tamil race. Devotee to Theru V.
Kalyanasundara Mundahar;
He went to live with him in
Royapettah. They fought against
Caste.

He told them of the Buddha's
Teachings. He translated them into
Tamil. He fought against religious
Fanaticism. He was writer, orator.
He planned housing, dwelt in
The slums. He wrote of their
Plight.

Are there only [sic] writer today? Should
We forget those who went before?
Ungrateful, O ye ancient Tamilian.
Look inward. Can we walk with
Heads high if not for people like
Ayodhyadasam?

The withering shoots require rain,
He said.
He told us that this country is ours.

He woke us from our sleep.
He roused the lazy
And all those who lived
On the fat of the land.
By what right do you
Sleep on cushions or use gold
And silver ware? He asked.
Without fear he waged war.
Let this brave man be remembered.

Education that is so ardently pursued has much part in the shift from village to urban life. This is only very indirectly a consequence of Buddhism. 'In Milind College, Aurangabad, it is noted that after students get their degree, they no longer fit in the society of their village, so they do not go black. They migrate to cities or towns like Aurangabad, and stay there if possible. In cities there is only 'underground discrimination'. The result is that the families of the educated do not benefit immediately from the education of the sons who leave them. Workers with good jobs, however, tend to keep in touch with their villages and families, or more often bring their parents to live with them—in their one room "apartment" in a Bomhay chawl, for instance.

Poverty at present prevents talented students from achieving eminence as musicians and artists, though "given an opportunity, they would be as good as any." (College principal —Buddhist). Those who do achieve success in some field, however, like Sohan Lal Shastri, in the Law Ministry, are well off, though again this is not because he is a Buddhist: "I'm not a victim of untouchability; because I'm a government scholar, my colleagues wouldn't dare do anything." As a lawyer said: "Now we are educated, we know how to fight with the Brahmins. We no longer can be insulted and be helpless against it." "There is evidence of a real movement upward. There are some very fine writers. Mr. Kharat, for example, is a fine man and a gentlemen; so is Khairmodey, a poet, a brilliant young man when I knew him first. But I don't think *Buddhism* has any part of this. It creates a new situation but also a new problem." (Brahmin intellectual).[14]

Some deny that any improvement has come from Buddhism. The Ven. Shanti Bhadra formerly of Milind College said:

> Either they will never be anything, not Buddhists, not Hindu, not Christian, this is a danger. Or they may yet take to Communism. They are trying now to hold to the Buddhist moral code, but have no monks, no trained people. They don't keep so well to not stealing, not lying etc. Sometimes I have to go to the police to get back a book or money I have lent.
>
> What will be the future? I don't know. When the boys get married, they get selfish, lose their ideals. It will take a long time.

Mr. Panchbhai of Nagpur claimed that:

> As long as varnas exist there will be no fluidity in society. Because of this practical difficulty, we are still Hindu, in custom, etc. And now because relgion is in the hands of politicans, we are getting more Hindu. Yet only politics will get us out of this. We need it for this, not just for opposition. The aim is to rule the country.

In the north, Mr. Bellay also sees little change:

> Coming up? Very little in the last ten years. We get facilities but they are still very poor. Here there is no aid for our schools and hostels, as in Maharashtra, due to a kind of corruption.

A sociologist (Brahmin) claims that there has been disillusionment since the Scheduled Castes are still not admitted to social acceptance by Hindus. "It is doubtful that conversion has helped or so many would not have gone back to Congress." He also points out that untouchables in North Mysore were long ago converted to the Lingayat Sect. According to the twelfth century prophet of the Lingayats, Basava, those who wear the phallus emblem are immune to pollution; yet they are still untouchable. So it is with the Christians in Ahmed-nagar. "In this district, 'Christian' means 'untouchable'. Even the cardinal has an inferiority complex." One's very name brands one. My name is now Desai, actually a Kshatriya but also a Brahmin name; it gives me more influence. "My father found in Church documents that 300 years ago that was our family name before it was changed to a Portuguese name." (A Christian priest). Hence there is question as to whether a new religious change will in the long run benefit the people, since centuries have failed to do so in these two cases and others. Principal Joshi of the new Buddhist college at Mahad feels that, "They are no better off because of a religious change." In one village the people admitted that there is no real eating together." At a funeral they send food here to us, if we invite them, they accept the invitation but don't come. Even if they would go to a wedding with us, they won't eat if it's in our village." In another village the Buddhist people were very abandoned. Formerly the village had been responsible for them, but now they need outside help. They asked a visitor for jobs for their children, and seemed deprived, frustrated, with no religious satisfaction. Now they feel exploited or neglected by their own leaders. A Brahmin, Kodanda Rao, said: "The present system of facilities perpetuates untouchability," and asked, "How many untouchables are accepted in marriage? Invited to eat in *homes*, not hotels? Never, in villages or even in towns."

Psychological Betterment

However there is, to my mind, a real psychological change in the attitude toward caste and its consequences. "Does Buddhism really better our position? Yes. We belong to the lowest group in Hinduism. When we leave it, we are no longer the lowest." (Buddhist in Jammu). "In Maharashtra, people are prouınd to say that they are Buddhists. They claim to be Buddhist even if they have not been formally converted. The simple declaration is enough." (Milind College). "In a 500 house village, five or ten houses are Mahar; whether converted or not, these call themselves Buddhists." (Pali teacher).

> We have also started to study what is Buddhism. We left everything of the Hindu religion, caste especially. Because of Buddhism, we gave up all that and are now stepping forward in thoughts, education, behaviour and everything.
>
> We believe in Buddhist equality. It is the best religion. There is nothing in Buddhism like Brahmin and untouchable.
>
> Unfortunately Dr. Ambedkar died too soon or there would have been a lot of changes in Buddhism especially. Since Buddhism, there has been change in everything; our thoughts, we no longer worship thirty-three scores of gods in blind worship. We couldn't enter temples yet in spite of that we worshipped. But not since Babasaheb Ambedkar. Now we throw the *murtis* into the river and do not keep any in our houses.
>
> (an Educated Buddhist)

"I am not a Harijan, I am a Buddhist." "Buddhism has much influenced our lives. Our inferiority complex is gone, the sense of being an outcaste. Dr. Ambedkar has given us this, to be proud of being Buddhist. Before we were not proud of being Mahars." (Buddhist lawyer). This is questioned by Dr. B. K. Bedekar: "Buddhism only gives *internal* advantage. Yet the Mahars and subjective freedom long before their conversion. From 1933 they no longer felt an inferior caste." However, the Mahars themselves are specific: "Our forefathers and my generation worshipped deities, especially Mariai; they believed in possession by deities, had shrines in each house, and offered sacrifices of goats and buffaloes. Now our people refuse to kill a buffalo on Dussehra Day. This has led to tension with Hindus but now we are no longer despised." (Buddhist lawyer). "When a priest (*i.e.*, a Scheduled Caste monk) speaks, we feel *light, united, polite* and honest. More than we ever felt before being a Buddhist. We now have a place and a time to sit and talk together, to tell our troubles to a priest who comforts us. We did not go to Brahmin priests before. We had our own and still respect them; there is no controversy, for they like Buddhism." (Buddhist government official). In Wai, for example, the former priest of Mariai is now considered a Bauddhacharya.

"The advantage of being Buddhist is that our blindness is gone. We have morally come up—no laying, no cheating, and we are well-united. We were so from the beginning, as being separated from others always bound us together, but Buddhism makes this stronger" (Hadapsar village). In the north, the reaction is somewhat different as yet, at least in Jammu:

> Those who are convereted feel some superiority. But do others treat them better? This is difficult. See the Sikhs. The Scheduled Caste Sikhs are still in Scheduled Castes. It is the same in Buddhism. We are still in Scheduled Castes. We now have access to wells, temples, etc. due to the constitution. Even when Buddhist, they still go to the temple if they want. In our houses, we have not yet reached the same stage as in Maharashtra (*i.e.* still have Hindu gods and do puja). So we still have to be awakened. (Buddhist leader).

A sociologist in Poona commented that:

> If Buddhists don't stress their conversion now, and don't show how they differ, they will be assimilated into Hinduism.
>
> Hinduism is changing now, at a behavioural level, in its ritual. Hinduism has already faded away. Everyone at least in cities ceases to observe worship of deities.

Even for cities, this is an exaggeration. In a very deprived village group where the shrine of Mariai was still kept, where the "Buddhists" also had joined the Salvation Army (apparently to get sewing machines or their use), where they spoke with cynicism of the leaders who came to them only at election time, yet one man said and the others agreed: "Before, I was a dirty rag; now I am a Buddhist. I am washed, I am clean."

In conclusion, then, it seems that caste for the Buddhists is the great enemy and caste for them means "Hinduism". Their effort to break away has been an heroic one. Its success so far is, as we have seen, very limited, but even so is of great significance to them. They realise that, as the Buddha said, they must be a light unto themselves. No one else will help them— and their new self-image, as Ambedkar had hoped, is undoubtedly the first step toward self-improvement especially as it is integrally linked to their push toward formal education and is the soure of new leaders. Their hope is in the next generation, their sons or even grandsons. The problem of the future will be what Isaacs points out—where, in India's elaborate caste system, will they fit? To whom will they belong? Their hope, since Buddhism is not, as in Buddhist countries, a strong establishment that gives status and prestige—is in international Buddhism which so far, save for a handful of devoted monks from Cambodia, Thailand, Ceylon, Japan, has done little for them. But even this would not solve their problem as long as the caste system survives in India.

NOTES AND REFERENCES

1. *See* a recent study, *The Untouchables in Contemporary India*, J. Michael Mahar ed., University of Arizona Press, 1972, and its bibliography on Untouchability, pp. 431 ff.
2. Owen Lynch, "Dr. B. R. Ambedkar: Myth and Charisma", *Untouchables*, pp. 99-104. *See also* David G. Mandelbaum, *Society in India*, Vol. 2 (Berkeley: University of California Press, 1970), p. 664.
3. Mahar, *Untouchables*, p. 428.
4. *See* Fiske, "Scheduled Caste Buddhist Organizations", *Untoucha-*

bles, pp. 113-42. *See also* Irawati Karve, *Maharashtra Land and Its People* (Bombay: Directorate of Government Printing, Stationary and Publications, 1968), pp. 32, 92, 105, 109, 140, for the Mahars.

5. *The Untouchables*, pp: 227-314.
6. *Ibid.*, p. 281.
7. *Ibid.*, pp. 276-77.
8. Cf. H. Isaac, "The Ex-Untouchables", *The Untouchables*, pp. 396-403.
9. Galanter, *Untouchables*, p. 242; Fiske, "Scheduled Caste Buddhist Organizations", *Ibid.*, p. 124.
10. L. Dushkin, "Scheduled Caste Politics" *Untouchables*, p. 168.
11. Andre Beteille, "Pollution and Poverty", *Untouchables*, pp. 416-20.
12. Karve, p. 32.
13. *Ibid.*, p. 106.
14. For detail on the educational organization in the People's Education Society, founded by B.R. Ambedkar, *see* Fiske, "Scheduled Caste Buddhist Organizations", *Untouchables*, p. 114; note 1, pp. 141-42.

Ambedkar, Bhimrao Ramji, *The Buddha and His Dhamma*. Bombay: Siddharth College Publication, I, 1957.

Fiske, Adele M., The Use of Buddhist Scriptures in Dr. B.R. Ambedkar's *The Buddha and His Dhamma*. M.A. Thesis, Columbia University, 1966.

Religion and Buddhism among India's New Buddhists. *Social Research*, 36: 123-157, 1969.

Isaacs, Harold R., *India's Ex-Untouchables*. New York: John Day, 1965 (Perceptive interviews with educated, urbanized Untouchables).

Keer, Dhananjay, *Dr. Ambedkar: Life and Mission*. Bombay: Popular Prakashan (2nd ed: 1962, with additional material), 1954.

Lederle, M. R. (S.J.), The Untouchable's Claim to Human Dignity. *Journal of the University of Poona*, Humanities Section, 19: 67-76, 1964.

Robertson, Alexander, *The Mahar Folk*. Calcutta: Y.M.C.A. and Oxford University Press, 1938.

Zelliot, Eleanor, Background of the Mahar Buddhist Conversion. In *Studies on Asia.* Edited by Report K. Sakai. Lincoln: University of Nebraska Press, 1966.

The Revival of Buddhism in India. *Asia* (New York) No. 10 (Winter): 33-45, 1968.

Dr. Ambedkar and the Mahar Movement. Unpublished Ph.D. Dissertation, University of Pennsylvania. 1969.

7

CASTE AS SOCIAL PROCESS

Caste is a peculiar institution with peculiar consequences. In order to investigate its implications for a broader understanding of social organization, I have previously developed a concept of caste organization which is intended to be cross-culturally applicable (Berreman 1960a, 1962, 1966, 1967a, 1967b). I have assumed that scientific endeavor requires comparison and that comparison requires careful definition of the phenomena to be studied/Caste systems were defined in terms of three dimentions: stratification, pluralism, and interaction. "A caste system occurs where a society is made up of birth-ascribed groups which are hierarchically ordered and culturally distinct. The hierarchy entails differential evaluation, rewards and association" (Berreman 1967a: 48, cf. Berreman 1965). In its interactional sense —the sense of differential association—a caste system is "a system of birth-ascribed groups each of which comprises for its members the maximum limit of status-equal interaction and between all of which interaction is consistently hierarchical" (Berreman 1967a:51), By reference to these definitions and their implications, castes can be distinguished from, and compared to, other types of social aggregates (*e.g.*, kin groups, classes, local communities), and caste systems can be distinguished from and compared to other systems of organizing people in societies (*e.g.*, pluralism, class, and homogeneity of culture and rank) (Berseman 1967a, 1967b). The types of aggregates and the systems of organization are not mutually exclusive. All of the dimensions vary along continua, and each of the difinitions is of the "idealtype' variety.

In conjunction with the definitional discussions, I indicated social and psychological concomitants of easte systems—ways in which the recurrent fact of caste organization affects those who live it. I suggested that these are common consequences of caste systems for the personalities as well as the social relations of members (Berreman 1960a, 1966, 1967a; cf. DeVos 1966). I sought to identify common behaviours and attitudes associated with caste systems and in fact proposed the utility of concept of "culures of caste organization", analogous to Lewis' concept of the culture of poverty (Berreman 1967a, Lewis 1959). These cultures share the distinctive combination of features common to people who live in caste systems.

Now I wish to move beyond that formulation of caste systems and, in response to the spirit of Levi-Strauss' recent critique of those who study kinship systems simply to classify into types and subtypes, "try to find out how they work, that is, what kind of solidarity they help to establish within the group ..." (Levi-Strauss 1966:8). I shall not dwell speculatively on origins, although statements pertaining to origins will necessarily appear. My focus will be on the functioning of caste systems in society—on how caste organization affects society. I will suggest that, among other things caste systems:

1. perpetuate and enforce social and cultural diversity,
2. articulate that diversity, and
3. protect privilege through the exercise of power.

Origins

To discuss social functions of caste is not an entirely novel undertaking. Many Indianists and historians have speculated on the origins of Indian caste and in the course of their speculations have implied or hypothesized functions which it serves. Anthropologists and sociologists have occasionally discussed origins or predisposing circumstances for caste in India and elsewhere. Sociologists have debated the functional implications of social stratification in discussions which have obvious, and sometimes explicit, relevance to caste stratification.

As *Pieris* (1952) has noted, Toynbee postulated that caste systems are one of "the three possible alternative outcomes of the impact of one society upon another—that is, extermination assimilation, and caste..." (Toynbee 1934:217). In the genesis of caste, either "an indigenous population may admit peaceful immigrants to live on sufferance in its midst...," or a population may be conquered by powerful invaders "who forbear to exterminate it and disdain to coalesce with it, and are constrained to toletrate it..." (*Ibid*))[1] In both cases the less powerful group is assigned low rank. Watson (1963) refers to a broad range of societies in which he believes caste organization occurs, and attributes its origin to intensified interdependence among formerly more autonomous social aggregates. Caste systems result from contact between social systems, and therefore he refers to them as a form of acculturation.

Nadel (1954) cites evidence, from Nupe in West Africa and Beni Amer in East Africa, of caste systems which have arisen as a result of ethnic heterogencity and conquest. He raises the question: "Is this the only way in which castes, *viz.*, as a side issue of government by conquest?" (1954:15). He concludes that while some caste systems arise in this fashion, others "arise from internal differentiation of societies, in the absence of any ethnic heterogeneity or any 'struggle of races" (1954:21). The conditions comprising the latter route to caste organization include:

1. a rigid division of labour,
2. a religious sanction for that division,

3. the fact that the tasks are vital in the society and inspire some feeling of awe (1954:22).

Watson rejects this explanation of the origin of caste systems, partly because "substantial cultural differences are initially necessary to permit and maintain a division on a wholly ascriptive basis between...segments of a composite community" (Watson, 1963: 368), and he holds that such differences do not occur within a single society.

Karve (1961;12ff.), addressing the same question, points out that anthropologists dealing with the origins of caste in India have been aware that some castes have long histories as castes, others are identified as immigrant groups, and some are recognized to have emerged as castes from tribal status. Yet, she points out, a dominant belief among students of the Indian caste system, exemplified in the work of Ghurye (1952) is that the caste system in its contemporary complexity arose out of the repeated fragmentation of previously unitary social grouping (probably beginning with the three, and later four, Aryan *varnas* of the Vedic period, and culminating in the thousands of *jatis* of today). The mythical Hindu "law-giver", Manu, set the precedent for this view when, 2000 years ago, in the first recorded description of castes in India, he ascribed their origin to the progency of *inter-varna* unions, the number of castes growing as the mixtures and permutation thereon increased in variety (cf. Karve 1961:53-57). Karve, in offering an alternative explanation, emphasizes the social and cultural distinctiveness of castes today (1961:28, 31ff.), and their mutual interdependence. She postulates that while Aryans did not have caste (*jati*), there nevertheless may have been castes in India prior to the Aryan period, and that the invading Aryans superimposed their *varnas* at the top of the hierarchy. In the process, some indigenous caste groups were incorporated into the *varnas*, but the majority of them were added at the bottom of the hierarchy to comprise a new, lower category—presumably the fourth *varna*. The "untouchable" category, sometimes regarded as a fifth *varna*, is often described as having a similar origin Karve notes that "the processes of castemaking were going on throughout history and are happening even at present" (1961:58). She speculates that pre-Aryan castes arose as a result of "tribe-like separateness"—of the cultural and social distinctiveness of groups which came together at various times and under various circumstances into a single society. She cites evidence wherein the same group has been incorporated into the society of different regions of India at different levels of rank (1961:58-69)/She thus sees fragmentation as a minor source of caste organization at most, and she, along with Watson (1963), sees the primary source to be in the coming together of disparate groups which remain distinct but which interact as components of a single hierarchy. For Ceylon, Pieris (1952) has provided evidence of such incorporation of disparate immigrant groups into a caste hierarchy. He concludes: "It seems therefore, that the dominant caste is originally a powerful invading group, and, once established as the governing caste, relegates all future immigrant groups to the ranks of the aboriginal inferior castes..." (Pieris 1952:414).

Speculations and inferences about the origins and development of caste systems in India and elsewhere are apparently immune to empirical verification, but the origins of particular castes, the conditions attending their origin, and the consequences of the occurrence of caste systems are not. Certainly the social functions of caste organization, once it has been established, are subject to analysis based on documentable instances. The accounts of origins cited above are relevant to such analysis insofar as they state or imply the functions served by caste organization. The following discussion is intended to be a more systematic, comprehensive, and explicit, but still preliminary, contribution.

Functions and Processes

Every system of social stratification allocates power and privilege in the society in which it occurs (Lenski 1966, cf. Mills 1963:305-323), and most if not all such systems are associated with some ranked division of labour (cf. Davis and Moore 1945;

Tumin. 1953). Caste systems are systems of social stratification which, although unique in that they are based on birth-ascription, share the general attributes of such systems. Like other stratification systems, they rank people, allocate power and privilege, divide labour, and promote interdependence. But an important point that has been largely overlooked by analysis is that caste systems are more than simply unusually rigid systems of stratification. They are also systems of cultural pluralism, maintained by enforced differential association among culturaly distinctive groups (Berreman 1967a, 1967b; Watson 1963; cf. Smith 1960; Benedict 1962). Consequently they have distinct and common attributes not shared by non-caste systems of stratification. The most important of these is that they serve to separate and coordinate culturally differentiated groups of people with the result that power and privilege are rigidly controlled.

Separation and Diversity

By restricting interation between groups, a caste system insures that the constituent groups will remain culturally distinct and may even become increasingly distinct (cf. Berreman 1960b). This results from the common culture depends upon learning via interaction Caste systems inhibit the opportunity for shared culture by restricting interaction. They also inhibit the expression of common culture, even where the opportunity for it exists, through sanctions enforcing caste-specific behaviour and attributes. One is not allowed to emulate his superiors, and one does not design to emulate his inferiors in caste-relevant ways. When a caste attempts to emulate its superiors it must be either prevented, punished, or promoted. That is, it must be made to desist or must be acknowledged to be of a rank appropriate to the behaviour and attributes of its members. Only thus can the system remain intact.

Each caste is a social and cultural entity and is expected to remain so and to occupy a rank position commensurate with the culturally prescribed evaluation of its distinctive attributes. Assimilation and acculturation are inhibited or prohibited.

Articulation (Coordination)

A plural society functions despite subcultural differences and social separation of its constituent sections because rules and mechanisms exist which facilitate interaction. Caste systems provide the epitome in regorous definition of behavioural rules, interactional mechanisms, and the contexts in which they apply. They permit, and in fact require, some kinds of interaction among groups while inhibiting the probable consequence of understricted interaction: cultural homogeneity and obliteration of cultural or caste boundaries. They thus articulate the activities of socially and culturally diverse sections of society without jeopardizing their diversity. They do so by providing, enforcing, and rationalizing precise rules of interaction, interdependence, hierarchy, and the allocation of power and privilege.

To do this a minimal consensus is of course necessary. As I have suggested elsewhere, members of different castes "agree on the objective facts of...who has the power, and how, under what circumstances and for what purposes it is likely to be exercised. They cease to get along when *this* crucil agreement changes or is challenged" (Berreman 1967a:55; cf. Berreman 1964b). But caste systems seem to depend far less on general consensus than do other systems of stratification and to rely mare heavy on behavioural conformity achieved through the threat or exercise of power in the context of socio-cultural diversity and minimal consensus. Caste systems are in this regard like other plural system, and they contrast in this regard with other systems of stratification to the degree that those systems are non-plural (cf. Berreman 1967a; Smith 1960). The emergence of broad consensus is inimical to caste organization, for it leads to common behaviour, common atributes, and common aspirations which threaten to blur or eliminate caste boundaries, caste prerogatives, and other distinctions crucial to the system. At the same time there is a constant possibility that conscneus will emerge because of the juxtaposition and potential interaction of castes. It fact, Watson

(1963:375) suggest that caste systems are for these reasons "inherently transitory"[2] These facts contribute to the heavy emphasis that is placed in caste systems upon social separation between castes and the readiness of those with power to exercise it, in order to maintain that separation and to enforce status maintaining differential power.

Protection of Power and Privilege

The castes with dominant power correctly see social separation and differential behaviocr among castes as necessary to perpetuation of the system and of their privileged position within it, for these features militate against combined action to challenge either the system or the position of those at the top of the hierarchy.

Distinct statuses and roles and attendant privileges are assigned to each group in a caste system according to the power it actually or potentially wields in the society. Once the group has been placed in the hierarchy, stability is sought through limiting the group's power to that which is regarded as consistent with its status.

Continuity: Power and Interdependence

Economic interdependence and relative economic non-competition among castes are aspects of the fact that caste systems are systems of sharply defined differential power. Goods, services, rewards, and obligations are distributed in large measure according to caste membership. Ideally every group is socially insulated, yet every group is dependent upon the other groups in society, and decisive power is firmly in the hands of those at the top. Caste is thus a conservative system whereby a status quo of rank can be maintained so long as the system is operational.

Caste organization not only protects the distribution of power; it is also dependent upon power. Sanctions are necessay to enforce adherence to the system (Berreman 1960a). Any change in the distribution of power leads to a shake-up in the hierarchy, if not in the very system itself. If any caste threatens to assume unwanted power, sanctions are at hand to reestablish the status quo. If these prove in effective, then alternative mechanisms must be available by which the caste's position (and hence the degree and nature of its legitimate claim to power) can be altered. If not, then the system is jeopardized, for power will not be denied—it leads to rank (cf. Lenski 1966). A powerful low caste or a relatively weak high caste is an anomaly, a dissonant element which normally leads to adjustments eliminating the dissonance (cf. Festinger 1957). Changes in power relations are undoubtedly the primary mechanism for change in caste systems.

In addition to conserving the allocation of power and privilege among groups, caste promotes the immediate self-interest of each group by providing a community of co-equals whose interests are defined by the system as shared and unique. The caste, therefore, is self-regulatory and self-promoting to a degree. Given the system, it is essenital that it be so; and it is perhaps inevitable that its members will define it as their refuge in a threatening world, their haven of equality in an environment of inequality.

The specialization and interdependence of castes has the effect of assuring that the jobs in society get done, just as it assures that no caste will be able to escape the system. Davis and Moore (1945; cf. Davis 1949:364-391) note that systems of stratification function to induce the members of a society to perform the various tasks required in that society. They maintain that this is done by means of differential rewards. "Social inequality is thus an unconsciously evolved device by which societies insure that the most important positions are conscientiously filled by the most qualified persons" (Davis and Moore 1945.243).

This view has evoked a storm of criticism and defense (Buckley 1958; 1959, Davis 1953, 1959; Levy 1959; Moore 1953; Tumin 1953; Wrong 1959). I would say that power is the factor most important in determining and maintaining any system of stratification—that sanctions are more important than rewards. The most common reward for people toward the lower end of a hierarchy is absence of painful consequences. The problem is not how to get people into positions of power and privilege, but how to keep them out—how to reserve such positions for the incumbents and their progeny, relatives, friends, or allies, and how to assure that someone will do those tasks that are necessary but undesirable being dangerous, dirty, poorly rewarded, and even defiling. Thus stratification is primarily a system for maintaining power relations and the status quo of privilege allotment rather than one primarily for insuring recruitment of the most qualified people for the most important jobs (cf. Tumin 1953; Buckley 1959).

A caste system assigns each group of people a particular amount of power and privilege and requires them to remain exactly where they are in the system of ranked groups. In the traditional context they must fill the roles they have always filled, acquire their accustomed rewards and no others, interact outside the group only in prescribed ways symbolic of their status, and be punished if they deviate from these patterns. The caste is organized, almost by definition, for promotion of its self-interest, for self-defense and for self-regulation. It is held responsible for the behaviour of all of its members and any sanction affecting one member may be extended so that if affects all. But the caste is not organized for achieving the broader interests of groups of castes or of the society at large except insofar as fulfilling its ascribed role may be assumed to benefit others.

As a self-interest group the caste is an effective kind of organization, functioning like a guild or union in many instances. But is does so within the confines of its intrinsic power relative to other castes.[3] This power is, for most groups other than the dominant one(s), quite weak. By fractionating society, a caste system makes each group dependent upon its own resources for its overall power in the society. Because caste members regard their own caste as having common and unique interests and a distinct culture, they are unlikely to identify their interests with the interests of others, and especially not with those who are closest to them in the hierarchy and who might be the most effective allies, for those are the very castes with which they are competing most avidly for status and other advantages. Each caste is too small, too isolated, too weak, and too preoccupied with its own position, and with jockeying for position and advantage with castes near it in rank, to engineer major changes. Those groups which are powerful remain so; groups which are weak are unlikely to combine forces to confront the powerful ones, so they remain weak. Power relations become solidified and are perpetuated.

If change occurs, it must be either through a major change in the power of a single caste (*e.g.*, loss or gain of land or clientele, access to office or to education) or through a change of the total socio-cultural environment (as in modernization and Westernization, when new avenues to power and prestige arise—avenues such as the vote—and when the old constraints decrease—constraints such as the importance attached to ritual status or traditional symbols of rank). Then people may be able to combine forces across the traditional caste lines or to mobilize themselves for certain purposes without regard to caste at all. Many of the currents of change in caste systems are of this nature. Within a caste system, it is true that the interests of each group are best served by remaining separate. If the system were to be challenged or altered, however, it would be likely to become advantageous or even necessary for some groups to join forces. A caste system imposes structural, cultural, and psychological impediments to this. The caste system therefore comprises its own barrier against threats to privilege and power, as well as being a mechanism for perpetuating the status quo of rank. Caste organization keeps power from those without privilege and privilege from those without power. It is not a benevolent system—at best it may be paternalistic—but it is in theory, and more rarely in practice, an efficient one.

Intrinsic Change

All social systems undergo continual restructuring and redefinition as a consequence of the fact that their definition and structuring are the products of human intercation; in fact, a social system is an abstract description of interaction.

While interaction takes place within the cultural and social framework of its participants, it concurrently conditions or influences that framework. This fact has been analyzed for social roles, for definition of the self, and for small-scale, face-to-face situations by those sociologists and social psychologists who are often collectively termed "interactionists" (*e.g.*, Harold Garfinkel, Erving Goffman, Tamotsu Shibutani), whose orientations derive from such men as George Herbert Mead, William I. Thomas, and especially Alfred Schutz. The same general fact has been analyzed for social structure on a broader scale by Edmund Leach, Fredrik Barth, and others. What this rather diverse collectivity of scholars share in their approach is a dynamic model of society emphasizing interaction and choice-making (what Firth terms "social organization" [Firth 1956:28ff., 40]) as crucial to that model.

Caste systems, as aspects of social structure, can be usefully analyzed from this perspective (cf. Marriott 1959). Interpersonal interaction is perhaps an even more conspicuous feature of social stratification, and hence caste, than of many other aspects of social structure. To describe a system of stratification, one abstracts from observations of interaction, from statements about interaction, and from statements or other evidence about the ideas and attitudes which condition interaction. A social hierarchy is continually redefined, affirmed, challenged and validated by interaction even as interaction is continually constrained by the hierarchy.

Continual adjustment is inevitable because the context as well as the precise nature of interaction continually changes. Power relations change as technology, demography, economy, polities, law, religion family, and other features of the overall situation alter. Moreover, individuals and groups do not define the hierarchical situation in identical ways. Hyman (1942) points out that subjective status may be quite different from accorded status, and either or both may be quite different from the status which would be assigned by objective application of status criteria. Also, the subjective view of status may be different depending upon whether the view is of "where I am in the hierarchy" or "where I deserve to be in the hierarchy", while accorded status may vary by the relative locations in the hierarchy of the ones judging and the ones being judged. These differential definitions of the hierarchical situation create what Festinger (1957) calls situations of cognitive dissonance, wherein there is a tendency to resolve the dissonance by bringing the various definitions into accord. The attempt to bring them into accord generates the strain, resistance, and striving characteristic of caste systems.

Mobility movements of various sorts are the most dramatic of the many manifestations of change in caste systems because they are international and are recognized as such both by those who stand to gain and by those who stand to lose. But every caste every day is engaged in validating claims and parrying threats, enforcing conformity within and managing impressions without. Even in the absence of mobility movements—in the absence of overt striving—adjustments routinely occur which result in change in the caste hierarchy through change in the idioms in which it is expressed, in the criteria by which it is defined, and in the order in which its constituent groups are ranked.

If one were were to indulge in the perilous pastime of drawing physical analogies, the caste system might be compared to a liquid whose constituent molecules are continually moving, testing the limits of their environment (the container, the pressures of air and gravity, the temperature), taking advantage of every fissure, responding to every change, and consequently reshaping the mass in response to the changing environment. Where the analogy breaks down conspicuously is in the crucial sphere of purposive action—of meaning, choice, and the reflexive charaeter of human interaction. Each human choice effects the conditions, the premises, for future choices, and in this manner the basic structure changes over time just as it varies in response to differing circumstances.

To study caste as social structure and to study its social functions, therefore, it is crucial that it be understood as a manifestation of interaction, of choices and decisions by people in situations defined by themselves in terms of their experience, their culture and society. That is, caste systems must be studied as social process (cf. Firth 1956:28).

Assimilation Versus Exclusion

When some sections of a plural society enjoy conspicuous privileges denied to others, those others seem inevitably to overcome that denial and will seek to do so if opportunity, as they define it, permits (cf. Berreman 1960a). If, as is the case in caste systems, assimilation to the high status groups and withdrawal from the system which accords them low status are both impossible, two means remain for acquisition of privilege; by a low caste:

1. by emulation of high status groups, *i.e.*, validating a claim to privilege through display of suitable attributes and
2. by organized power, *i.e.*, validating a claim to privilege through exercise of political, economic, physical, or other power.

Orans (1959, 1965) has described as "the emulation-solidarity conflict", the dilemma of a tribal group in India faced with the choice of either emulating the dominant society in the expectation of achieving success on its terms (at the cost of loss of cohesion and distinctive group identity) or alternatively, maintaining the distinctiveness and identity of the group in order to achieve the power and intrinsic rewards which result from group cohesion (at the probable cost, in the short run at least, of losing out or being accorded low status is the dominant society). This is the common dilemma of the socially mobile or acculturating group any society (cf. Berreman 1964a). The dilemma is especially acute in a caste situation when, as in the case of Negroes in American society, emulation of some aspects of the dominant culture is encouraged but fails to accomplish assimilation and when, on the other hand, solidarity is discouraged as a means to bring changes in the hierarchy of power and privilege.

The contemporary plea for "black power" represents an awareness of this dilemma by Negroes—the recognition that without power, their struggle for privilege (even the privilege of equal treatment) is doomed. It includes the plea to members of the group that group interest be recognized as the way to achieve the power or influence which will serve that interest. This grows out of the awareness that the dominant group has long equated its group interest with self-interest and has long used power to serve those interests, and that it has equally long encouraged emulation rather than solidarity as the road to salvation for the very groups to which it has denied the reward which emulation is designed to achieve, namely, assimilation. That is, whites have used power to achieve their own ends but have discouraged or prevented its acquisition or use among Negroes, *i.e.*, among those whose disadvantage they have defined as advantageous to themselves. The drive toward black power thus grows out of the experience that where assimilation is effectively denied, emulation in the absence of power simply leads to perpetuation of subordinate status and precludes the kinds of changes which would change that status or would challenge the system upon which it is based.

Here there is an important difference between caste systems and other systems of stratification. In a non-caste system, where power and privilege accompany achievable status, emulation is at least potentially effective and assimilation is a realistic goal, as most ethnic groups in America, for example, have found out. But in a caste situation, where these rewards are ascribed by birth, emulation is ineffective as long as the system persists and assimilation is impossible, as Negroes in America, for example, have found out (unless, of course, one can successfully conceal his identity and "pass" as a member of a high status group).

The only hope that a minority has of moving up in a caste hierarchy or of challenging the system is in the acquisition and exercise of power relative to other groups or relative to the society at large. This is true of castes in India just as it is of Negroes in America. In India upward mobility of castes is sought, validated, and rationalized through emulation but is achieved only in combination with power (cf. Bailey 1957: 200-226; Cohn 1964; Lynch 1966:103ff.; Rowe 1960:56ff., 299ff., 1963; Sinha 1959, 1962; Srinivas 1956, 1966:1-45, 89-117).

The current split in tactics advocated by different segments of the civil rights (or black liberation) movement in America, exemplified in the contrasting approaches of the National Association for the Advancement of Coloured People and the Student Non-violent Coordinating Committee, represents primary reliance upon emulation and upon acquisition of power, respectively. It is not surprising the latter choice has become widespread more recently than the former, for it is an outgrowth of frustration encountered in following the first choice. It is also not surprising that the second choice is more feared than the first—that it generates expression of a "white backlash"—for it has the potentiality of effectively challenging the hierarchical status quo which emulation did not, Precisely the same principles have been manifest in South Africa, in India, and other regions where the caste has confronted alternative values.

A mobile group's dilemma of emulation versus solidarity

might be described, from the point of view of the dominant elements in society, as the 'assimilation-exclusion conflict'.. Caste organization is a recurrent means through which that conflict is resolved by the dominant group. A group which is new on the scene need not be assimilated into an existing group nor be excluded from participating in the society; it can be incorporated as a socially and culturally distinct entity, interacting with other groups in the society in ways which are rigorously defined by its assigned place in the hierarchy. The ways in which interaction is permitted are so defined as to keep the caste unassimilated (and unassimilable) into other groups as well as unexcluded (and unexcludable) from the society.

The caste mechanism thus contrasts sharply with the method of enforced conversion, assimilation, or acculturation characteristic, for example, of Christianity and Islam, of Western imperialism, and of the Inca state. The ideology of caste is antithetical to the ideology of assimilation although it is perfectly possible for both ideologies to be expressed in one society with reference to different groups. It is precisely because they were regarded as unassimilable that Negroes in America have remained a caste while other ethnic groups, those regarded as assimilable, have disappeared into the "melting pot".

In a caste system, groups are incorporated essentially by being quarantined, each being assigned a private and exclusive cell in the established hierarchy, there to perform their role of interdependence with the larger society without contaminating or infringing on the social space of others, there to elaborate their own distinct culture and to accommodate to the cultures of others.

Redefinition

Wherever caste organization occurs, it is acutely jeopardized by modernization and nationalism. The reason for this is that under the impetus of these processes there is uprecedented pressure for, and the means to, cultural homogeneity; the direction is toward conformity, consensus, and the "replication of uniformity" in place of the traditional pluralism or cultural diversity (cf. Wallace 1962:26-29). Through such mechanisms as mass media and universal education, this pressure achieves results. McLuhan (1965:5) has noted that in America today the Negro, the teenager, and some other groups "can no longer be *contained*, in the political sense of limited association. They are now *involved* in our lives as we in theirs thanks to the electric media." This becomes increasingly the case with reference to caste groups in most societies today as modernization, accompanied by universal education and exposure to mass media, occurs. Cultural diversity diminishes; pluralism is undermined.

Common sources of information, common role-models, and common opportunities lead to common aspirations and expectations, common reference groups, common values, common attitudes and behaviour. The diversity and dissensus requisite for caste systems are replaced by the homogeneity and consensus which are their nemeses. The threat of increased homogeneity in a caste system is likely to be resisted both from within and without particular castes. From without, it is resisted by the society at large (on behalf of the privileged castes who dominate it) as a threat to the system—to the hierarchical status quo. It is resisted from within particular castes as a threat to the organized efforts of the caste to promote its self-interest, *e.g.*, to be accorded higher rank.

Under conditions of increasing cultural and social homogeneity, caste, as traditionally defined, becomes decreasingly relevant, appropriate, and effective as a mechanism for protecting self-interest, because the society and ideology within which it arose and to which it was adapted are redefined. Individual mobility becomes possible and desirable and the intertia of the caste group becomes a handicap. Individuals demand and achieve the means to acquire power and privilege by routes independent of caste organization whether these be individual routes or routes involving groups other than castes. These subverts the basic principle of caste, that of birth-ascribed hierarchy. Caste becomes defined as an impediment to aspirations which can be realized if it is ignored or destroyed. The sanctions which functioned to maintain it weaken as the circumstances which supported them disappear. The recent history of the American Negro is a case in point. Attempts to change or eliminate caste systems bring conflict, this does not mean that the former system was enfunctional, but only that it protected major vested interests and that their beneficiaries are loath to relinquish them. One man's (or caste's) eufunction is another man's dysfunction.

These facts do not mean that castes simply disappear when the cultural and social environment changes, but that under these conditions castes inevitably alter their structures and functions. Whether or not they remain castes is a matter of definition and of time, for caste organization is an ideal type at one end of a continuum along which any particular group or society may move through time. "Like other structures", Watson suggests (1963:374), "they change, waxing, waning." Accordingly, we see that in India today, castes (*jatis*) join together, particularly in cities and in the context of contem-prary electoral politics, to form associations with political, economic and social power beyond the capability of any single caste (c.f. Lynch 1966: Rudolph and Rudolph 1960). This is an effect toward the exercise of power by increasing the size and solidarity of the contending groups. In some instances in India the traditional *jatis* remain functional at the familial and marital level after they have diminished in relevance in other spheres (cf. Bailey 1960:240). Cultural diversity seems to diminish in many modern, urban contexts, while structural distinctions between groups remain important, although the composition or boundaries of those groups are often redefined (*e.g.*, caste associations in place of *jatis*). Thus, *jatis* may well disappear before caste does; caste boundaries are likely to be redefined, their identifying characteristics changed, and their functions altered or adapted, while the hirarchical, segmentary, group-interest-promoting, power building principle persists.

At the other extreme we see avenues to individual mobility replacing traditional efforts at raising the status of the entire caste when assimilation is defined as possible. Individuals move from untouchability to high secular status, for example, entirely outside of the constraints of caste (cf. Isaacs 1964). People move out of villages into cities where traditional caste is less important in day-to-day social relations, employment, etc., where caste roles are less clearly defined and less relevant, and where the division of labour and economic and social interdependence are less closely tied to caste. In the United States, Nagroes leave the South, become educated or join the army, and in this manner escape some of the more painful aspects of their caste status, by leaving the contexts in which it is most relevant.

People thus come to see traditional caste as irrelevant to new concerns. Those who benefited from it, of course, object to the changes and resist them. The confronation of equalitarian and caste ideologies is a source of powerful conflict, for it threatens a basic change in social organization—an upsetingt of heavy vested interests, a changed relationship among individuals and groups, a change from the articulation of diversity based on social separation and enforced by the free use of power to the replication of uniformity based on common experience, pervasive communication, and intensive interaction. This is the source of the explosive results wherever caste system have been challenged by equalitarianism.

Conclusion

Caste organization has been viewed by many scholars as an integrative mechanism in society and as non-conflictive, based upon consensus and mutual respect. Thus, it has often been explicitly or implicitly adjudged individually and socially eufunctional, giving it as does to each individual a place in society and a sense of social worth. This tends toward the 'conservative thesis' regarding social inequality described by Lenski (1966:5-17).

The view advanced here is that caste systems are held together by power, concentrated in certain groups, more than by consensus; that they work (and in that sense are functional) by facilitating the articulation of culturally diverse groups; that they are enabling devices for cultural pluralism and for the protection of privilege. They are threatened and they inevitably change when power relations change and also when consensus becomes the primary basis for social integration, for then pluralism—an essential ingradient of caste systems—is threatened or disappears. This approximates the view of social inequality which Lenski calls the 'radical antithesis' (1966:5-17). That caste system often succeed in articulating the activities of diverse groups does not mean that for individuals and groups such systems may not be starkly dysfunctional by limiting opportunities, thwarting aspirations, and precluding effective alternatives. Ultimately caste systems are likely to lead to overt conflict as mass media and other appurtenances of modernization afford opportunities for those who suffer denigration under caste organization to challenge it or throw it off, and as these opportunities are interpreted by other groups as threatening.

Caste is thus a means for ordering the relations among disaparate groups. As a form of pluralism, it is an alternative to assimilation or eradication of groups in contact, as Toynbee has noted, although it is not the only alternative. Non-hierachical pluralism is another possibility, but how often such pluralism in fact occurs is a moot point; perhaps hierarchy almost inevitably develops if pluralism persists, for power is never held equally, and group identity, loyalty, and self-interest may tend to cause it to be passed on within the group, *i.e.*, frequently by birth. Caste organization can be effective in achieving ordered relations among groups for a time, but its ability to withstand universal education, mass media, equalitarian ideologies, and the elimination of monopolies on power which these engender is highly doubtful.

NOTES AND REFERENCES

1. I would suggest that pluralism, rater than caste, is the third alternative, and that caste is a common (perhaps the most common) means of organizing pluralism—it articulates the distinct sections of society in a hierarchy and defines their membership by birth, This view and its implications are elaborated below.
2. "Having argued the vary profoundity of inter-group differences when a caste system is at full tide, we may not seem consistent in asserting that caste systems are inherently transitory. Nevertheless there is both theory and fact in support of this view. If stratified differences of a caste order cannot arise solely from within one socio-cultural continuum, it is reasonable that, except under most favourable (and therefore inferequent) circumstances, such differences would be too great to endure for very long periods within a single continuum" (Watson 1963:374-375).
3. Lynch (1966:3), in his study of an untouchable caste of Agra, notes that "Caste is an adaptive structure through which its members can relate and rerelate themselves to members of other castes in terms of the potentialities provided to them by the socio-political environment in which they interact."

Bailey. F.G. (1957). *Caste and the Economic Frontier*. Manchester: Manchester University Press.

(1960), *Tribe Caste and Nation*, Manchester: Manchester University Press.

Benedict, Burton (1962). Startification in Plural Societies. *American Antropologist*, 64:1235-1246.

Berreman, Gerald D. (1960a). Caste in India and the United States. *American Journal of Sociology* 66:120-127.

(1960b). Cultural Variability and Drift in the Himalayan Hills. *American Anthropologist*, 62:774-794.

(1962). Caste, Racism and Stratification. *Contributions to Indian Sociology*. 6:122-125.

(1964a). Aleut Referenee Group Alienation, Mobility and Acculturation. *American Anthropologist*, 66:231-250.

(1964b). Fear Itself: An Anthropologist's View. *Bulletin of the Atomic Scientists*, 20:9:8-11.

(1965). The Study of Caste Ranking in India *Southwestern Journal of Antropology*, 21:115-129.

(1966). 'Caste in Cross-Cultural Perspective,' in *Japan's Invisible Race: Caste in Culture and Personality* (ed. by G. DeVos and H. Wagatsuma), pp. 275-324. Berkeley: University of California Press.

(1967a). 'Startification, Pluralism and interaction: A Comparative Analysis of Caste,' in *Caste and Race: Comparative Approaches* (ed. by A. de Reuck and J. Knight), pp. 45-73. Boston: Little, Brown and Co.

1967b 'The Concept of Caste,' in *International Encyclopedia of the Social Sciences*. New York: Crowell, Collier and Macmillan Company (in Press).

Buckley, Walter (1958). Stratification and the Functional Theory of Social Differentiation. *American Sociological Review*, 23: 369-375. (1959). A Rejoiner to Functionalists Dr. Davis and Dr. Levy. *American Sociological Review*, 24:84-86.

Cohn, B.S. (1954). *The Camars of Senapur: A Study of Changing Status of a Depressed Caste.* Unpublished Ph.D. dissertation, Cornell, University, Ithaca, New York, (Also, microfilm, University of Michigan, Ann Arbor, Michigan.)

Davis, Kingsley (1949). *Human Society*. New York: The Macmillan Company. (1953). Reply. *American Sociological Review*, 18: 394-397.

(1959). The Abominable Heresy: A Reply to Dr. Buckley. *American Sociological Review* 24: 82-83.

Davis, Kingsley, and Wilbert E. Moore (1945). Some Principles of Stratification. *American Sociological Review*, 10:242-294.

DeVos, George (1966). 'Motivational Components of Caste', in *Japan's Invisible Race: Caste in Culture and Personality* (ed. by G. DeVos and H. Wagatsuma), pp. 325-384. Berkeley: University of California Press.

Festinger, Leon (1957). A *Theory of Cognitive Dissonance* Evanston: Row, Peterson. Firth, Raymond (1956). *Elements of Social Organization*, 2nd ed. London: Watts and Co.

Ghurye, G.S. (1952). *Caste and Class in India*. New York: Philosophical Library.

Hyman, Herbert (1942). *The Psychology of Status*. New York: Archives of Psychology no. 269.

Isaacs, Harold R. (1964). *India's Ex-Untouchables.* New York: The John Day Co.

Karve, Irawati (1961). *Hindu Society: An Interpretation.* Poona: Deccan College Postgraduate and Research Institute.

Lenski, Gerhard (1966). *Power and Privilege: A Theory of Social Startification.* New York: McGraw Hill.

Levi-Strauss, Claude (1966). The Disappearance of Man. *New York Review of Books*, 7:1:6-8.

Levy, Marion J. 1959 Functionalism: A Reply to Dr. Buckley. *American Sociological Review*, 24:83-84.

Lewis, Oscar (1959). *Five Families: Mexican Caste Studies in the Culture of Poverty*, New York: Basic Books.

Lynch, Owen M. (1966). *The Politics of Untouchability: Social Structure and Social Change in a City of India.* Unpublished Ph.D. dissertation, Columbia University, New York, New York.

Marriott, McKim (1959). Interactional and Attributional Theories of Caste Ranking. *Man in India*, 57:171-222.

McLuhan, Marshall (1965). *Understanding Media: The Extension of Man.* New York: McGraw. Hill (paperback).

Mills, C. Wright (1963). 'The Sociology of Stratification', in *Power, Politics and People: The Collected Essays of C. Wright Mills* (ed. by I. Horowitz), pp. 305-323. New York: Ballatine Books.

Moore, Wilbert (1953). Comment. *American Sociological Review*, 18-397.

Nadel, S.F. (1954). Caste and Government in Primitive Society. *Journal of the Anthropological Society of Bombay*, 8:9-22.

Orans, Martin (1959). A Tribe in Search of Great Tradition: The Emulation-Solidarity Conflict. *Man in India*, 39:108-114.
(1965). *The Santal: A Tribe in Search of Great Tradition.* Detroit: Wayne State University Press.

Peiris, Ralph (1952). Caste, Ethos, and Social Equilibrium. *Social Forces*, 30:409-415.

Rowe, William L. (1960). *Social and Economic Mobility in Low-Caste North Indian Community.* Unpublished Ph.D. dissertation, Cornell University, Ithaca, New York. (also microfilm, University of Michigan, Ann Arbor, Michigan.) (1963). *The New Chauhans: A Caste Mobility Movement in North India.* Center for South Asia Studies, Institute of International Studies, University of California, Berkeley (mimeographed).

Rudolph, Lloyd I, and Susan H. (1960). The Political Role of India's Caste Associations. *Pacific Affairs*, 33:5-22.

Sinha, Surajit (1959). Bhumi-Kshatriya Social Movement in South Mahbhum. *Bulletin of the Department of Antropology* (Calcutta), 8:2:9-32.

(1962). State Formation and Rajput Myth in Tribal Central India. *Man in India*, 42:35-80.

Smith, M.G. (1960), 'Social and Cultural Pluralism,' in *Social and Cultural Pluralism in the Caribbean* pp. 763-785. Annals of the New York Academy of Sciences, vol. 83, art 5.

Srinivas M.N. (1956). A note on Sanskritization and Westernization. *Far Eastern Quarterly*, 15:481-496.

(1966). *Social Change in Modern India*. Berkeley: University of California Press.

Toynbee, Arnold J. (1934). *A Study of History*, vol. 2. London: Oxford University Press.

Tumin, Melvin M. (1953). Some Principles of Startification: A Critical Analysis. *American Sociological Review*, 18:387-394.

Wallace, A.F.C. (1962). *Culture and Personality*. New York: Random House.

Watson, James B. 1963 Caste as a Form of Acculturation. *Southwestern Journal of Anthropology*, 19: 356-379.

Wrong, Dennis H. (1959). The Functional Theory of Stratification: Some Neglected Considerations *American Sociological Review*, 24:772-782.

8

CASTE DYNAMICS AND COMMUNITY DEVELOPMENT PROGRAMME

I

The Community Development Programme was launched by the Government of India, on 2nd October, 1952 with a view to achieving the total transformation of the Indian social order from the folk to the secular. An attempt is made here to discuss the impact of the Community Development Programme on the caste relations in Basavpur and Rajhalli.

It is very difficult to define precisely the form and content of the Community Development Programme in India. But an attempt can be made in this regard in terms of the formulations given by scholars from time to time. Batten (1957) considers the field of Community Development Programme, "to include any action taken by any agency and primarily designed to benefit the community." (Quoted by I.T. Sandars: In the *International Encyclopaedio of the Sociol Sciences*, 1968). Dunham (1960) has enumerated the elements involved in the consideration of Community Development Programme as

(a) a planned programme,

(b) the encouragement of self-help,

(c) techical assistance, and

(d) the integrating of vorious specialities in order to help the community, (*Ibid.*, p. 171).

Nelson, Ramsey and Verner (1960) regard Community Development as an "Education-for-Action Process." (*Ibid.*, p. 171). Sandars emphasizes two major ideas in Community Development; the first is the conscious acceleration of socio-economic change and the second refers to planned change in a village, town or city, etc. The development of such a movement in the context of a democratic social system presupposes certain facts, that there are limited resources, that there is enough haman labour available, that the planned change is to be brought within a prescribed period and that the people's participation in the programme is necessary.

Basavpur was covered by the Community Development Programme in its first phase of implementation in this region in 1953. This village was chosen to be made a model village. The change aimed at an all-round development of the village in the field of education, agriculture, health and sanitation, cooperative societies. housing and other facilities. The programmes executed in the village were the construction of a gymnasium, a gram kendra, a school building and the establishment of a yuvak mandal, a poultry farm, and a mahila mandal. The *amber charkha* center drew men belonging to almost all castes together. Within a span of 10 years most of the programmes were completed.

The effects of the Community Development Programme on the people of Basavpur reveal a differentiated impact on the various castes and, subcastes of the village. The agricultural castes were the first to be exposed meaningfully to the influences of change; while the others participated in the programmes, they were unable to benefit from the facilities to the same degree.

Discussing the impact of the Community Development

Programmes on intercaste relation , M.S.A. Rao in his study of Yadavpur, holds the view that

> there is an affirmation of the status quo of the caste ranks. The dominant caste (here I should say the subcastes) exploited all the opportunities and became rich. It should again be stressed that this consequence is not entirely due to the Community Development Programme. But it is due to the manner in which the Community Development programmes were launched. The differential distribution of benefits of the programmes has along with other administrative measures contributed to intercaste conflict and community life without the emergence of a new basis. (1962, p.. 11),

We find that the Community Development Programmes in Basavpur are mainly responsible for minimizing the hegemony of the old body of elders who took decisions on all important matters whether they were disputes or problems connected with the day-to day life of the different groups of people. At present, a new class of people has emerged comprised of rich landowners, educated persons, members of the pauchayat committee, yuvak mandal members, political leaders, village officials, and those who have greater contacts with urbanites. Though by itself Community Development Programme cannot be treated as being responsible for change. it has, to some extent, facilitated the processes of urbanization, modernization, and secularization. It has made the community more and more dependent on the world outside in order to satisfy their growing needs and requirements. Though in the initial stage the people of this village showed some shift from their traditional way of life, they have gradully accommodated the changes in their traditional idiom of living. As Patnaik has pointed out. "the flow of modernization and the people's involvement in it are obstructed by many dykes built by cultural tradition, worldview, value, attitude and socially approved habits and practices." (1969, p. 67).

Moreover in the earlier phase of the Community Development Programme there was a kind of temporary dislocation of the traditional institutions that deprived the so-called village caste and subcaste elders of their privileges. At present the responsibilities are divided between the village officials and the members of the panchayat committee. Though in the earlier period of the Community Development Programme, the village showed a considerable degree of cooperation and homogeneity, such a situation no more exists today. The community appears to be more divided that ever and the competition between the major subcaste factions is also gradually increasing. During the latter phase of the Programme no significant activity could be undertaken in which the entire mass of the village could be involved. The one programme in which all the village participated was the cleaning of the silt in the village pond. The new institutions which have been brought into the village by the Community Development Programme simply withered away for lack of participation and support.

To what extent has the Community Development Programme brought about a relaxation in socio-cultural norms and the traditional value system? We find that it has brought about some minor relaxation in caste norms, though the people continue to retain the old identities with their prescriptive role. The transformation of the socio-cultural order from prescriptive to achieved is still not within sight. On the other hand, it cannot be denied that each caste/subcaste group is becoming more and more aware of interests beyond the village. This greater awareness however, is accompanied by a growing reverence for the traditional value system rather than a new rationality, as emphasized by M.S.A. Rao (197). In the day-to-day activities and decision-making they tend to observe traditional norms whether they be marriage customs, or commensal restrictions, etc.

It may be argued that we should not restrict our inquiry to the role of the Community Development Programme alone in analysing the forces of change that have impinged on the rural population. Community Development has been "a fraction of the total process of modernization that is taking place in rural India today." (Lalit K. Sen and Pradipta Roy, 1967, p. 49). There are several other forces which have to be taken into account in order to understand the extension of the process of modernization in rural areas, *e.g.*, the spread of money, economy, irrigation, land reform, flood control, migration new job opportunities, electricity, movies, health, education, population pressure, the disappearance of malaria, state-initiated programmes of development, etc. Many of these have been affecting the way of lives of the people of Basavpur for the last two decades.

An objective evaluation of the effects of the Community Development Programme on Basavpur reveals that there has been little departure from the traditional framework of the social order. Strict observation of caste, subcaste, and sect endogamy, the absence of occupational mobility in the village, the rationalization of the principle of hierarchy, the popularising of festivals at the family level, a tendency to increase ritualization, a phenomenon described by M.N. Srinivas as "Sanskritization," the extension of relations with the outside world on the basis of caste, the increasing urge to maintain group identity, the preservation of commensal restrictions at the village level, the segregation of Harijans as all level and their continued apartheid, the dependence on kinsmen, the observance of rituals on the occasion of the crises of life, the creation of more opportunities for the common man to attend to religious discourses the involvement of the youth more and more in fairs, festivals and cultural functions, the revival of religious sentiments the increasing role of spiritual leaders all over the region, all show that the traditional social framework is hardly disturbed by the Community Development Programme. Nevertheless some change is visible in a few areas. More education, the relaxation of commensal rules in the city environment, the utilization of chemical fertilizers, tractors and other improved implements, agricultural prosperity for a few rich land-owners, the emergence of a new leadership on a new basis, the use of material goods like radios, cars, scooters, the wearing of new styles of dress, the acquisition of new modes of sophistication in speech and manners may be said to be said to be the results, of the Community Development. But these, we must remember, have mainly affected the upper strata of Basavpur.

Rajhalli was brought under the Community Development Programme in 1958. Already 18 years have elapsed, but the Community Development Programme has not achieved many substantial results except for a school building, an approach road to Dharwar which is now under heavy repair, the construction of a well for drinking water, a Mahila Mandal which is now defunct, a *Sarvajanika Vachanalaya,* a public library and Yuvak Mandal. Despite the efforts made by the Government through the Community Development Programme, the people of Rajhalli did not make any significant progress. Due to their relative isolation, the lack of direct contact with the city market and the lack of transportation facilities, the people were not as directly exposed to the forces of modernization, as those of Basavpur although regarding the relationship between the caste groups, the situation in Rajhalli is no different than that of Basavpur.

The Community Development Programme in the two villages attempted to alter the socio-economic situation by developing a few village industries such as poultry farming, spinning, etc., without any success. The development of viable cottage industries might have injected a new dimension to the village economy. In fact, for an adequate structural change, the development of cottage industries seems to be a major economic imperative and that is why the progress made so far in both the villages in the fields of agriculture and education have tended to be in the direction of organizational rather than structural change.

II

The paper attempted to determine the pattern of behaviour and relationships of an individual with respect to various types of activities and situations. Each head of the family was interviewed and facts about his total interaction in the community in the village and outside were recorded. Likewise his attitudes and opinions about the desirability of certain changes in relationships were also enquired into. As a result of this mode of attack the following groups were found to be important.

A person in a village has generally a given sort of neighbours in terms of his caste. The habitation areas of all the villages are divided between two main areas, one inhabited by those who are traditionally called touchables and the other by those who are known as untouchables. Within the touchable area 5 or 6 castes may either live intermixed, or in separate clusters. In the area in which untouchables live, there is a sharp demarcation of habitation areas of different castes. Wherever one finds a Muslim family in the village, it occupies a marginal position between the two areas but nearer to the touchable area. Whether or not the habitation area is of a nuclear or a dispersed type, it does not affect the caste pattern of habitation, except in terms of attitudes. Thus we found that in the dispersed village of Karul, people did not seem to mind the caste of the neighbour as far as attitudes and opinions were concerned. However, as far as actual habitation is concerned, the neighbours were caste fellows. Within each habitation area houses belonging to the same clan tended to cluster. Such a cluster sometimes contained some houses belonging to clans connected by marriage. To sum up, it can be said that in a village man's nearest neighbours tended to be the agnates or the affinal kin. The larger circle of neighbours consisted of caste fellows. Then come the touchables. On the other hand in the untouchable area a man's next door neighbour would be his agnatic or affinal kin or his caste fellow. The other untouchable castes were as far away as the touchable cluster. In Wadi—an experimental co-operative farm—it was found that habitation area did not follow the caste pattern in as much as people living on the farm, lived intermixed in the houses provided by the society. Of course there was not a single untouchable member of the society.

The total number of families interviewed were 343, spread over 21 castes. Most of these people, except for Wadi, were residents of the village concerned for over two generations. The educational attainments were very poor. The total percentage of literacy was 37. Of these the majority were just literates, less than 10 could read and write English. The touchables were comparatively more literate than the untouchables and the tribals. The family type was more or less the same in all the villages, the predominant pattern being husband, wife, children and husband's relatives living together.

Except for Ahupe where there was no school, there were primary schools in all the villages. In Varkute less than 50 per cent of the children of school-going age went to school. In Vasti and Karul about 2/3s of the children go to school, while in Wadi, over 90 per cent go to school. In Varkute the majority did not send girls to schools. In other villages both girls and boys were sent to school. Answers about the wish to educate children showed that the aspirations were modest and realistic, hardly going beyond middle school education. The majority wanted their sons to follow the traditional occupation. However, where change was desired, it was in favour of white-collared occupation. The major occupation of the villagers was the traditional occupation followed by a particular caste. The majority belonged to the farming castes. The next service-men and artisans. There were a few castes which followed a profession.

In most of the villages except Karul, the landlord and tenant belonged to the same caste. However, in the majority of cases, where people worked for some one, they did so outside their own caste except in Ahupe. Among those who had borrowed money, the majority had to go outside their own caste to borrow money. We have seen that the boundaries of kin and caste were transcended in types of interdependence entailed by economic relationships, still a cousiderable minority did not go outside the caste. Economic interdependence did nor seem to imply social intercourse, like hospitality, etc., on a footing of equality.

There was another kind of economic interdependence which is reflected in 'Balutdari-system'. Each village contained a large number of heads of families belonging to agricultural castes. These received certain types of traditional services from the heads of the families of other castes. Some of the services were rendered by touchable castes like Nhavi (barber), Gurav (temple servant), etc. and the other services were rendered by untouchable castes like Mahar, Mang, Ramoshis. This kind of interdependence was bound up with certain types of obligatory hospitality reflecting caste hierarchy. In such intercourse agriculturists were the gives and the receivers were service castes.

Direct questions on social relationships were asked to heads of families. As regards hospitality, in almost all the cases meals were given without any special occasion only to kin. On some occasions meals were served to people of serviee caste. There were only seven cases where food stuff was received from lower castes.

Occasional hospitality involving perhaps the receiving and giving of a cup of tea, was also confined to kin and caste. At the time of marriage, however, meals were served to almost the whole village by the agriculturists and professionals, while this activity was confined to kin and caste entirely among untouchables, almost entirely among the other service castes. This pattern was not significantly affected by factors like age, education, nearness to city and contact with the outside world. In Wadi, however, the caste pattern of hospitality does not obtain.

Help as regardsagricultural operations was generally received from people of own caste. There were a few occasions of help outside the caste. As regards borrowing of money for short period and without interest, there were a number of cases of such borrowing outside the caste. As regards help during sickness help involving personal attendance was confined mostly to kin and sometimes to caste. Help involving giving of medicine etc. was given freely outside the caste. Help given and received at thetime of funeral followed traditional pattern. Even occasional help was confined to caste. In time of calamity help was rendered by caste and kin if it involved giving of a little food stuff or some other thing. Giving of contribution was expected from all who could contribute, irrespective of caste.

Most of the friendships are with persons of own caste, except extremely few genuine friendships across the caste. Friendship involved mutual visiting, even partaking of food, but only by the lower caste at the house of higher caste. At such time the vessels were cleaned by the persons concerned and kept separately. Friendships across the caste among children were rarer than among adults and no feeding of any type was involved. As regards friends outside the village, they were mostly confined to one's caste. Travels and visits did not involve intercaste intercourse. The majority of occasions for going out of the village were weekly visits to the market town. Other travels did not involve putting up with other people.

Almost every family had entertained guests. These were mostly relations by blood or marriage, In Varkute, a mother visited her married daughter over fifty times, almost every week in a year. Most of the guests came from neighbouring villages in Varkute, Ahupe and Karul. Thus guests cannot be said to have provided urban influence. In Wādi and Vasti people went often to Poona and entertained guests often from Poona.

Most of the persons interviewed said that they liked to travel but very few linked to leave the village for good. Majority of the villagers said that they would not like to leave the village, even if their children settled elsewhere. The reasons given were, attachment due to long association, lower cost of living, the feeling of belonging and being respected in the village.

As regards factions and quarrels, those involving inheritance, field-boundaries etc. were among kin. There were other quarrels about leadership, personal differences and tresspassing. These involved different castes. Quarrels about inheritance, etc. generally went to the law courts and involved disputes lasting over long period. Other quarrels were generally sought to be amicably settled either by relatives or friends, or more formally in the village Panchayat (village council). The persons who took lead in compounding quarrels belonged generally to the higher castes, though sometimes persons from the lower castes also mediated. Surprisingly enough, qnarrels and especially factions were not based on caste rivalries. Nor were they based on economic groups like landlord-tenant. employer-employee, money-lender-borrower and Balutdar-Non-Balutdar.

In none of the villages did the untouchables have access to wells and temples situated in the touchable areas. In Varkute, where everybody used the water from the stream, untouchables filled water down the stream so that the water used by touchables was not polluted. Even in common festivals, where work was assigned to every person in the village, the caste pattern was maintained in as much as cooking and fetching water was done by the higher castes and menial duties of bringing fuel, sweeping the ground, were assigned to the persons of untouchables castes. Participation in road building and allied activities were such that the higher castes mostly contributed money and little physical labour whereas the lower castes contributed physical labour only.

Thus we find that most of the intercourse of an individual was confined to kin-groups. And the inter-group intercourse was regulated by the caste code.

The attitudes and opinions confirm the behavioural pattern in terms of social distance and nearness dictated by the caste system. In fact the finer shades of social distance and nearness were brought out by the responses regarding attitudes and opinions. It is true that among the many factors such as age, education, external influence sought to be correlated with behaviour and attitudes, only education seems to have some impact on behaviour, attitudes and opinions. It was only in Wadi that a great measure of liberal attitude was enviced. However, even in Wadi there was by and large a great deal of conforming to the caste pattern in terms of social distance and nearness.

Going into the questions of system of beliefs and values that sustained the type of behaviour and opinion described above, we found that by and large the traditional values about the caste system, the system of age-grades, etc., continued to define the status system even now.

As for the position of the scheduled castes, concrete suggestions have already been made, *viz.*, that so far as they do not have a place in the rural economy, it is very difficult to uplift them. Even certain public utilities were meant to be used by all, the untouchables were prevented from doing so. This of course was due to the stigma attached to untouchability. However, the fact that the untouchable had more or less ceased to be a functional element in the village system, cannot be ignored. For example, the untouchables had ceased to drag dead cattle of the farmers.

To sum up, it should be noted that as regards the major groups, which define and delimit personal and social intercourse in rural communities, are the kin and caste groups. Of course groups based on economic interdependence also bring about relationships and contact, but such groups fail to bring about any significant personal or social intercourse. Further it must be noted that by large there is a correspondence between the economic strata and the social strata. Therefore, again it is not merely the economic groups which bring about personal or social intercourse. But the system of social stratification defines and delimits personal and social intercourse. The exhaustive investigation made, apply proves the point.

The major hypothesis about kinship, caste and locality as the determinants of interpersonal and intergroup relatioaships has been by and large proved. Likewise the methodological experiment has largely proved to be successful in-so-far-as the nature of the material elicited by the use of the various methods and techniques is concerned.

III

Intercaste relations have reveral dimensions. The religious order in Basavpur and Rajhalli is viewed in terms of the rites of passage, fairs and festivals. Attempts have been made by earlier scholars to examine them in the social, economic, religious and educational contexts of rural life. An attempt has also been made to examine the emerging pattern of caste relations in the context of rural life by taking into account the life crises and/or life cycle rites which have been more often regarded as "rites of passage." (Van Gennep, Arnold, 1960), rites performed at the time of birth, initiation, marriage and death in any society. These occasion in the life of each individual are marked with great significance because they bring about transformations in the living status of the individual. Van Gennep collected evidence from different societies in order to show that there is an occurrence of ritual sequences whenever a passage from one stete to another occurs, whether in the status change of an individual, or in the transformation of a community (quoted from Mitchell, *Dictionary of Sociology*: p. 148; L. Mair, 1965; J.H.S. Bossard and L.S. Boll, 1950).

There has been a long-drawn controversy among classical sociologists, anthropologists, and philosophers regarding the nature and position of rituals and beliefs. There were some Robertson Smith, Edmund Leach and Durkheim who argued that rituals preceded beliefs while Tylor and others suggested the opposite. It has now been proved beyond doubt that rituals precede the beliefs in any religion. The rites connected with life-cycle occasions have been categorized broadly into three stages, *viz.*, the separational, the transitional and the incorporational. These rituals encompass a greater domain of religious activities in the context of the family. Moreover, these rites are repetitive in the sense that each individual is required by rule to undergo them in order acquire the privileges, rights and responsibilities of a full-fledged member of the community.

Rituals refers to a category of standardized behaviour (Quoted in Mitchell, p. 148; Goodey, 1961, pp. 142-64). Nadel makes similar observations in his writings (quoted in Mitchell, p. 148: *Nupe Religion,* 1954, Chap. 3rd and 4th). There are some social anthropologists who favour the views of Levi-Strause that ritual procedures from an integral part of the processes of thought. Ritual, according to Leach, serves to "re-affirm the status differences which are created as a result of the complex net work of relations in a society. Ritual serves to remind the congregation, just where each number stands in relation to every other and in relation to a large system." (From "Ritual," in *International Encyclopaedio of the Social Sciences,* Vol. 13, 1968, pp. 520-26).

Rituals have been regarded as having a communicative power. It is through these rituals that one becomes familiar with the norms of the society. Ritual from the point of view of the actor can have the power to alter the state of the world because it involves power. The actor and the others involved in such ritual procedures have confidence in their power to bring about the desired effects.

Life-crisis occasions in an Indian village are very closely connected with the network of intercaste relations, though these need to be further riewed in the context of the family. These life-crises are governed by the more stable and enduring arrangement that existed between families that have interacted for several generations. The inter-familial relations between food-producing and servicing castes have been described as Jamani relations by Weiser (1936). Jamani relations in the organization of a village life incorporates all the or facts of life, namely, religious, social and economic. A close observation of the organization of life reveals the importance of the principle of cooperation and interdependence. On occasions such as birth, initiation (*diksha*), marriage and death, the families cannot by themselves undertake all the roles which are necessary to meet the requirements of the situation. These are several activities which are undertaken by other kinsmen, other castes, friends, and special institutions. Hence, the study of life cycle rituals involves a consideration of the relations between the families belonging to the same as well as to other castes. All the castes in a village can be categorized as:

(a) those who receive the service, and

(b) those who render the services.

Even in such relationships, the principle of superordination and subordination is given prominence. If a high caste member has to perform certain duties in respect to a low caste family, he seems to be favouring them by his act. When a low caste member renders any service to a high caste family, he performs a duty. Such is the understanding between the persons actually involved in such relationships.

Life for the villagers is regarded as a round of rituals and ceremonies (Majumdar, 1958, p. 36). It is these rituals and ceremonies that bring individuals, families, subcastes and castes together. Such rituals and ceremonies extend the bonds outside the village. On these occasions the kinsmen living outside their village renew their bonds, re-affirm their relations and maintain the continuance of such relations. The family level ceremonies acquire social significance when individuals belonging to different caste groups contribute their success. The role played on such occasions by specialists goes on increasing as one moves up the level of the hierarchy (Brijraj Chauhan, 1967, p. 99). The concept of "dominant caste" as developed by Srinivas and Majumdar needs to be reviewed in the context of further empircal data now available. Our field investigations indicate that the concept of dominant caste should be extended to include subcaste dominance. The Lingayats no doubt are the dominants caste in the two villages; but more significant sociologically are the dominant subcastes in the two villages. The Panchamsali and Kudavakkaliga are the dominant sub-castes in Basavpur; and the Banajiga, Ganiga and Panchamsali are the dominant subscastes in Rajhalli.

Life Cycle Rites and Caste Relations in Basavpur

Birth, initiation (*diksha*), marriage and death have been regarded as occasions when different families belonging to different castes come together and renew their faith in the structural order of the society. The data collected regarding these occasions reveal an emerging pattern of relations between the castes of the village. These relationships are examined against the background of the rites performed earlier and at present, their nature, their manner of performance and the alterations, if there are any in their performance.

Birth

Prior to the birth of a new-born, a pregnant woman has to observe several taboos such as not crossing a river, not moving in the village at odd times, standing below certain trees, observing restrictions on certain varieties of food (especially, when it is the first birth), etc. The ceremony of *kubusa maduvadu*, (the offering of a bodice to the pregnant woman) is performed in the fifth as well as in the eighth month. *Simantha* (blessing the prospective male child with a safe birth) is performed during the eighth month. These two ceremonies are performed at the time of the first pregnancy only. Later, the female members of the family take all precautions to ensure a safe delivery. In Basavpur, there are expert *sulagittis* (midwives) present at the time of birth, who belong to the Lingayat and Muslim community. Irrespective of caste and religious affiliation, they always extend their full cooperation to those who are in need, however their services are not extended to low castes such as the Talwar and Harijans. The latter have to make their own arrangements. In contrast, village studies have shown that this function is exclusively undertaken by a particular caste such as the Nai (Barber), (Atal, 1968, p. 16).

The population of this village is more than 80 per cent Lingayat. Hence, our study has been largely preoccupied with the Lingayat rituals. We foung that the birth of a baby in a Lingayat family provides an opportunity to the kinsmen, friends, washermen and Jangams to extend their services to the family of the newly born. A new born baby in the family is first incorporated into the family and then into the caste by the Jangam priest who performs the initiation rites and gives it *diksha.* The ritual involves the washing of the feet of the Jangam. the purification of the house the performing of *abhisheka*, and the tying of the Lingam around the neck of the new-born. The birth is celebrated by a dinner given to the kinsmen, friends, the Jangam, the gardener and the washerman. The Jangam, the gardener and the washerman are paid for their services in addition to the *Aya* given at the time of harvest.

Such rituals reveal the economic condition of a family. A rich agriculturist, will celebrate the birth of a male child on a large scale inviting friends even from the nearby city. A less affluent person will limit himself to his close circle and the manner of celebration will also be very simple. A few of the wealtheir persons tend to go to hospitals in the nearby city for the first delivery and as soon as they return, the usual birth ceremonies are performed.

In Rajhalli the washerwomen and the kuruba women attend deliveries and get payment in return for their services. The birth and initiation rites follow the same pattern in Rajhalli as in the case of Basavpur. However, there are minor differences in the manner of the performance of the rites depending upon the priest. Thus, if the priest is an elderly person he is more particular about the performance of the rites, however the same seriousness is not observed if the priest is much younger. For instance, in Basavpur, one of the Kudavakkaliga priests is quite young, only 20 years old and is not adept in rituals;

hence they are not performed elaborately; while in the case of Rajhalli, the priest is a senior and serious-minded person who performs the rites more conscientiously. Again, as we move towards rich families, the ceremonies are more eleborate even though the priest remains the same. Family traditions also count in respect to the manner of celebrating the occasions. A complete response from the servicing castes can be seen only when the family concerned is rich and influential. In Basavpur and Rajhalli the rites performed at the time of birth are more or less same. But owing to economic backwardness and other problems, elaborate ceremonies are not within the reach of the Rajhalli villagers.

Marriage

Marriage is an important occasion in the life cycle of an individual. Right from the beginning of the arrangement of a marriage to the end of it, the family concerned interacts with other families, caste groups and the entire community at one or the other stage. There are four important stages in the marriage ceremony:

(a) the engagement,

(b) the betrothal,

(c) the *arisina* day ceremony,

(d) the wedding rites.

In each stage, again there are several rites or practices which are observed of practised in order to complete the ceremony.

Several rites which were observed prior to Independence still continue to be observed. Thus, the tradition of consulting village elders, senior kinsmen, the tallying of the horoscopes, etc., are still in vogue. However, some changes are noteworthy. The bridegroom has some degree of choice in the bride. Secondly, while bride was the earlier rule, today in the case of the rich, the bridegroom's family expects a handsome dowry. For instance; one Kudavakkaliga bride's family has paid as much as Rs. 10,000/ as a dowry to the bridegroom. *Teruyu* (bride price) is slowly disappearing even among the lower strata. The change is also noticed in the mode of performing the marriage rites. Most of the performance today are sysmbolic. On certain occasions the absence or presence of other members of one's caste, the servicing castes or one's kinsmen makes little difference. The role of kinsmen in organizing activities on such occasions is not affected by the economic prosperity of the agriculturists. The tradition of giving honour and respect to village customs is continued.

The Role of the Service Castes at the Marriage Ceremony

It is in the life-crisis occasions that we can observe the interaction of families belonging to different castes and how they reaffirm each other's status and role in the social structure of Basavpur. Since a large number of agriculturists who own land come from the Lingayat community, all the other service castes show a greater association with the ceremonies performed by them. As they *Aya* and *Aligal* to the service castes, the entire network of relationship can be examined around the activities of those agricultural families where there is mutual dependance.

Service castes such as the Madiwalar, Bariker and/or Walikar, Hadapad, Hugar, the Jangam priest and the Midiga, are essential on certain occasions owing to their specific roles and privileges. The services of the Kattimani and Metimani are availed of. On the other hand, if the Lingayats neglect to ask for their services, it is treated as a serious lapse on the part of the erring family and is publicly criticised as being a deviance from the norm. While none of these castes insists on being employed, it is traditional to honour the long-standing customs and it shows respect to the traditional system of values. Even the rich do not go against the established pattern of performing marriages. In fact, the rich and educated people give greater importance to the respective roles of the service castes, thus acting as the custodians of the traditional order.

At engagement and betrothal, ceremonies apart from the

kinsmen, lineage elders and elder members of the family, the caste elders and other friends are invited. It is an occasion for re-affirming mutual trust and good feelings towards each other. The Jangam, the family priest, the village elders (village officials), the Kattimani and the Metimani are invited to be present on the occasion. Special mention needs to be made of the role of the Kattimani and the Metimani in the rituals. The village in this part of the country are unique in that they have perpetuated the institutions of the Kattimani and Metimani who belong to the Langayat community. These families of Kattimani and Metimani are invariably invited to any social function in the village. Their task is also to assist the family in arranging the functions and their word carries a great weight among the rural population. Though these families are still honoured and obeyed, there is a visible change in the intensity and degree of such honour and obedience accorded to them. Some two generations ago, the Kattimani and the Metimani were considered to be very powerful in the village affairs. They had the rights to even punish offenders in the village and no one had the courage to defy their words. Obedience was total. But now, such a degree of obedience is not entertained. But still these institutions are respected and people honour them as a matter of tradition, and deviation is considered to be a departure from the social norm. Thus, the Kattimani and the Metimani are sent to invite the kinsmen for the ceremonies and it is they who take the first *vitlya* (betal nut and pan) as a token of honour.

At a wedding, one finds members of different castes helping with the ceremony. The *Barkers* (Walikar) clean the vessels and the *Madaru* sweep the pandal and maintain cleanliness. The *Kumbar* (potter) provides *magis* (special type of pots), needed for the occasion. The goldsmith prepares the *tali*, (the gold cups in the *mangalsutra* needed at the time of a wedding). The role of the goldsmith is gradually diminishing because people tend to buy *talis* from the city. There are only a very few families at present who employ the services of the goldsmith for this purpose. But the people in the village still observe *bab* (the privilege of offering) *sidha* (food) to the goldsmiths even if they get *talis* from the city. The florist provides flowers and garland needed on the occasion. His family also provides the *patri* (sacred leaf), required to perform *pooja*. At the wedding the florist provides the *bhasinga* which is to be tied on the forehead of the bride and bridegroom. It is an occasion for the family priest to officiate at the rituals performed on the occasion. All the other caste members are paid for their services in the form of cash and kind; this is apart from *Aya* given on the occasion of harvesting. In the case of Basavpur, the people from other villages are also invited to perform certain services such as the *bandwallas*, the *sanai ooduvaru*, the pipe players, and painters. Marriage provides an opportunity not only to one's own kinsmen and/or castemen but also to the other service castes, from outside the village. Thus, at the social level, it promotes a solidarity among different caste men, reinforcing and renewing the group bonds, The functional role of each caste in the ritual situation conforms to the ideal pattern which constitutes the rural social structure. So far, no other caste family or any outside agency has ever undertaken those traditional. Economic prosperity and education in Basavpur have not in any way reduced the adherence to such a pattern of caste relations.

The form of marriage ceremony amongst the Lingayat families in Rajhalli is more less the same as at Basavpur. Some differences, however, can be noted. For instance, there are no families of *Kumbar* (potter), *Hugar* (florist), *Bariker/Walikar* (dish-washers) etc., in Rajhalli. Their activities to be undertaken by other caste families or else have to be done by alternate arrangements. The Jangam performs rituals and the role of the Mathapati is sometimes undertaken by another Jangam, or else, a Mathapati from the neighbouring village is invited. Sometimes for such services, the people of Rajhalli depend on persons from Amminbhavi. The poor Muslims, Bajantris, and Walikars may undertake the dish-washing at the time of marriage. There is no goldsmith in this village, hence, the people go to the goldsmiths of Amminbhavi or

Dharwar. The marriage of a rich person at Basavpur is usually attended by people belonging to different occupational classes of urban areas. Whereas in Rajhalli this is not so; as the distance mher in more difficult. In both villages, however, subcaste endogamy is strictly observed and intercaste marital bonds are almost out of question. The kinsmen play several roles in the performance of marriage. The relatives from the mothr's family (uterine kinsmen) prove more helpful financially and otherwise. There are not more thon 5 to 6 cases among the Lingayats where *teruvu* (bride price) is taken even to this day. Though this was a practice in the past, it is now given up.

The several Lingayat subcaste in this village cooperative with each other whenever a marriage is performed in a Lingayat family. Except for the Hadapads they interdine with all other subcastes. There are certain families which perform the marriage of their daughters or sons in temples such as the Basavanna Temple of Basavpur and the Ishwar temple of Amminbhavi. Sometimes, the marriage may be celebrated in the city temples where all the facilities are available. The Uluvi Basappa temple at Dharwar is one such place. Even when marriage takes place outside the village, the persons belonging to the different service castes and the families associated with them are taken there to perform their services. Thus, one sees that the performance of the servicing castes is continued even outside the village.

Death

Death is another crisis in the life cycle. It is an occasion when the different castes voluntarily come forward, forgetting their status differences for a while and participate in the disposal of the dead. Except for the castes who cremate, the rest bury the dead. It is the practice in this region that whenever death occurs in any family, except that of Harijans, at least one member from each family accompanies the procession and participates in the ritual known as *mannu koduvadu* (covering the dead body with earth). Kinsmen from other nearby villages also rush to the family of the breaved to express their sym pathy.

Economic prosperity in Basavpur enables rich agriculturists to spend more money in performing the last rites and offer a good-amount of *dana* (charity); this is a matter of status symbol. But the poor people at Basavpur are not able to spend much even on death; some times they have to borrow money for the funerary rites.

The Role of the Servicing Castes in the Funerary Rites

As in all other crises of life, death is also an occasion where several other castes are involved (See Sociogram No. 3) and affrm their allegiance to the deseased family. The kinsmen, lineagemen, castemen friends, and other servicing castes come express their condolences with the family.

After a death a Hadapad and/or a Madiga is sent to inform the kinsmen of the deceased who are living near the village. Men of low castes, the Walikars or the Madigas dig the grave; the Kumbar provides the required pots; the Badiga helps the *viman* (the carrier of the dead body); the Jangam officiates at the rituals the florist provides the *patri* (scared leaf and flowers); and other low caste people help in carrying the dead body. The relatives perform other ceremonies such as throwing coins and *churumuri* (fried rice) around the *viman* or *sidagi* (the carrier) which is collected by the children of the Madiga and other low castes. The servicing caste families receive *babs*, privileges and gifts in return.

It is almost an obligation to attend a funeral. Any negligence is considered a deviation from the norm. Economic prosperity and education in Basavpur have not brought about any change in this tradition and the rich and the educated in the village continue to maintain it. Among the rich people it is now becoming a practice to solemnize the memory of the deceased by donating money/or by constructing some rooms either in a hostel or a school.

The rites or practices described for the Lingayats of Basavpur are equally applicable to the Lingayats of this village. A Jangam is invited to officiate at the ritual and the Bajantris play music on the occasion. Since this village has no florist, potter or Madiwalar, their services are undertaken by other men of the same castes from nearby villages, otherwise by Muslims or Marathas or Walikars from their own village. Thus the traditional functions are maintained. In Rajhalli the death of village official, a rich person, a panchayat member, or a member of a respectable family is mourned by the entire village. People from all families attend a funeral and show their allegiance to the dead and his family.

As with Basavpur, the people of Rajhalli village forget their differences at the time of death. Many poor families in this village have financial troubles and are either depend and on their relatives or the rich people in the village. It is a norm that if a person comes with such a request he is normally not refused. The regular financial worries that accompany these life crisis rites have made several families, including the big agriculturists, feel handicapped. Be it birth, marriage or death, the families find it difficult to overcome the crisis unless they seek outside financial help from someone. They often turn to the rich at Dharwar for financial help. According to one estimate, the agriculturists of Rajhalli have borrowed in all, not less than 2 lakhs of rupees from the government and/or rich businessmen of Dharwar. Such a huge amount cannot be easily repaid in view of their poor crops and the continued impoverishment of their soil. During the last decade, the agriculturists of Rajhalli have shown a gradual reduction in agricultural output. The loans multiply and re-multiply and even if the loan amount is paid, the interest cannot be paid and hence they become life-long debtors.

The importance of the rites of passage cannot be minimized in the context of evaluating the structural change. These provide visible opportunities for the interplay of several roles in any given caste order. Much depends on the economic and social position of the family in observing rites and rituals. The greater the economic and social position, the greater will be the desire of the family to make the occasion more prominent because of the element of prestige involved in it.

Owing to the difficulty of making arrangements for a longer stay for the guests and due to the problem of time the duration of the ceremonies is now shortened. Thus marriage rituals are completed within a day or two, but mutual understanding and good will is maintained even though it is for a short time. Intercaste relations hips with all their obligations and duties are still honoured and respected. It is observed that greater economic prosperity in the case of Basavpur has resulted in the observation of the rituals (such as on the occasion of Basava Jayanti) in greater detail.

Fairs and Festivals

The impact of fairs and festivals, on the hierarchy, of inter-caste relations in the two villages, Basavpur and Rajhalli, completes our analysis of religious organization.

Fairs and festivals occupy an important place in rural India as they are special occasions for one and all. The fairs and festivals in Basavpur and Rajhalli are classified into national, regional and local. The observance of festivals and fairs is part of religious activity. E. Washburn Hopkins has observed that "all Hindu festivals were religious: and this is not due; solely to the fact that the literature itself is religious...all celebrations of a public nature consisted partly in feasting and partly in religious exercises"[1] Several festivals of ancient times have been discarded and some are now observed differently. Hopkins maintains that the

> "chief local festivities today are associated with places and deities unknown to the ancient world of India; but the seasons remain the same, and the celebration of the advent

of spring, for example, does not differ in reality from the old spring festival. To whom the honour is paid is of less importance than that the festivity should be celebrated. The rites in honour of one Gold have passed over to another without materially altering the celebration and sometimes even today the same celebration is held in honour of different Gods...One thing is to be remarked in regard to modern festivals, as compared with the old, namely, that whereas the old seasonal festivals such as those of the New Year, spring and autumn, were degraded into ritualistic observances, so that in many cases it is hard to recognize the original intent, the modern festivals have thrown off Brahamanism as far as possible, and are more clearly celebrations of seasons devoid of priestly ritual self-sufficiently...Most of modern festivals celebrate seasonal changes, or are held in connexion with pilgrims to some holy place, the shrime, or the river *tirtha*.[2]

Except for the Basavanna fair, the rest of the festivals are celebrated both in Basavpur and Rajhalli. As mentioned earlier, these villages form part of the North Karnataka region of Karnatak state and the Lingayats form the bulk of the population in this region. The contention of Ishwaran[3] that Lingayats are essentially different from Hindus is untenable as can be seen in the celebrations of the festivals in these villages. The Lingayats in these villages celebrate most of the festivals with the same religious fervor and observe all the important rites as do the Hindus. However, there are some festivals such as the Narsimha Jayanti, Vaisnava—Ekadeshi, Asadhi, Narikela Purnima, Rishi-Panchami, etc., which are not observed by the Lingayats. However, the major festivals are common to all and hence it is difficult to see the Lingayat community as being outside the mainstream of Hindu religious life.

The villagers still perform most of the festivals and observe rites as before, although new trends are discernible in the manner of observing some of them. For instance, in the festival of Basav Jayanti, unlike as in the past there are popular lectures and the taking out of a procession with the photo of Lord Basaveshwara. The young people play a major role in organizing such festivals in these villages. It is also observed that some festivals do not attract the entire mass of the village; for instance, celebrated some Muslim festivals such as Moharum which was previously celebrated by all in Basavpur, today seems to be exclusively the affair of Muslims; while in Rajhalli the young men from the Hindu community still participate in this festival, though the elders have ceased to participate since the last two decades. The same is true about the participation of Muslims in some of the Hindu festivals.

Fairs and festivals in rural communities regulate the religious life. In festival after festival, people renew their faith in the traditional order. The elders are honoured and their faith in the religious values and norms of society is reinforced. It is observed that some festivals like Diwali and Kara-hunnive in these villages have been losing significance, but nevertheless they are observed by most in the villages. Though the educated youth and some rich families do not observe the rituals and consider them as traditional and outmoded, but they do not take any anti-traditional stand.

The Basavpur fair is an example of how the people, irrespective of their status and achievement, are very keen to celebrate it with pomp and show. Offering food to the deity, obtaining the services of the servicing castes, holding feasts, inviting the family priest and offering prayers to family deities are done on such occasions. The ritual order is rigorously maintained and the contribution of the women is of special significance as they meticulously observe the rituals with great religious interest.

The celebration of festivals and fairs cut across religious and caste/subcaste barriers and brings individuals of different castes together, fostering a sense of village social solidarity. It is observed that these festivals and fairs go a long way in reinforcing the structure of the caste system and that adherence to it becomes automatic with the celebration of each occasion. The greater interest evinced by the people in the performance of some festivals clearly shows that it is one of the ways in which the caste system is being reinforced.

REFERENCES

1. *Encyclopaedia of Religion and Ethics*, Vol. 5 (1964), p. 867.
2. *Ibid.*, pp. 868-70.
3. (1968), p. 32.

9

CASTE AND COMMUNITY AMONG INDIAN JEWS

One of the more interesting facts about the sociology of South India to the existence of Jewish communities in Malabar, reported by travellers from Europe and from Near Eastern lands from the twelfth century onward. Their peaceful, compatible status among their neighbours became so widely known among European Jews that when Menasseh ben Israel in 1655 petitioned Cromwell to readmit Jews to England, he cited the case of the Cochin Jews in support of his argument. The local Jewish tradition in Cochin tells that Jews first came there in consequence of the dispersal following the destruction of either the first or the second Temple. Be that as it may, there are two copper plates in the possession of the community which certainly antedate the earliest travellers' reports by several centuries, and constitute a grant of privileges of nobility to one Joseph Rabban.

The relatively detected and substantial reports, dating from the sixteenth century on, depict a people devout in their Judaism, observant of Judaic ritual as they knew it, yet unlike Jews in other parts of the world in certain respects. They divided themselves into separate groups that were quite like the caste group of their Indian neighbours. Those of one group did not intermarry with those of another, they did not usually worship together, each group maintained its own burial grounds.

The experiment in human history that the example of the Cochin Jews provides can be viewed from several perspectives. One approach examines the broad question of what it can tell us about the nature of Judaism. Another view looks to the light it can shed on the nature of Indian civilisation. Yet another considers the understanding it can yield on such aspects of the human condition as social stratification. The two latter approaches I take up in greater detain in a forthcoming paper. In the present discussion we focus on the relevance of the study of the Cohin experience to an understanding of some aspects of caste and of Judaism, both in earlier centuries in the Indian milieu and, in recent decades, of their social relations in Israel.

The Early History

An early centre of Jewish settlement on the Malabar coasts was in a place some twenty miles north of the present Cochin City. The opening line of the charter inscribed on the two copper plates states that it was granted while the Raja was in residence at Muyirikodu, now a village cluster called Cranganore and referred to as Shingli or Shinkali by the Cochin Jews.

The receipient of this patent of regal favour was Joseph Rabban, a Jew, who was thereby granted the guild (or principality) of Anjuvannam and all its revenue, together with certain perquisites of nobility. The inscription on the plates does not indicate why these rights were bestowed. One can infer that neither Joseph Rabban nor his fellow Jews were then newcomers to the region and that they had performed and were expected to continue to render valued services to the Raja. At that period the Raja has just begun a major defensive war. My own review of the analysis of the copper plates led me to conclude that the consensus of the experts pointed to the year

1020 as the date of the grant (Mandelbaum 1939: 425, footnote 2; the other bibliographic references in my earlier study of the history of Cochin Jewry need not be repeated here). But more recent studies have established the date as the year 1000 (Narayanan 1972: 29, 81-82).

A more define date but a less clear location is given in the account by Rabbi Benjamin of Tudela whose chronical notes that in 1167 he came to a city and Island called Khulam in a pepper growing country. This may well be the modern Quilon, a town to the south of Cochin. He wrote that there were several thousand Isrealites there who were black in skin colour like the other inhabitants. "They know the law of Moses and the prophets and to a small extent the Talmud and Halacha." Marco Polo also made a clear reference to the Jews of Malabar in 1295, Ibn Batuta did so in 1324, and other travellers of the thirteenth and fourteenth centuries noted the existence of Jewish communities along the Malabar Coast (Fischel 1967: 231 fn. 7).

A more weighty dating is from the earliest Jewish tombstone yet found in the Malabar region. It bears the date, in Hebrew characters, of the year corresponding to 1269. The inscription on the stone marks the grave of Sarah, daughter of Israel, and includes a quotation from Deuteronomy 32.4, which apparantly is not inscribed on Jewish tombstones elsewhere. The French servant, Sylvain Levi characterised the inscription as the work of an ignorant person, but it provides clear evidence that in the thirteenth century the Jews of this part of India knew Hebrew and scripture but that their learning may have been somewhat defective, perhaps because of their remoteness from centres of Jewish learning.

In the year 1341, great floods impelled a shift of population in Cochin, including most of the Jews. The harbour of Cranganore, to which Roman traders had come regularly and where an ancient Christian as well as a Jewish community had long existed, became silted up and useless while the harbour at Cochin was improved by the force of the flood waters of the river Periyar. Three years later, in 1344, a new synagogue was built in Cochin, the Angadi synagogue, which still bears a mural slab inscribed with the date of its completion. Other congregations may have moved at about the same time; two of the names of synagogues in and near Cochin, the "Riverside" and the "South of River" synagogues seem to be carryovers from their location in Cranganore rather than in Cochin (Rabinowitz 1952: 102).

Another turn in the communal experience of the Cochin Jews began in 1498 when Vasco da Gama led the first Portuguese expedition to find a route from Portugal to the Malabar Coast. Once the route had been charted, succeeding expeditions followed in rapid succession, its members motivated by the great profits to be had from cargoes of pepper and other spices, by the vision of capturing vast hoards of gold, and by the incidental urge to convert the heathen. The Portuguese set up trading posts, military establishments and missions. They conquered some of the local kingdoms, dominated others, made converts instantly by the sword or later by persecution. Eventually they were ousted by the Dutch who in turn were replaced by the English. The Portuguese kept their enclave at Goa, north of Cochin, until finally ejected after Indian independence.

When Vasco da Gama first landed on the shores of India he was met with a coal reception from the inhabitants and had to stop at the off-shore Anjedive Islands to repair and refit his ships. There he was visited by a grandly attired personage who, surprisingly, spoke the Venetian dialect well and presented himself as the emissary of a powerful Muslim prince. He himself, so he related, had been born a Christian in the Levant, had come to India as a young man, and there had been converted to Islam. All this was poppycock. Hereally was a Jew from Posen in Poland who had drifted about until he somehow made the long journey to Cochin and had managed to marry a Cochin Jewish girl there. For da Gama, however, he was just the interpreter ond intermediary he needed. Moreover, since he promptly became a Christian with da Gama standing as godfather to baptise him as Gaspar da Gama, he was also living proof of the religious yield that might be expected in this far land.

When the newly-christened Gaspar returned to Cochin in 1502 he tried to persuade his Cochin wife to embrace Christianity as he had done. She promptly insisted on a Jewish divorce and got it. The Portuguese established their first trading post in Cochin and to it in 1505 came a Portuguese Marrano with a chest of Hebrew books that he offered to sell to the Jewish community. The books, perhaps including some Torah scrolls, had been collected after the destruction of the synagogues in Portugal and the expulsion of the Jews there in 1497. The bargain was struck in 1506 with the aid of Gaspar's former wife and the Jews of Cochin received a fresh infusion of Judaic knowledge (Fischel 1962: 39; 1971: 18, 48).

Portuguese incursions along the Malabar Coast pushed the scattered settlements of Jews to Cochin where successive Rajas steadfastly extended their protection to refugees from Portuguese depredations. Thus those Jews who had still remained in Cranganore finally fled about 1565 when they found themselves living on a battleground between the Portuese invaders and the Muslim ruler who opposed them. The Raja of Cochin had a brigade of Jewish soldiers in his forces and once, in 1550, when he was in temporary alliance with the Portuguese, he refused Portuguese plans to attack an enemy on a Saturday because, as he told them, the Jewish soldiers would not fight on that day and they were the best warriors he had raised (Amzalak 1923: 15-16).

The concentration in Cochin of Jews from various parts of the Malabar coast was further hastened by the institution of the Inquisition by the Portuguese over the people of the areas they controlled. There was also an influx of Jews who had fled from the terror against them in the Iberian peninsula to this enclave of tolerance on the Indian peninsula. (Rabinowitz 1952: 98-99).

There was some trickle of Jews into Malabar before the Portuguese came, as is suggested by the presence of Gaspar (his original Hebrew name in his Polish birthplace is not known) to meet da Gama's expedition. Similar indication is given in a genealogical account of the leading families of Cochin Jews that was compiled by a research team of Dutch Jews led by Moses Pereyra da Paiva. In his report of 1686 to the Sephardic Jewish community in Amsterdam, da Paiva wrote that the first Spanish Jew came to Cochin in the year 5272 (1511) but that "the first foreigner in Cochin" was a Jew from Jerusalem (Amzalak 1923: 6-7).

Not many years after sea voyages from Europe and the Levant began to be made regularly, Jews from these regions came to settle in Cochin along with the older settlement of Malawar Jews. Difficulties than arose among the Jews of Cochin, a kind of controversy that is reported periodically for more than four centuries thereafter, indeed up until the migration of most of them to Israel (see Fischel 1973: 42, footnote 74).

About the year 1520, a leading Rabbi of Egypt received a series of questions from certain of the Jews of Cochin. He wrote a responsum in which he sketched the Cochin problem, no doubt as it had been portrayed to him by the not urbiased questioners. The Rabbi, David ben Solomon ibn Zimra, wrote that there were nine hundred Jewish heads of families in Cochin of whom one hundred are Jews, original and genuine. The rest, he continues, are offspring of slaves, or of unions between Jewish merchants and native women, or are converts. Those of the hundred families of Jews, "original and genuine," called *meyuchaism* (those of lineage) do not intermarry with the others and because of this the others have unlimited grievances.

The Rabbi explained the difficulty on the grounds that the Cochin Jews had not known of the Talmudic laws concerning the liberation and full enfranchisement of former slaves. He noted that reports from Cochin had reached Egypt only since the Portuguese arrival in India and that the Cochin Jews had requested books because they had not possessed copies of the Talmud, Mishna, or the codes.

The Rabbi's decision was that the meyuchasim could intermarry with the other Jews, provided the latter first performed the rite of tebila. A similar decision was arrived at a generation later, in another responsum by Rabbi Jacob de Castro of Alexandria, the pravious Rabbi's pupil and successor. This Rabbi the soothing comment that it is no difficult thing to bathe in the daytime and in the presence of three persons. But the meyuchasim, the ancestors of those later called the white Jews, were not convinced and continued to exclude the others, who came to be called the black Jews (or Malabar Jews) from marital relations with them and from close contacts of any kind. Three centuries later, in 1882, the Malabar Jews addressed their grievances to another famous sage, the Grand Rabbi of Jerusalem, Rabbi Phanizel. He resurrected the decision of Rabbi de Castro, quoted it, and came to the same judgement which was similarly disregarded by the meyuchasim. In 1952, another learned Talmudic scholar visited Cochin, Rabbi Louis Rabinowitz (then of South Africa), and he was posed with a question relating to a case of the marriage of a man and woman of two different Jewish caste groups. His analysis of the case and his judgement is a remarkable example of Talmudic reasoning, but he concludes his account of it with a pessimistic note that he cannot hope to remove the "deep-seated, emotional prejudice" any more than could the opinions of his great predecessors, from David ibn Zimra in 1520 to Abdul Somekh in 1888 (Rabinowitz 1952: 113-114, 116-120).

About 1570 a Jewish traveller, Zechariah ben Se'adyah, described his journey from Yemen to Cochin. By then the division had become clearly fixed; he tells of a Sephardi community and congregations of black Jews. Though Pereyra de Paiva's relation of 1686 notes at least two families of the meyuchasim whose ancestors had been among the original Malabari inhabitants of Cranganore (where, as I learned on a visit there in 1937, the local villagers still can part of the area the Jews' quarter), it is highly probable that most of the white Jews are descended from immigrants of the sixteenth and later centuries from Europe and the Near East, while most of the other Jews of Cochin are descended from the older settlements at Cranganore, Quilon, Calicut and other parts of Malabar. Some also, as we shall note, are the descendants of more recent converts.

The immigrants, fluent in European and Levantine languages, skilled in commercial and diplomatic relations, became close advisers and intermediaries for the Rajas of Cochin. One Raja helped establish their synagogue, the handsome *Pardesi* synagogue of 1568 that is still one of the principal landmarks of Cochin, immediately adjacent to the grounds of his palace and his temple. Each of his successors similarly found these Jews to be useful to the realm and trustworthy to his person. A Dutch traveller, Van Linschoten, needed in his report of 1584 that these Jews were rich merchants, the Raja's nearest counsellors. They speak good Spanish and "they observe the Saboth, and other judicall ceremonies and hope for the Mesias to come..." That hope was, with the rise of Zionism, translated into mass movement to Israel, particularly by the Malabar Jews.

The Portuguese had their own fortified quarter in the town, though the Raja controlled the main part of the town and the state. No love was lost on the Portuguese, so when a Dutch contingent attacked the Portuguese fort, they were helped by Jews. During a temporary setback of the Dutch they had to retreat and Portuguese soldiers forthwith pillaged and burned the Jewish quarter (Fischel 1962: 41-42). But the Dutch counter-attacked, won the day and replaced the Portuguese as the principal European power in Cochin from 1663 to 1795.

Efflorescence During the Dutch Regime

Both by reason of their knowledge of Jews in Holland and

their experience in Cochin, the Duch merchants and soldiers had every reason to work harmoniously with the Jews of Cochin and so they did for one hundred and thirty-two years. This was a prosperous era for the Cochin Jews. Dutch interests were focussed on trade, especially in pepper. Unlike the Portuguese, whose national self-image rated conquest, conversion, and booty at least on a par with trade, the Dutch were quite content to concentrate on trade. The ruling Rajas of Cochin (most of them quite old men since the succession was matrilineal and went by seniority through a line of the sons of a set of sisters, and then through the sons of the previous Raja's sisters) were also content to allow the Dutch to provide a trade opening to the West and they employed Jews as advisers, interpreters, and intermediaries in that trade. Each Raja appointed a *Mudaliar* for the Jews, an official spokesman, but the day-to-day government of the Jewish community was in their own hands (Fischel 1971: 20).

We have several brief but relatively reliable accounts of the Jews of Cochin during the period that the Dutch were ensconced there. Notably there is the report of Pereyra de Paiva's delegation, who visited Cochin in 1686 and were accorded considerable ceremonial honours by the Dutch commandant. They published their report, together with answers to a questionnaire of 46 questions, in 1687. De Paiva was impressed by the upper caste of Cochin Jews, noting that though their skin colour is brown ("caused no doubt by the climate") they are *bahale Torah*, learned in Torah. They keep themselves entirely separate from the Malabar Jews, do not intermarry with them, and do not even count them as one of a *minyan*, the minimal number of ten for congregational services. Yet despite this separation, the two groups observe the same Judaic rites and ceremonies and these are essentially the same as the practice in Amsterdam. The latter observation may testify to the regular visits to Cochin by travelling scholars and to the importation of Hebrew books, an inflow that was accelerated through Pereyra de Paiva's help. The report mentions the copper plates which had also been noted in a Hebrew letter from Cochin to Amsterdam in 1676, but, rather strangely, were not mentioned in any of the known earlier accounts (Amzalak 1923: Fischel 1967b; 232-233).

A letter describing the Cochin Jews was w itten in 1723 by a Dutch Chaplain, Jacob Cantor Visscher. By then the terms "white" and "black" Jews were in common use. Visscher observes that the white Jews, though fewer in number, are much wealthier and more powerful than the black. There is supposed to be no intermarriage among the two "although these sometimes take place." The men of the upper group are involved in commerce with the Duth East India Company and trade in the more valuable commodities. The black Jews are mainly petty traders, in poultry, eggs, and butter. Some also, according to Adriaan Moens *Memorandum* of 1781, are cultivators and cattle traders.

Visscher notes that when a cantor (he uses the term "Rabbi" although they had none) of the white Jews enters a synagogue of the black Jews, he must have the honour of leading the sacred service, but reciprocal honours are not accorded by white Jews when a black Jewish cantor visits their synagogue. The friction between the two groups continued; Visscher reports that the black Jews agitated to compel white Jewesses to keep their heads uncovered as their own women did. They appealed to the Raja who handed down a sage judgement that in this matter the women of each side could attire themselves as they pleased.

Jews of both groups, Visscher notes, own slaves who wear the Jewish skullcap. Those slaves who have been fully admitted to their religion by performance of the customary rites, can never be sold to a stranger. The documents of manumission, duly made out in the orthodox form, as we shall note later, provided for complete enfranchisement of a freed slave as a Jew with full Jewish rights, but apparently this was not made clear to the liberated, nor perhaps understood by the liberators.

For about a third of the duration of the Dutch period, the leading Jewish personage in Cochin was Ezekiel Rahabi (1694-1771), whose career Professor Fischel has reconstructed from the evidence of numerous documents. From 1726 on, Rahabi is referred to as the chief merchant, the *Judische Koopman*, of the Dutch company and in their name he negotiated complex treaties, monetary transactions, and trade arrangements with a vast congeries of Malabar rulers for the whole complex array of commodities that by then had become part of the India-Europe trade. More than that, he acted as a clearing house for information. In Professor Fischel's words, "He kept the Company steadily informed about world affairs, military, political, and economic events and changes, about movements of the ships of the English and French companies, about troop movements of the king of Zamorin (Calicut), about the outbreaks of wars of European nations...and last but not least, on the fluctuation of money prices, piracy, confiscations and the repercussions of the European conflicts upon the Indian scene" (Fischel 1971 : 27). He conducted negotiations with English merchants as well as with indigenous rulers. When the local Malabar Christians wanted to import a Bishop from Basra, it was Ezekiel Rahabi who made it possible. He was helpful to other Christians as well, aiding Catholic Carmelites as well as Danish missionaries. His aid was extended also to Muslims and Hindus (*ibid.* 34-35). An Englishman, Edward Ives, who wrote of his visit to Cochin in 1757 made particular note of Ezekiel Rahabi as "a man of consequence, and his word is held in high estimation: he is a lover of science and understands astronomy" (Fischel 1962 : 50).

For all his international and inter-religious dealings, Rahabi never presented himself as anything but a steadfast Jew. Professor Fischel examined much of Rahabi's voluminous correspondence and many business contracts and found that Rahabi always signed his name in Hebrew characters, a practice that his Jewish predecessors and successors in Cochin also followed (1962 : 54-55).

His correspondence includes answers to enquiries from Jews in various parts of the world. In 1768 he wrote a history of his community in the form of answers to 13 questions sent to him by Tobias Boaz, a Jewish merchant and banker of Amsterdam. (A similar epistle was written in 1790 by the Cochin Samuel Abraham to Solomon Joseph Simpson of New York.) He restored the Pardesi synagogue, was involved in providing it with a clock tower and the famed Chinese tiles, saw to it that Hebrew books kept being sent from Holland to Cochin, purchased lands for some of the Malabar Jews, built a synagogue for some of them and supported it as long as it was in use (Fischel 1962 : 52-56).

In one of his letters to the Jews of Amsterdam, written in 1731, he gives an account of the number of Jewish families in the seven synagogues that then existed. There were 40 families of white Jews, 370 of black, making 410 Cochin Jewish families in all. In 1686 de Paiva had estimated a total of 460 families, and in 1781 the Dutch Governor, Moens, had given a figure of 422 families. It would seem that through the Dutch period the total population of Cochin Jews was between two and three thousand people.

Moens wrote his *Memorandum* for his successor to the post of Governor and he comments that the Jews of Cochin are not at all like the stereotype of Jews in Europe, a stereotype that he may have known better than the actuality. He wrote that the Jews of Cochin are honest, as clean in their houses and persons "as we," distinguished from the other nations of the land only by their dress and physical appearance.

By then there were other Jews in India. The earliest Jewish tombstone as yet discovered in Madras is dated 1687. And to the north of Cochin along the coast near Bombay there had long existed scattered settlements of Jews, known as *Bene Israel*, whose early history has not yet been well documented. Only when many of them moved to Bombay City at the end of the eighteenth century are there well-based records about them. Dr. Schifra Strizower writes that in an unpublished family history in Cochin, written in Hebrew, "I have read that a member of the family, David Ezekiel Rahabi, went to western India in the middle of the eighteenth century, in the course of his work for the Dutch East India Company, there encountered the Bene Israel, and revived the Judaism he found existent among them" (1971: 36). Walter Fischel found that the first Bene Israel synagogue in Bombay was established in 1796 by one of their leaders, Samuel Ezekiel Divekar, who had been an officer in the East India Company's army (1967a : 205). During that same year, according to a tombstone of 1796 in a Cochin Jewish cemetery. one Samuel been Eliezer Diveker Cammodan had come to Cochin to purchase a Torah scroll for the Bombay community. He died while praying in the synagogue.

The impact of the Cochin Jews on the Bene Isreal, Walter Fischel wrote, was again manifest from 1826 when, "a group of pious and learned Cochin Jews moved to Bombay, not to enter the military service or to engage in trade and commerce, but to instill in that community cut off for so many centuries from Jewish life, a new Jewish spirit." They helped to establish schools and prayer halls, taught Torah and Halakhah (1972 : 6).

From British Rule to the Migration to Israel

When, in 1795, the English displaced the Dutch as paramount European power in Cochin, the status of the Jews there went into a decline. Although the Rajas of Cochin still ruled the state and were to do so for another century and a half, they were very much under the control of the British rulers who gradually brought all of India under their regime early in the nineteenth century. In that century, the port of Cochin became less important for overseas trade and the English did not maintain close and cordial relations with the Cochin Jewish community as their Dutch predecessors had done.

The circumstances of the Cochin Jews were described in a book of 1832 by Rabbi David D'Beth Hillel. It is an account of his far-reaching travels and was published in Madras with encouragement of the Anglican Archdeacon of Madras at that time. He related that although the white Jews were then much sunk from their former prosperous state, their marriages were nonetheless celebrated with great expense and in grand style "like those of the Hindus." The black Jews maintained six synagogues and were well versed in Hebrew scripture, "which they readily translate into Malayalam and as far as circumstances allow them they walk according to the Law." There were no priests or Levites among them. Most were artisans, few were poor by local standards, they are "respectable for moral character." The old quarrel continued, the Malabar Jews claiming to be descendants of the original Jewish settlers in the land, the white Jews countering that they were the descendants of slaves (Fischel 1973 : 113-114).

By then there had come into being a third caste group among the Cochin Jews who actually were the descendants of manumitted slaves or of household servants who had asked to become converts to Judaism. They were called meshuhrarim (or meshuchrarim), the "manumitted." There were only about thirty of them in 1937, but they too entered zestfully into their own struggle for impressed status. Known in English as the "brown" Jews, they worshipped in the forecourt of the white Jews' synagague (There may have been a comparable group liberated by black Jews and affiliated with their synagogues but there is only the barest mention of them in the literature.) These meshuhrarim were permitted to approach only to the main entrance of the Paradesi synagogue, looking in and listening through the doors and windows. They could not participate as equals in the service and the white Jews forbade intermarriage with them.

This despite the documents of manumission which faithfully followed the form specified in the Talmud that specifically gave manumitted slaves full legal, religious, and social rights as Jews. Rabbi Louis Rabinowitz examined two such documents in Cochin, one dated in the Hebrew year corresponding to 1826, the other 1835. The former documents liberated the house-woman, Hannah, and added a clause noting that her sons would be counted as part of a minyan. The latter was for Simeon "hitherto our houseborn slave" and followed the explicit Talmudic formula "And thou art permitted to enter into the Holy Congregation of Israel, and to marry a daughter of Israel, and to mingle with Isreal, and thy children are permitted to be taught the Torah, since of our own free will we have emancipated thee."

But, as Rabbi Robinowitz was told, the emancipated ones were given to understand that the manumission was according to the custom of Cochin which transcended the written formula and forbade intermarriage and the right to full religious participation. A group of the meshuhrarim in 1848 were sufficiently outraged by this to move to the section of Cochin City directly controlled by the British. There they built a prayer hall, established their own cemetery, and conducted themselves as a fully independent congregation. But an outbreak of plague diminished their number later and they had to return to their former homes in the Jews' street of Cochin. In the Paradesi synagogue they were allowed to be called up to the Reading of the Law only on Simchat Torah. They had full rights of participation only on the two Seder nights of Passover when they joined their employers or former masters at the Passover table (Rabinowitz 1952 : 110-115).

Throughout the period of British rule, the vigorously argued differences among the three caste-like groups continued. the Malabar Jews and Meshuhrarim asserting their rights to equal status as Jews, the white Jews regularly denying their claims. There was no rejection of the common frame of Judaism. All acknowledged their common religious heritage, their shared identity as Jews.

Yet the contention continued, as is exemplified in the case of the burial of a highly respected teacher of Talmud. He was a Jew from Poland, named Abba Isaac Joffe, who came to Cochin about 1880, perhaps one of the emissaries from

Talmudic study centres in Jerusalem. (Somo came with packets of earth from the Holy Land that were placed in the coffin of a deceased Jew, one packet under the head, so that his final rest could be on a bit of the sacred soil.) Abba Isaac Joffe decided to settle in Cochin so that he might help enhance Judaic learning. Finding a keener interest in such study among the Malabar Jews, he moved across the harbour to their quarter in Ernakulam. He became the revered teacher in the synagogues there. When he died, the Malabar Jews buried him with great honour in their cemetery and set up in his memory a marble slab with a long commemorative inscription on it. But since he had been a European Jew by birth, if not by choice of latter affiliation, the white Jews considered him to be one of their own. They raided the cemetery in Ernakulam, unearthed the body, and reburied him in their own cemetery (Rabinowitz 1952 : 127-128). They were apparently still influential enough with the secular authorities to bring off this sortie.

And yet they all share a common style of life and shered in each other's worship on certain (though not frequent) occasions. When in 1877 the first Hebrew printing was done in Cochin, six booklets were produced that dealt with the distinctively Cochin hymns, prayers, and *piyutim* used in all the seven congregations. These hymns and prayers were noted as being according to the "*minhag Shinkali*", the custom of Cranganore, the place they had left in the fourteenth century. Their usual pronunciation of Hebrew, Rabbi Rabinowitz observed, is in the Sephardic style used by other communities of Indian Jews, but for festive occasions they use the Ashkenazi (European) pronunciation which they call the "Shingli" mode (1952 : 109).

Their songs and cantillations have been studies by the musicologist, Dr. Johanna Spector. She finds no relationship in them to European Sephardic influence but does find considerable likeness to the musical styles used by Bagdadi, Yemenite, and Kurdish Jews. The songs specifically called "Shingli" are most like those sung by Jews from Yemen (Spector (1971 : 180-185).

All three groups of Cochin Jews were attracted by the Zionist movement. There is a letter of 1901 from a leader of the white Jews to Theodore Herzl in Vienna in which the writer expresses support for Herzl's cause and offers to collect funds for it from the seven congregations of Cochin Jews. By 1903 the first Zionist organisation was formed in Cochin (Fischel 1971: 59-61). The "hope for the Mesias to come" that van Linschoten noted among them in the sixteenth century was transmuted to the emigration of most Cochin Jews to Israel in the twentieth century.

The Cochin Jews in 1937

In 1937 I spent a few weeks, from Rosh Hashonah through Simchat Torah, with the Jews of Cochin. My observations and interviews showed that Jewish life in Cochin had not greatly changed from its character as described in accounts of the nineteenth century, nor indeed was it vastly altered in its essentials from the way of life described in the seventeenth century. I need not repeat here the ethnological dates that were summarised in my article of 1939.

The continuity with their past was apparent in both their internal and external relations. The caste-like division among the white and Malabar Jews persisted. There was also the third group, the *Meshuhrarim*, the manumitted. Their leader for several decades was a remarkable man, Abraham Barak Salem, who fought vigorously for full Judaic rights for his group. He was a lawyer, a "High Court Advocate" who held local political office and was also active in the Congress Party's struggle for Indian independence. He was a dedicated Zionist, visited Israel, and was one of the most learned of Hebrew scholars among the Cochin Jews (*see* Mandelbaum 1939 : 44-450; Rabinowitz 1952 : 116-120; Elias and Isaac 1963 : 85-86).

The Malabar Jews were not then actively carrying on this kind of struggle with the white Jews although, to a man, they were sure that they were descendants of the original Cochin Jews and were entitled to all their rights as pious Jews. There were between thirteen and fourteen hundred of them in all; most earned a living as peddlers of poultry, eggs or fish, by keeping small shops, or by working as artisans (*see* Kushner 1973 : 18-20). Ther were only 125 white Jews by my count, one family of merchants was fairly prosperous; twelve of the thirty-three employable men of the white Jews derived their livelihood from this family's business activities. Their one professional man then was a physician recently retired from the government medical service. There was a good deal of illness, physical and mental, among the white Jews. The Malabar Jews were, on the whole, poorer but seemingly less stricken by illness.

The three groups in Cochin town lived on Jews' Street, the Malabar Jews at the bustling lower end, the Meshuhrarim in houses generally along the middle of the street, the white Jews in larger houses at the quieter, upper end of the street at the head of which stands the Paradesi synagogue situated next to the Raja's ancient palace grounds.

Each of the seven synagogues was the centre of society and the focus of culture for its congregants. It was the men's daily meeting place, the clearing house for news and gossip, the community's centre for all of its functions. It was each person's symbol of identity as a Jew and of his unity with his own kind in Cochin and with Jewry around the world. A man achieved status and validated his prestige, mainly through his synagogue participation; every meaningful stage of his life cycle was celebrated in the synagogue. It was so for a woman to a somewhat lesser degree though the woman's gallery of the synagogue was important in ther life. Each person's aesthetic satisfactions were attained in the synagogue, in the staging of the rites and ceremonies, in the artistry of song and cantillation, in the richness of decoration of the synagogue interior and of the dress of the participants during the holy days.

The people, except for a few, were poor but the synagogues were, by comparison, rich, Each synagogue had been endowed by the pious of past generations, with lands, investments, and ornaments of gold and precious stones.[1] The income was used to educate the young and to give aid to the aged and indigent of the congregations, as well as to keep the cemetery and other community projects (cf. Kushner 1973 : 20-21).

Though internal contention and factionalism were as common among the Cochin Jews as among many other groups in India, or among other groups of Jews for that matter, the mutual participation in synagogue activities seems to me to have had a soothing and smoothing influence. The high holy day services were conducted with a mutuality of common concern; Sinchat Torah was celebrated with joyous gusto by all the Jews. Rabbi Rabinowitz's observation of Cochin Jewry attests to the impression they gave (at least to one who visited them briefly) of the zest of their way of life. "Poverty-stricken and primitive though they are, they seem to go through life with a song in their hearts and on their lips." At a reception in his honour he learned that all the Jews there knew each of the 175 hymns witten in one of the manuscripts of their hymns that he examined. When all assembled at the reception participated in singing one of the hymns that he requested, he asked how many knew all of the large corpus of religious songs, S.S. Koder, one of their most eminent men said: "There is not a man, woman, or child in Cochin who does not know the words and tune of every hymn by heart" (1952 : 135-136).

Moreover, the Jewish ritual calendar provided a rhythm for the life of a Cochin Jew and for all his community. That rhythm not only produced the kind of personal security that is commonly absorbed from willingly observed religious calendars but also was a completely different life rhythm form those followed by their non-Jewish neighbours. A Jew's day, his year, his life-course were all apportioned, divided, accented, celebrated in his synagogue according to scriptural injunctions embellished by local Jewish custom.

The relations of the Cochin Jews with their neighbours were cordial but not close. An example of that lack of animosity was told to Rabinowitz. In the usual drinking done by young men of the Cochin Jews on Purim, a group of them once became more than usually tight. They entered a Catholic church, carried off a statue of the Virgin Mary, and burned it as an effigy of Haman. On hearing of this; the leader of the white Jewish community "went post haste to the priest, who passed off the incident with an understanding joke" (1952 : 137). The priest's light-hearted dismissal of this incident was, if the usual practice was followed, encouraged by a liberal and immediate donation to the church. But where deep-rooted animosities between religious groups in India exist, no donation could have averted a costly, perhaps bloody, retaliation for so sacrilegious a misdeed.

There was a particular bond among the long-settled Christians, Muslims, and Jews of Malabar, each considering the others as "people of the book" like themselves. I saw an example of this during World War II. When the allied forces entered Rangoon, I searched for the Jewish synagogue there, knowing that some Cochin Jews had settled in Burma. I found that all but three Jewish families had fled when the Japanese troops captured the city. But these three families had lived in the synagogue during the Japanese occupation, and had managed to keep the Japanese authorities from learning about the considerable treasures of the synagogue, particularly the gold-crowned and silver-encased Torah scrolls. They told me that they had succeeded in keeping Japanese patrols from inspecting the synagogue closely and from finding the room with the treasures in it, because their Muslim neighbours on the street had helped them in diverting the attention of the Japanese and in guarding the Jews' secret from the occupying force.

The cordiality in Cochin was part of the Indian tradition under which each endogamous group is expected to have some cultural uniqueness. This traditional Indian tolerance could be freely manifested because the Cochin Jews were a very small community and did not pose a threat to the incomes or to the caste status of other groups. The Jews were very much like the other people of Cochin in speech, in physical appearance (except for some of the fairer of the white Jews), and in dress, though the males always wore a skullcap that identified each one as a Jew wherever he might be. Their methods of trade and their craft skills were quite like those of other shopkeepers and artisans of Cochin. Yet the rhythm of their lives and the content of their domestic and community rites set them quite apart from the other people of the region.

Life in Israel : Bet Avi in 1961-62

Indian independence was attained in 1947 and, like most other ethnically distinctive communities in the land, the Jews of Cochin were both elated at the political victory and uncertain about their future in the new regime. So when they heard, in 1948, of the establishment of the State of Israel and of the plans for the ingathering of exiles, the fulfilment of the ritually expressed hopes of all the generations of their forebears in Cochin, most of them had no question about what to do. A delegation promptly appeared at the offices of the Jewish Agency in Bombay. Soon a Jew from Bombay, F.W. Pollack, the trade commissioner for Israel in India, visited them. After talking with them, he found that they held highly unrealistic views of their future in Israel. He concluded that a good many of them would be making a serious mistake in emigrating, but "I have had no option but to report to the Government of Israel that there is no power in the world which will stop them. They are possessed with a Messianic fervour of the most exalted order" (quoted in Rabinowitz 1952 : 90).

Within a year several families came to Israel. In 1952-54 a few hundred children between the ages of 12 and 16 were brought by the agency devoted to youth immigration and placed in their centres so that they might be acclimated enough to act as guides for their elders later. Most of the Cochin Jews came to Israel during 1953-55. When I visited Cochin for a day in 1964, only the white Jews were still resident in sufficient numbers to carry on full synagogue activities. The great majority of the Malabar Jews were in Israel.

In 1961-62, some eight years after the bulk of the Malabar Jews from Cochin had arrived in Israel, an American anthropologist, Gilbert Kushner, studied one of the villages in which they had been settled. Bet Avi, the pseudonym he uses for it, then held 203 Jews from Cochin, who had come there in 1954 when immigrants from Yemen were also living in the village. But the Yemenite Jews soon shifted to a nearby village where other Yemenites lived, and the village residents were practically all Malabar Jews. The village is in the Judean Hills, some 45 minutes by bus from Jerusalem and clearly visible from the Jerusalem-Tel Aviv road.

When the Jews from Cochin landed in Israel they were told that they could be settled either in a *kibbutz* or in a *moshav olim*, the latter a type of settlement with considerable governmental guidance and aid, presumably to be organised by the villagers along cooperative patterns, but without strong communal ownership and sharing that characterise the kibbutz type of organisation. But the Cochin Jews had heard that the Kibbutzniks were not religious, that they worked on the Sabhath and ate non-kosher food. So they all opted for the moshav. None of them wanted to be farmers; exceedingly few of them had been cultivators in India; but the officials gave them no choice about that. For reasons of state, of military security, of national development, of ideology, those who were in charge of settling them were sure that they should be and could be farmers.

When Kushner was in Bet Avi, most of the villagers were not very good farmers. For one thing, the soil they had to till was not fertile. The village was administered as a "managed farm" for the first four years of its settlement by Cochin Jews, with the settlers working for wages, and official instructors teaching them how to raise the main crops of tomatoes and cucumbers as well as planning all agricultural operations. But, the agricultural instructor complained, his charges "apparently learned nothing during the managed farm phase of the village's lifetime" (Kushner 1973 ; 70).

The villagers had the reputation, among the instructors and other Israelis assigned to work with them, of tiring easily, of being irresponsible about the imperative schedule of tasks necessary for efficient agriculture, and of frittering away valuable time in weekly visits to Jerusalem to sell their produce and in overlong domestic and religious celebrations. For their part, the residents of Bet Avi were, in general, not happy with their assigned work as farmers. The physician who came twice a week to the village thought they were "too weak for agricultural life, given their general light body build, suspecting this as a significant influence on their capacity to work which the village instructors ignored" (Kushner 1973 : 75).

Before they had left India, the immigrants had imagined that in Israel they would find a blessed break from their placed lives in Cochin, that they would live as authentic Jews, given wholly over to pious observances, undistracted by the economic and social tribulations of the *galuth*, the exile. They did experience sharp discontinuities, but not of any kind they could have forseen.

In Isreal, the small details of daily life were different. Their diet changed radically, they could have a greater variety of foodstuffs than in Cochin and ate more bread, vegetables, milk products. They learned to like beer. The visiting nurse urged mothers to wean their babies at the age of six months rather than continuing breast feeding for a year or two. The men continued to wear the distinctive Cochin type of pillbox hat. "In Cochin their caps helped identify them as Jews, and in Israel they were equally significant in setting them apart from other Jewish men." But on visist to Jerusalem, most men replaced the traditional Cochin headcovering with the cone-shaped hat popular in Israel or with a beret (Kushner 1973 : 73). It is as though the Cochin cap served as a mark of special group identity for them while they were among their fellow Cochin Jews, but in Jerusalem they wanted to be identified only as Israelis The women still made the Cochin caps for their men, but women now had important farming chores to do, as in caring for the chickens, and the division of labour among men and women was becoming quite different from the division they had known in India.

They were having to change the fundamental rhythm of their lives. They had followed a religiosly-oriented life style within a pluralistic society under a princely state controlled by a remote colonial power. Now they were asked to follow a work-oriented life style in a welfare dation-state whose leaders were trying to forge a homogeneous culture. They received only occasional encouragement for their own predilection from the religious agencies and religious political parties that operated within, and almost as part of, the state.

A central change was that their work had become not only different in kind but also more complex and demanding; it required more planning, discipline, and sweet than had been needed in Cochin. Work became far more important partly because of official pressures, partly by the example of other farmers about them, and also because hard work was the principal avenue toward acquiring possessions, a goal highly sanctioned in the new cultural environment.

The villagers told Kushner that making a living in India was very easy, at least by comparison with earing a livelihood in Bet Avi. A man would buy a small stock of chickens, eggs or fish and could sell them in a few hours. "Once the goods were sold, he would return home for the remainder of the day, visiting with friends, sitting in the synaggue, or going to a shop with friends and relatives to drink." If a day's sales were especially good, a man could stay home for a few days and go back to the market-place when money was again needed for household expenses. In the Malabar area, few material possessions were needed, especially by those at their socio-economic level, and were not difficult to get. All were quite clear "in pointing out the high desirability of the 'merchant' life, with free time, clean hands, and reliance on verbal skills to talk up a good sale" (Kushner 1973 : 19-20).

In Bet Avi, by contrast, they felt the work to be so hard and demanding that there was just not enough time or energy to devote to ritual practices as they would have liked to give. The time schedule of a farmer, with its early-to-bed and early-to-rise routine, interfered with late evening prayers and religious celebrations. All the villagers agreed "that they had never realised that they would be less strict in their ritual observance in Israel than in India" (Kushner 1973 : 77). But from the viewpoint of their Israeli guides, they spent far too much time in celebrating marriages, *bar-mitzvot*, and circumcisions, even though these celebrations were considerably curtailed from the Cochin practice where, as is not uncommon among Indian groups, a wedding might cost about half of a family's annual income. For these rites of passage, friends and relatives came from other Cochin settlements and stayed for about a week of visiting, drinking, and general celebration. All work, except the most essential, stopped during such weeks. "The instructors pointed out that this was obviously not the way for a 'good' farmer to behave, work ought not to cease for any reason" (*ibid* : 75).

The latter phrase illustrates the great difference between the ethic which the Cochin Jews were inculcated in their old homes and that which was urged upon them in the new. In Cochin a man and woman had only to maintain their family at a simple level, consort pleasurably (occasionally factiously) with fellow Jews and, above all, glorify God. In Israel, they were asked to glorify work in order to achieve more for their family and to help maintain the state. The state was a community of a sort in their eyes, but vast, disparate, strange.

They still observed the Sabbath and the Holy Days in their old manner. All the families managed to revert to their marchant style by making weekly visits to Jerusalem or other places where they could sell their produce and again enjoy the interaction between buyer and seller. Yet somehow, the glorification both of work and of God did not go well with them and most of them were not happy, at least in 1961-62, with that aspect of their lot in Zion.

The synagogue was no longer the central stage of their lives nor was it in centre stage during most of their days. It was only one of a set of ramshackle service buildings. While the original wood and tin houses for families built for the settlement had been replaced, by 1962, with concrete houses, the service buildings were still the original flimsy structures. These service buildings indicated the new kind of community organisation and functions that had to be maintained in the new land. They included a general store, a recreation centre, equipment and produce sheds, an armoury, a weapons, storehouse, a dispensary, a bathhouse (*mikvah*), a kindergarten as well as the synagogue. True to the nation's values, the kindergarten building was the best maintained of the wooden structures. The teacher was a *sabra* graduate of the Hebrew University and was zealous in her mission of helping raise her 22 charges as true Israelis. The older children were bussed to a religiously oriented school. There the children from Cochin were among children from diverse Jewish backgrounds and were generally making normal educational progress, although the Cochin parents seemed quite disinterested in their children's education (Kushner 1973 : 72). Perhaps this was so because its form and content were so alien to anything they had experienced.

The social and political organisation of Bet Avi was also quite different from that of the Cochin community. Caste stratification and caste contention were gone; a new kind of social stratification was developing. Within the village, formal authority was in the *vaad*, the elected village council. In 1961-62 the council consisted of five young men, average age 26, "all of whom spoke Hebrew well and were among the most successful farmers in the village" (*ibid* : 80). The synagogue elders came to them for help and advice; secular capabilities rather than ritual concerns had become the standard for leadership and prestige.

The council served as the chief liaison between the villagers and state officials; especially with the instructors who had been assigned to induct them into their new way of livelihood and life. The secretary of the council drew a salary and was supposed to be, in effect, the chief executive officer of the village. The first paid secretary, though of Cochin origin, had no close relatives in the village and had lived in Bombay before his emigration. His wife was the most highly educated woman in the community, and for a cluster of reasons, she was accused by some of the women of sorcery, an accusation not unknown in Cochin. He was soon replaced as secretary by a young man of the group who had just completed his military service (*ibid* : 80-81).

The more successful farmer, those who were stronger, worked harder and had young wives and children to help with the farm tasks, earned more and were able to buy the household furnishings that were much desired. They had refrigerators, washing machines, gas cookers, chairs, couches and other things beyond the minimal furnishings provided by the Jewish Agency for each family. The wealthier families seemed on the way to forming a new upper stratum in the community's social stratification.

The four instructors posted to the village (for home economics, poultry, vineyard-almond orchard, and a general instructor) were not very satisfied with their jobs or their achievements. Their formal roles, at least at that period, had not been well defined, they had little training for their duties and their meagre pay was supposed to be augmented by their sense of mission. But, Kushner writes, "All of the instructors, in fact, were very unhappy with the Cochini and their seeming lack of "progress" (*ibid* : 82). The Cochin Jews, for their part, were dissatisfied with the Jewish Agency's handling of their assets, especially the synagogue properties, in Cochin. Most of them believed that much more money was involved that the Agency accounted for and that the Agency had simply kept it instead of using it to subsidise the settlement of Cochin Jews more substantially that had been done (*ibid* : 23). They saw the instructors and the planners as all-powerful agents of the state who, nonetheless, would somehow make sure that no one was left without a livelihood, playing a role something like that of the synagogue trustees in Cochin.

Yet despite their feelings of unwanted dependence, the older people's disppointment with the pace and focus of their new life, and the ineptitude of many of them as farmers, the settlers of Bet Avi admitted that conditions in Israel were, on the whole, batter for them than in India. They had more amenities, better health care, more property than they had in Cochin. All had electricity, piped water, showers, more housing space than in Cochin, many had radios, some had an array of home appliances and farm machines. The could readily go by bus to a metropolis that was also The Holy City. Young couples were pleased to be freer of domination by their elders. A few marriages with spouses of non-Cochin origin had been made.[2] The children were getting an education that would enable them to cope with modern conditions as full Israelis. Both the children and younger adults spoke Hebrew among themselves although Malayalam was still used at home and in discussions in the synagogue (*ibid* : 70-72, 76, 87).

In all, this account of the people of Bet Avi in 1961-62 gives us a view of a community in the process of change, confronted with the familiar predicaments of homecoming to Israel while being absorbed into the new national culture that itself was in the process of being formed. I recall that when I was once travelling from Bombay to Tel-Aviv and beyond, there happened to be a party of immigrants on the plane, Jews from Bombay. They were mostly in family groups, each person flanked by his close kin and familiar neighbours. Each had with him a little bag of familiar, favourite possessions. They felt that they were going to their true homeland, the holy land of their ancestors, the cradle of their faith. But they were also encased in a vehicle none had even ridden before. It was hurtling them in a cultural direction that neither they nor their ancestors had ever taken before. They were being catapulted into a society that was in the land of their hopes but was also in a stage of development whose conditions they could not have realised before. The journey was one they dearly wanted to make, the arrival would inevitably bring on new perplexities and problems. These perplexities and problems were shared by many of the immigrants, including those depicted in the account of Bet Avi in 1961-62. The problems were not insignificant, but they were also being surmounted and adaptations were being made, especially by the children and young adults.

Some Reflections on the Cash Example of the Cochin Jews

When then, can we learn about the nature of caste and of Judaism from the experience of the Jews of Cochin? Certain negative answers are clear. Opposition, persecution, enforced segregation are not at all necessary for the long-continued existence of a Jewish community. None of these conditions seriously affected the Cochin Jews. Even when the Portuguese conquerors bore down on Jews in the Malabar area, they did not conquer the Raja of Cochin who gave shelter and favour to the Jews in his realm. Their long residence along Jews Street in Cochin was a matter of their choice, not of outside pressures.

They were devoted to the Torah but were not, with only rare exceptions, notable scholars either in Hebrew or Malayalam. The usual religious offices of Judaic society were not maintained among them. They had no rabbis. The Malabar Jews did not even any one men who could, by hereditary right, perform the ritual duties of *Kohen* (priest) or Levite.

Nor were they generally imbured, at least for the past century and a half, with any inner urge toward hard work that has sometimes been accounted a Jewish characteristic. Work, for many of them as for a good many other people of the world, was necessary and even meritorious in its proper time and place, but was a practice that should not stand in the way of ritual devotion or of pleasure.

Jews who live as a small section of a larger society in which they are amiably accepted, are supposed, according to some conventional wisdom, to be particularly liable to assimilation into the main culture. The conventional farecast is that they will seep gradually into the larger society until no viable, distinctive Jewish community remains. That has indeed happened in some places, as it did in China. The Indian cultural milieu both favoured and discouraged such a process. The emulation of the ritual practices of higher groups by those of lower rank, in order to raise their status, is a process widespread in Kerala as in all India. And the competition for status is, among most caste groups, keen and continuous. But the process of social mobility is best done by whole groups rather than by solitary members attempting to pass to a higher level.

The struggles of the Malabar Jews and of the Meshuhrarim for equality with the white Jews were much like the common similar struggles with a *jati* (an endogamous caste) of Hindus. When the section of a previously intermarrying set of families, perhaps prospering more than the others, are able to take on appurtenances of higher ritual rank, they may set themselves apart from their previous jati brethren and refuse to intermarry or interdine with them as indication of their new higher rank (*see* Mandelbaum 1970 : 487-499). But while this typical internecine struggle went on among the Cochin Jews, all of them were quite aware that together they formed a special entity. However divided they might be on status rank, they were united in wanting to be regarded as Jews. The Malabar Jews' appeal to Rabbis of other lands over several centuries and the white Jews' counter-appeals to rabbinical authority give indication of their common culture and identity despite their social distinctions. Another example of this is the offer of 1906 to collect money for Zionism from *all* seven congregations of Jews in Cochin.

That common culture and sentiment was built through their common immersion in synagogue activities; each congregation on its own but all conscious of the shared rhythms of their lives, so different from those of their non-Jewish neighbours. It was this great disparity in the life timings, perhaps as much as the content of otheir Judaic culture, that made them feel set apart from the non-Jews with whom they interacted quite cordially in the market place. Their domestic and synagogue rites were indeed vastly different from those of Hindus, Muslim, and Christians, though in certain matters, as in making offerings to local shrines or in witchcraft accusations, they observed similar ritual practices and beliefs.

The Jewish rites were both symptoms of certain deeply ingrained values and also were acts that reinforced these values. Among a congregation's men, for example, all were rigorously equal in certain respects and fiercely competitive in others. All men in a congregation (the Meshuhrarim apart) were equally entitled to participate in sacred services; unless a minimum of ten men came together to do so, a congregational service could not be held, in Cochin as everywhere in Jewry. Yet those ritual prerogative that brought personal prestige, as the carrying of a Torah scroll in the Simchat Toral procession, were matters of keen competition that were resolved by auction that awarded the privilege to the highest bidder. Thus the synagogue was at once the locale of each one's equality, th arena for dramatic competition, and the financial benefact of that personal competition. If a Jew did not attend syr gogue services he could not have opportunities to strive the personal prestige that was so precious to most. Senior in age and ability to chant the services elegantly also ga respected status and these avenues to prestige did not requi special financial resources. In any event, there was not much differentiation by wealth within a Malabar Jewish congregation, given their occupatios and reluctance to encourage habits of unremitting work. As artisans and merchants, they preserved the independence they prized, since very few were bound into the local agricultural system as labourers tied to a patron, or even as cultivating landowners dependent on maintaining *jajmani* relations with a variety of specialist villagers. Their verbal skills were prized in the synagogue and were useful in making their living as merchants and peddlers.

Women were formally subordinate in the synagogue, but were frequently powerful influences in their homes. The women's gallery in each synagogue was high above the main floor and hidden by a lattice. A feature that is not found elsewhere, according to Rabbi Rabinowitz, is that on the gallery, but in front of the lattice, is a reading desk from which the men read important sections of each service (1952 : 129-130).

No small part of the continuing sense of Jewish identity was their firm belief in the God of Israel who, in His good time, would redeem them and would repatriate all Jews to the promised land. Until that glorious day, a Cochin Jew accommodated to the peoples and cultures among whom he lived. Some of the minor accommodations were ritual ones. Thus they made vows and offerings at the tomb of a Jew from Yemen, who came to Cochin at the beginning of the seventeenth century and died there in 1616. He was learned in the mystic ways of the Kabala, and clearly made a great impression on the Cochin Jews since they built an ornate grave marker for him. The anniversary of his death, the 25th day of the month of Kislev, was observed as a day of pilgrimage to his grave. A lamp was affixed to the grave structure by Syrian Christians, "who kindle it for the repose of his soul." Hindus also participate in praying for benefactions at this tomb : both Hindus and Christians make votive offerings to the synagogues (Rabinowitz 1952 : 125-126, 137-138). Shrines to holy men and votive offerings at holy places are common among Indians of all faiths; the Cochin Jews would sometimes make vows for immediate benefits, such as the cure of a sick child, not only at their own sacred places but also at the shrines of other religions (see Mandelbaum 1970 : 411-412)

A more significant accommodation, at least since the influx of Jews from abroad in the early sixteenth century, was the accommodation to the Indian caste system, with its rigid rules against intermarriage and interdining among different jatis. Caste divisions are extreme forms of social stratification. The self-classification of Jews into higher and lower categories is no new or unique phenomenon. In Cochine, the more prosperous Jews accepted the Indian mode of social stratification. Those Jews whom they deemed lower in caste status objected vigorously; this was also in the Indian mode whereby lower groups often fiercely contest the claims to higher rank of those just above them in the local caste ranking.

Zionism provided the Cochin Jews with a cause around which they could and did unite, despite all their local adaptations, divisions, animosities. Their feeling for *Kehila*, community, of Jews everywhere had been repeatedly reaffirmed for Cochin Jews through the centuries, especially since the sixteenth century, by Jewish visitors from abroad and by the Hebrew books they had received. They reacted as Jews have generally responded when they felt that the Kehila of Jewry was gravely endangered, or that it could be rebuilt in a newer and stronger way. Whatever codes of specific conduct they may have adopted, in their final judgement Jews have usually chosen to support the maintenance of the Kehila rather than to insist on upholding patterns of particular adaptations.

Paradoxically, the Jews of Cochin became much better known in India generally and of some symbolic significance to Indian polity, after most of them had migrated to Israel. The 400th anniversary of the building of the synagogue of the white Jews as cetebrated in 1968. Under the leadership of S.S. Koder, it was done with great eclat and nation-wide publicity. Leading luminaries, academic, religious, and political, of Kerala State participated. Guests from abroad attended, including Professor Fischel who gave the main historical address. And the Prime Minister of India, Indira Gandhi, came and made a thoughtful, well-phrased inaugural address.

She began by saying that this occasion was not her first visit to the ancient synagogue, "Each visit is a reminder of the long history of our country with which the Jews of India and, certainly, the Jews of Cochin are associated and also of the tradition of religious and cultural tolerance, which is our very great heritage." She noted how that tradition had been proclaimed by the Emperor Asoka in antiquity and by the Emperor Akbar in later times. The founder of Indian independence, Gandhi, had vowed to srrive for equality of all religions; her father, India's first Prime Minister, Jawaharlal Nehru, "believed that tolerance is the basis of our unity and indeed the foundation on which world peace can be built." She went on to discuss the contemporary emphasis on secularism by the Government of India. "Secularism in India does not mean animosity toward religion. It implies equal respect for all religions and a separation of church from State." Mrs. Gandhi then touched on India's contemporary problems and concluded gracefully with a "mazel tov" to the Jewes and good wishes for all the people of Kerala (Indira Gandhi 1971: 5-8).

The symbolic gesture of her attendance had to do with the problems of maintaining a secular state. Her father had insisted on this during the negotiations for independence and had to agree to the partition of the subcontinent into secular India and Islamic Pakistan. Through all the ensuing years, India's leaders have had to keep a close concern for the country's very large Muslim population, to keep them relatively content with a secular state. This led to a foreign policy that stressed cordial relations with Muslim nations, a policy that was later reinforced by the politics of oil. So the Prime Minister's attendance at the synagogue celebrations was more than a purely political gesture since there is scarcely a smaller minority in India than the Jews. It was rather a symbolic reaffirmation of a basic principle of national policy. The Jews of Cochin offered a useful case on which, for a moment at least, to focus and restate that principle. Other political leaders, in other places and at other times, have similarly taken the example of Jews and Judaism to illustrate fundamental values they wanted to declare.

The Cochin case illustrates the old saying that the Jews kept the Sabbath and the Sabbath kept the Jews. For about a millennium, perhaps even longer, the Cochin Jews faithfully kept the calendar of holy days and held close to the synagogue as the significant focus for their lives. But when their Millennium did come and they flew to Israel, they had to change a good deal of their traditional way of life if we ean take the account of Bet Avi as typical. The pulse of that life had to be altered and they were no longer a small band of true believers marching together to the same rhythm and in the same cultural direction while their non-Jewish neighbours marched in different time and with some different cultural values. In Israel they were influenced by powerful institutions other than the synagogue—the schools for the children, the army for the young men, the other agents and agencies of the State. And they were exposed to the impact of the experiences outside the synagogue, from the Saturday night movies in the recreation hall to periodic trips to Tel-Aviv and Jerusalem, so different from Cochin and Ernakulam. Their previous work ethic and work habits were under challenge. It was much too soon, in 1961-62, to assess the depth of change, even in the one small settlement of Bet Avil. If the generations there follow the central values of their ancestors, they too will quite flexibly adapt to local conditions and circumstances but will not cling to any particular adaptations if that signifies to them danger to the existence of the community. Then they will stand firm for Kehila over any particular code. But that remains to be studied, now and in, the future.

NOTES AND REFERENCES

1. Torah scrolls in Cochin are encased in metal cylinders, which are opened on longitudinal hinges when a Torah portion is to be read. These cylinders are usually of silver alloy, but one of the synagogues in Ernakulam had a cylinder of solid gold, The Paradesi

synagogue in Cochin City possesses several crowns for Torah scrolls that are made of gold and set with gems. One was the gift of the Maharajah of Travancore in gratitude for the aid of the Cochin Jews in saving the life of his friend, Colonel Macauley (Rabinowitz 1952 : 126-127, 131).

2. The Jews from Cochin did not meet with difficulties about marriage with other Jewish communities in Israel that some families of Bene Israel immigrants from Bombay encountered (*see* Eisenstadt 1967: 312-314).

Amzalak, Moses Bensabat, 1923 Notisease dos Judeos de Cochin mandados por Mosseh Pereyra de Paiva. Lisbon : Museu Comercial.

Eisenstadt, S. N., 1967 Israeli Society. New York : Basic Books.

Elias, E. and E. Isaac, 1963 Jews in India with Who is Who. Ernakulam: Indo-Israel Publications.

Gandhi, Indira 1971 Great Heritage. In Commemorative Volume, Cochin Sybagogue Quatercentenary Celebrations, P. S. Velayudhan *et. al.*, editors, pp. 4-8. Cochin: Kerala History Association.

Fischel, Walter J. 1962 Cochin in Jewish History. Proceedings of the American Academy for Jewish Research, 30 : 37-59.

1967a The Indian Archives—a Source for the History of the Jews of Asia (from the Sixteenth Century on). In Seventy-fifth Anniversary Volume of the Jewish Quarterly Review. A.A. Neuman and S. Zeitlin editors, pp. 192-209. Philadelphia: Jewish Quarterly Review.

1967b The Exploration of the Jewish Antiquities of Cochin on the Malabar Coast. Journal of the American Oriental Society, 87 : 230-348.

1971 The Contribution of the Cochin Jews to South Indian and Jewish Civilization. In Commemorative Volume, Cochin Synagogue Quatercentenary Celebrations, P.S. Velayudhan *et. al.*, editors, pp. 15-48. Cochin : Kerala History Association.

1972 The Literary Activities of the "Bene Israel" in India. Jewish Book Annual 29 : 5-11.

1973 Unknown Jews in Unknown Lands. New York: Ktay.

Kushner, Gilbert 1973 Immigrants from India in Israel. Tucson : The University of Arizona Press.

Mandelbaum, David G. 1939 The Jewish Way of Life in Cochin. Jewish Social Studies 1 : 423-460.

1970 Society in India, Berkely and Los Angeles : University of California Press.

Narayanan, M.G.S. 1972 Cultural Symbiosis in Kerala. Trivandrum : Kerala Historical Society.

Rabinowitz, Louis 1952 Far East Mission. Johannesberg: Eagle Press.

Spector, Johanna 1971 The Music of the Jews of Cochin with Special Reference to Singli Tunes. In Commemorative Volume, Cochin Synagogue Quatercentenary Celebrations, P.S. Velayudhan *et. al.*, editors, pp. 177-185. Cochin: Kerala History Association.

Strizower, Schifra 1971 The Children of Israel; The Bene-Israel of Bombay. Oxford : Basil Blackwell.

10

THE EXPERIENCE OF MODERNIZATION

A.S. FELDMAN & C. HERN

Abstract

The nature of the change in value patterns that precede, accompany and are consequences of modernization is an important and durable issue for students of industrialization. This paper investigates mobility from rural and/or traditional occupations to urban and/or industrial occupations and attempts to relate this mobility to different estimates of value change. The date come from re-interviews of a simple of Puerto Rican heads-of-households originally interviewed in 1954. The specific data reported herein are from the first 104 pilot-study re-interviews. Our results challenge many of the popular assertions re the kinds of value changes accompanying the experience of modernization, *e.g.*, the modernizing mobiles are less likely to value education as an avenue of mobility for their children. Thus this

Reprinted from Feldman and Hern, "The Experience of Modernization", *Sociometry*, Vol. 29, No. 4 (December, 1966), pp. 378-395, by permission of American Sociological Association.

polit study finds, once again, that a consistency between value and position at any point in time should not be extended to the interaction of these two factors in the course of social change.

Modernization refers to those social changs that generate institutions and organizations like those found in advanced industrial societies.[1] Difinitions of modernization all tend to include a similar list of these institutions or the processes through which they come into being, *e.g.*, urbanization, bureaucratization, political mobilization, etc.[2] However, the various conceptions of modernizations differ with regard to which of the processes are considered especially salient (primary, most basic, most difficult, etc.). For example, Lerner emphasizes personality change, Moore and Feldman concentrate on labour force commitment, Hagen argues the primacy of family socialization as the agency for inculcating need-achievement, and Bendix focuses on the changes which alter the normative basis for the legitimation of authority.[3] Thus, no matter how defined, modernization necessarily involves an experience of social change for the modernizing population. People must change their personality and/or their occupation and/or their values and/or their loyalties.

Modernization, than, involves widespread popular participation. Yet the experience of participationts in modernization, and the pre-requisites, concomitants and consequences of this experience are little studied and less understood. Rather, most assertions about the experience of modernization are derived and deduced from institutional data and relationships.[4] Indeed it may not be excessively hyperbolic to state that while most of the sociological assertions about modernization employ a rhetoric of behaviour, the data are hardly over observations of behavioural changes.[5] One consequence of this state of affairs is that the sociology of modernization tends to describe actors as representative of the institutions and communities to which they belong, or to whose norms they are subject.[6]

This state of affairs is perhaps best illustrated by what may be labelled "the industrial man" hypothesis.[7] The normative and organizational structures of industrialism are projected upon the population, and the thesis seems to be that people are determined (perhaps over-determined) by the social milieu within which they live. Their economic roles are all technically specialized, bureaucratically coordinated and allocated in terms of achievement or performance. Their values are affectively neutral, universalistic and diffuse.

This hypothesis—as much parody of self as other—is employed as the presumed route of modernization. Modernization, it is asserted, involves changes in social structure that culminate in the organizations and ideologies previously sketched. Of course, this much is true by definition. Unfortunately this kind of analysis is quite limited. Few modernizing societies seem to be travelling the route explicated in the "industrial man" hypothesis. Rather, organizational and normative variation is all too frequent.[8] More important for purposes of this paper, the populations of modernizing societies do not experience institutional change evenly or uniformly. Thus theories of structural change are of limited utility for the study of what happens to people as they experience modernization.

The Problem of Sequence. The issues involved are brought into sharper focus when we examine the sequence of changes that are asserted to characterized modernization. For the analytical distance between the assertions of sequence at the institutional level and the sequential experiences of participants in modernization is particularly striking.

For the most part, the sequences asserted to take place during modernization are derived from the presumed functional connectedness of various institutions or social structures. Sequence is not dealt with as the consequence of social mechanisms that relate various changes through time. Rather sequential statements describe the change from one constellation or configuration of institutions to another. Thus, rather than assertions about processes of change, there are assertions about stages of change, each stage presumably involving a different institutional configuration.[9]

When put into a behavioural vocabulary, the experience of modernization is, then, also perceived as stage-like. One receives the impression that the population of modernizing societies consists of so many Stage I, Stage II, and Stage III people. Full modernization exists when everyone, or almost everyone, is a Stage III person.[10]

Often, it is argued that only part of the population experiences the full number of stages. This is a situation wherein only that segment of the population which has moved from Stage I to Stage II and finally to Stage III is thought to be participant in modernization. But another way, since the stages are defined as configurations of social properties, this type of perception of modernization attributes a maximum of social consistency to persons at the different stages. Rural populations are perceived as stereotypically traditional, and urban populations as stereotypically modern. Transitional populations are thought to be marginal, subject to strains, anomic, etc.

Thus, the sequential tone of stage theories of modernization imparts an excessive consistency to the participating actors at any one time. The actors come to represent the stages to which they presumably belong. The stage to which they belong is typically judged by their occupation (whether it be agricultural or industrial), and the mode of and time of recruitment to the occupation (whether it be as result of some significant sector mobility or whether it was already part of their mikleu). The content of the stage for the participant is the consistency of others factors—mostly value or normative—with his occupation, *e.g.*, family, polity, residence, etc.

Now, even assuming that the high positive correlation between position and value, between occupation and belief, exists at different points in time, their joint development is surely problematic. At the very least there should be some specification of how this consistency comes about or whether it comes about. Otherwise, the theories of modernization will remain more magical than empirical.

Narmative and Distributive Change. This is the issue that will be investigated in this paper, *i.e.*, the relationship of occupational and value change in the course of modernization. The sequential relationship between these two factors is, of course, a classic sociological concern. The concern is a two-fold one, which we will call:

(a) the problem of primacy, and

(b) the problem of consistency.

Primacy. The primacy issue is an old one. At the institutional level, it is represented by the statements of a Marxian vs. a Weberian conception of European industrialization, and by extension, contemporary modernization.

At the behavioural level, this same issue is critical for theories of social mobility, *i.e.*, the role of anticipatory socialization vs. determinancy of social structure. Are mobiles self-selected or are they carried along on societal tides of various kinds? These questions are particularly salient for societies experiencing modernization. Mobiles in these societies are likely to be the first or second generation of their kind. In this sense, they represent a crucial departure from the pre-modern society. Equally important, mobility—residential as well as occupational—is the prime observable experience of modernization. Thus, understanding the nexus between mobility and other changes is crucial for any theory of modernization.

A recent statement of the primacy issue is represented by the work of McClelland and his associates in general, and more particularly by the use of this work in relation to modernization by Hagen and Rosen in particular.[11] Unfortunately, the manner in which n-achievement is asserted to be generated makes a direct test of the validity of these theories most difficult. To begin with, n-achievement is thought to be a most primordial characteristic implanted during early childhood. Hagen argues that its genesis in modernizing societies takes place among minorities who have previously suffered from status withdrawal. Thus, a most difficult trait to observe, must be observed over several generations.

What we can do is observe the value characteristics of people who are mobile in a traditional to modern manner. We can observe the extent to which, and the ways in which, they were distinctive *before their mobility*. And while this hardly tests the ideas put forward by n-achievement theorists, such an investigation does bear on, and may sharpen the issues involved.

Consistency. The second problem regarding distributive and normative factors in the course of modernization is that of consistency. The issue here concerns the normative consequences of modernizing mobility. The nexus of distributive and normative change is central to most sociological theories of modernization, and it has many themes. As mentioned earlier, consistency is important for what was labelled the industrial man hypothesis. Indeed, it is the scale for judging the degree of modernization attained institutionally and behaviourally.

Yet there is little study of how, behaviourally, consistency is or is not generated in the course of modernization. The effect of modernizing mobility on values has rarely been studied longitudinally. Rather most of our information is cross-sectional (*i.e.*, it shows how migrants differ from non-migrants, etc.).[12] Generally it is assumed that modernizing mobility generates or reinforces modern values.[13] However, the analysis seems more a matter of sociological cliche (the avoidance of strain, the social pain of inconsistency, etc.) than a consequence of empirical study.

The Study

In this paper we will examine empirically both the issue of

primacy and of consistency. Before presenting the data, let us briefly describe ther source. In 1954, a survey of 1000 wage-earning, heads of households was carried out in Ruerto Rico. The study was subsequently reported in *Social Class and Social Change in Puerto Rico.*[14] In 1965, the resurveying of the original respondents was begun. The data reported herein are based on a first wave of re-interviews. Eventually, all original respondents who can be located will be re-interviewed, as well as a sample of their sons.

The 104 cases on which this paper is based have been employed as a pilot study for the more complete survey, which is now in the field. Some 300 additional cases have been interviewed, although they are not analyzed as yet. In any case it should be clear that the present results are tentative.

Once the first 104 cases were available, we selected for intensive scrutiny a small number of those who experienced the most distributive change. In conjunction with Professor Bernard Beck of Northwestern University, we compared the 1954 and 1965 interview schedules in detail and prepared lengthy case studies. These case studies were used to generate coding frames as well as to find the main themes or hypotheses to be tested via the remainder of the 104 cases and then the full re-interview sample. Many of the findings reported herein are, then, actually hypotheses for fuller test, derived inductively from the case studies. The tables reported herein are to be considered as tentatively confirmatory of the themes located by the case studies.

Problem of Occupational Change. The 104 cases were selected so as to provide as much spread as possible across the diverse segments of the population. Since occupational change was our principal variable of location, we divided the cases into four groups as reported in Table 10.1. The criteria of classification used are, of course, the occupational status in 1954 and the occupational change between 1954 and 1965.[15] Thus we have these four groups:

TABLE 10.1

Characterization of Sample Groups

Variable	Group 1 (N=29) Non-mobile, Low Status	Group 2 (N=42) Non-mobile Higher Status	Group 3 (N=11) Tradit ional to Modern Mobility	Group 4 (N=8) Mobile within Modern System
Occupational mobility previous to 1954	19 of 29 changed jobs but only 8 also changed category	31 of 42 changed jobs and 25 changed category	6 changed jobs but only 3 category changes	6 job changes and 5 category changes
Occupational mobility since 1954	13 of 29 changed jobs	8 of 42 changed jobs	Only 2 were mobile by promotion or continuous mobility	4 of 8 were mobile through promotion or continuous mobility
Age: (X yrs)				
1954	40	40	36	37
1965	51	51	48	49
Income: (X weekly)				
1954	23.62	52.71	32.91	62.00
1965	39.96	89.14	65.00	120.50
Education: (X yrs)				
1954	5.2	8.0	6.3	12.2
1965	5.5	8.2	6.7	13.4

Note: See text and footnote 16 for discussion of "category change" and "continuous-discontinuous" mobility.

1. unskilled mannual workers in 1954 with no significant mobility between 1954 and 1965;
2. a somewhat higher status group in 1954 (skilled and white collar) showing no significant mobility;
3. a group with low status and traditional occupations in 1954 (mostly rural) who shifted to modern, urban occupations in 1965; and
4. a group who had higher status, modern occupations in 1954 and who were mobile into a still higher modern occupation by 1965.

A number of comparisons are possible. Comparing groups 1 and 0 of Table 10.1 with groups 3 and 4 involves a comparison of no-mobility with mobility, at two status levels. Comparing groups 1 and 3 with 2 and 4, involves a status comparison for mobiles and non-mobiles. The comparison of greatest interest for modernization is group 1 (traditional and low status at both times) with group 3 (traditional to modern mobiles). Obviously, the variable N's and especially the law N's for groups 3 and 4, make the statistical result a matter of caution, especially the percentages. But given the rarity of longitudinal data the statistical risk can be afforded, especially if the results are used as instruction rather than proof.

The last three rows in Table 10.1 roughly confirm our interpretation and use of the four groups. Note that mobiles were younger than their status peers (*e.g.*, group 1 compared with 3, and 2 with 4) had somewhat higher education before their mobility (more pronounced in the 2 with 4 comparison), and had somewhat higher income than their status peers previous to their mobility. Of course, they increased their income much more markedly than the non-mobiles between 1954 and 1965. This is especially true of the modernizing mobiles, eight out of eleven of whom (73%) at least doubled their income, while for their status-of-origin peers in Group 1 only 5 out of 29 (15%) at least doubled their income.

The first two rows in Table 10.1 report the occupational

experiences of the sample, and we have looked at this matter in greater detail. These data raise the most vexing methodological problem of a study such as ours. We want to investigate the relationship between occupational and value change at two time periods. Roughly eleven years separate our observations. Presumably any number of other changes of consequence could also be experienced in the interval. Thus, the connection between the occupational change and value change is quite tenuous and vulnerable. In addition, it is not at all certain that the value change between Time I and Time II is not related to developments previous to Time I. For example, some of our respondents experieneed significant mobility (termed "category change" in Table 10.1) previous to 1954. The value change measured between 1954 and 1965 may reflect these, or still earlier, changes. The small number of cases makes any further cross-classification inefficient at this time. But even many more cases would not solve this problem. This potential number of changes would always exceed the number of cross-classifications possible.

We cannot stop to examine this vexing issue fully at this time. We merely want to state it and note its magnitude. Thus group I although stable in terms of occupational category between 1954 and 1965, contained 8 of 29 (28%) members who changed categories previous to 1954, another II who had job change previous to 1954, and 13 of the 29 had a job change between 1954 and 1965.[16] The number and proportion of category changes previous to 1954 is even higher for group 2 (25 of 42) as might be expected of a higher status population. The same occupational lability previous to 1954 holds for groups 3 and 4.

There was also considerable lability between 1954 and 1965, with group 1 showing the greatest amount as might be expected. The 1954-1965 results for groups 3 and 4 are somewhat differently labelled. Since all of these people experienced category change, they were distinguished by whether the change was continuous with the 1954 occupation or whether it involved a discontinuity, *e.g.*, a sector shift, etc. Again as might be expected the higher status mobiles had a more continuous shift.

All of this highlights our difficulty: we can associate occupational and normative change, and we can make before and after comparisons; but we clearly cannot assert causal connections.

Results

We speak above of objective occupational change, but our ability to relate this to value change is aided if we can show some respondent awareness of the occupational change. The data clearly suggest that those who experienced occupational change also changed their self evaluation of occupational status, though these data need not be presented here in detail. In both 1954 and 1965 the interviews contained a picture of a three-runged ladder. The respondents were asked to say at which part of the ladder their occupation was located. Whereas there is very little change in the responses of group 1 (low status, non-mobiles), there is noticeable change in group 3. For the former, exactly the same percentage (60.7%) rank themselves as being "low" on the ladder in both years; while in group 3 (traditional to modern mobility) 7 of 11 (64%) place their occupation in the lowest third of the ladder in 1954, as compared with 7 of 11 who place themselves in the *middle* third in 1965. While the small N's are most inhibiting, the results appear to justify the interpretation that those who experience occupational change are aware of it. This interpretation, if allowed, we feel makes succeeding connections between distributive and normative changes somewhat more plausible.

Ambitions. The next two Tables (10.2 and 10.3) report on the ambitions of respondents. These data bear on two issues. First, as was the case with the respondent's self-evaluation of occupational change, if mobiles are aware of their success, or if they perceive the occupational change as indeed upward

TABLE 10.2

Responses to Question an Ambitions, by Occupational Change Groups, for 1954 and 1965

Occupational Change Group	*Year*	"More than" *Number*	"More than" *Per cent*	"Same as" *Number*	"Same as" *Per cent*	"Les than" *Number*	"Les than" *Per cent*
Group 1: Non mobile low status	1954	1	3.4	17	58.6	11	37.9
	1965	3	10.3	15	51.7	11	37.9
Group 2: Higher Status non-mobiles	1954	8	19.0	21	50.0	13	31.0
	1965	10	23.8	26	61.9	6	14.3
Group 3: Tradi-tional to modern mobility	1954	0	0	6	54.5	5	45.5
	1965	0	0	10	90.9	1	9.1
Group 4: Mobile within modern system	1954	0	0	8	100.0	0	0
	1965	1	12.5	6	75.0	1	12.5

Note: The N's in each group are as given in Table 10.1. The full question reads: "World you say you have achieved your ambitions more than, the same as, or less than most other people?"

mobility and at least relative success, they should become somewhat more affirmative regarding the extent to which they have achieved their ambitions in 1965, compared with their response to the identical item in 1954.

Table 10.2 indicates, although moderately, that this is indeed the case. Whereas there is remarkably little change for group 1—the consistency of the "less than" response is particularly noteworthy—given a tendency to opt for a middle, more neutral response, there is again a marked improvement in groups 3 (the traditional to modern mobiles). Approximately half of these 11 people move to an "improved" response between 1954 and 1965. The interpretation again is that this indicates the plausibility of a connection between distributive and normative channe in that those who are mobile from traditional to modern occupations raise their evaluation of the extent to which they have achieved their ambitions.

The comparision between higher status mobiles and non-mobiles (groups 2 and 4) does not lend itself to this interpretation. There is a small to moderate upward change in group 2 and minimal change in group 4.

Of course, any interpretation of response change concerning perceived ambition achievement depends upon the content of the ambitions involved. Thus, the change noted for group 3 in Table 10.2, could mean a number of quite different things. For example, it could mean they have a happier home life, more children, have remained happy, etc.; but it could also mean they are making more money, have a better occupation, or are more able to give their children an education. Obviously, the interpretation of the increase in perceived achievement depends upon the ambition content involved.

Table 10.3 reports this information, for ambition achieved and (independently) ambitions not achieved. Since the table reports on ambitions mentioned, the N's are variable and are higher than the N of respondents.

TABLE 10.3

Instruments Vs. Cousummatory Ambitions: Number and Per cent of Instrumental Ambitions Achieved, and Not Achieved, by Occupational Change Groups, for 1954 and 1965

Occupational Change Groups	*Year*	*A Achieved*			*B. Not Achieved*		
		Number Instrumental	*Per cent Instrumental*	*Total Number of Achieved Ambitions*	*Number Instrumental*	*Per cent Instrumental*	*Total Number of Unachieved Ambitions*
Group 1: Non-mobile low status	1954	15	23.8	63	17	51.52	33
	1965	16	26.2	61	25	55.56	45
Group 2: Higher status non-mobiles	1954	37	37.4	99	46	80.70	57
	1965	41	39.4	104	38	74.51	51
Group 3: Traditional to modern mobility	1954	7	28.0	25	11	64.71	17
	1965	9	34.6	26	13	72.22	18.

Group 4: Mobile within modern system	1954	6	33.3	18	10	76.92	13
	1965	10	47.6	21	5	71.43	7

Note: The total N's reflect multiple mentions (for respondent N's, see Table 10.1). Consummatory mentions (for both achieved and not achieved independently) make up the reminder of the 100 per cent (*e.g.*, 76.2 per cent consummatory in group 1 above; 48 achieved consummatory mentions as the counterpart to 23.8 per cent instrumental). See text discussion of the instrumental-consummatory distinction.

We divided the specific ambitions into two categories labelled consummatory (*i.e.*, family life, health, home life, etc.) and instrumental (*i.e.*, job, salary, education, etc.). For ambitions achieved (Table 10.3 A), there is little variation between 1954 and 1965 within the four groups, and little difference between groups. All respondents say they have achieved their consummatory ambitions more than their instrumental ambitions. This is true for both time periods. The main change between 1954 and 1965 is a slight increase in the mentioning of instrumental ambitions achieved. Groups 3 and 4, the mobiles, report the largest percensage change of this kind.

The data on ambitions not achieved is somewhat more informative. As one might except, the higher status groups (2 and 4) mention a failure to achieve instrumental values more often than consummatory values. Although the changes are slight, the overall pattern is that groups 2 and 4 decrease the mention of instrumental values not achieved, and groups 1 and 3 increase their mention. The one noticeable change in the percentages is in group 3 (the traditional-to-modern mobiles). In 1954, this group is midway between those they most resemble in initial status (group 1) and the higher status, more modern groups (2 and 4). In 1965, they were quite like groups 2 and 4 with respect to ambitions not achieved.

Thus in 1954, the traditional-to-modern mobiles were more oriented to instrumental ambitions than group 1 in both respects, *i.e.*, in achieved as well as not achieved ambitions. But they seport the most *percentage* change towards increased awareness of instrumental ambitions between 1954 and 1965—28 per cent to 34 per cent for ambitions achieved, and 65 per cent to 72 per cent for ambitions not achieved. Thus, although the modernizing mobiles are somewhat more instrumentally oriented than other low status respondents before their mobility, the experience of mobility seems to augment this awareness.

These data on ambitions are, unfortunately, quite ambiguous. The traditional to modern mobiles show a relatively slight change between 1954 and 1965, and one might well question the utility of making and interpretation given the low degree of absolute change in the various categories. However, the direction of change appears consistent; and we feel that the interpretation, although fragile, is nevertheless quite suggestive.

This change is in the direction of differentiating group 3 the modernizing mobiles, from their status-of-origin peers (group 1). In the interval between 1954 and 1965, group 3 respondents become more optimistic about the extent to which they have achieved their ambitions, they increase their percentage of instrumental ambitions achieved, and they also increase their mention of instrumental ambitions not achieved. Thus, there is slight but consistent evidence that they become more sensitive to instrumental ambitions generally. Assuming that the differences between 1954 and 1965 are a consequence of modernizing mobility, this status change apparently had a consistent impact on the ambitions of those to whom it happened. At least to this extent, normative change is produced by distributive change. Of course, the modernizing mobiles were also normatively different preceding their mobility.

These ambition questions were asked retrospectively. Thus, these data give us some idea of how the experience of modernization affects the evaluation of previous experiences. And our modernizing mobiles in 1965 thought that they had done better, particularly with respect to instrumental ambitions, although more of them also felt that they had failed to achieve instrumental ambitions than was the case in 1954. One possible interpretation of these findings is that mobility not only satisfies previous ambitions but generates new and primarily instrumental ambitions. And in that sense, mobility is a teachar of modern values.

Aspirations. We can now examine the estimates of our respondents with respect to the future. With respect to aspiration, we should expect some effect from aging. Our samples are all in the fifty-ish category. And one would expect that the decade. belween the ages of 40 and 50 is accompanied by some attenuation of occupational aspirations. But we have two additional aspiration questions: income aspiration and aspiration for the children's style of life.

Table 10.4 reports on occupational and income aspirations, *i.e.*, whether or not respondents "expect to be able to get a better job" in the future, and whether they "think it is realistically possible to double" the amount they report as their present earnings per week.

The first and most noticeable finding here is that all groups (both mobiles and non-mobiles) are less optimistic in 1965 about getting a better job than they were in 1954. In 1954, most respondents felt that they would get a better job, the lowest proportion being in group 2 (53%), and the highest proportion in group 3 (90%). The 1954 results clearly discriminate non-mobiles from mobiles. And even before their mobility, the mobile respondents (in groups 3 and 4), were noticeably more optimistic about getting a better job than the non-mobiles. So if these results are to be trusted, the mobiles were anticipating their mobility regardless of status in 1954. Of course, group 3 (the traditional-to-modern mobiles) are particularly noteworthy. Ten of the eleven members of this group said they could get a better job, and they did.

The 1965 results, also point to the difference between group 3 and the others. They remain the most optimistic about future mobility. Indeed, they are the only group wherein over 50 per cent (6 of 11) feel that they will get a better job. The other three groups look remarkably similar; roughly 65 per cent feel that they *cannot* get a better job. Thus with respect to the chances for occupational mobility, the modernizing mobiles are almost completely optimistic before their mobility and continue to be more optimistic than the others after their mobility. Put another way, they start highest and remain highest in this respect.

With regard to the income data in Table 10.4, only the

TABLE 10.4

Per cent Estimating Favourable Prospects (% "Yes") for Getting a Better Job, and for Doubling Income, by Occupational Mobility, 1954-1965

Occupational Change Groups	*Year*	*Better Job*		*Double Income*	
		Number	*Per cent*	*Number*	*Per cent*
Group 1: Non-mobile low status	1954	17	58.6	21	72.4
	1965	11	37.9	10	34.5
Group 2: Higher status non-mobiles	1954	23	54.8	29	69.0
	1965	14	33.3	21	50.0
Group 3: Traditional to modern mobility	1954	10	90.1	6	54.5
	1965	6	54.5	6	54.5
Group 4: Mobile within modern system	1954	6	75.0	7	87.5
	1965	3	37.5	4	50.0

Note: N's as in Table 10.1. See text for specific wording of questions.

latter part of the previous sentence is true, *i.e.*, group 3 remains highest. The modernizing mobiles are the least optimistic about doubling their income in 1954. And while they show no percentage change during the interval, in 1965 they are the most optimistic in this regard. Group 1 (the low status, non-mobiles) show the greatest shift on this item. They start quite high (21 of 29 in 1954) and finish the lowest (10 of 29 in 1965) with regard to the expectation that they can double their income.

We venture to suggest that the traditional-to-modern mobiles turn out to be much more realistic, both before and after (but especially after) the fact of their mobility. This gain in realism could account for the difference between the 1954 position of these mobiles on occupational and income mobility. Their universally shared optimism on occupational mobility is not matched by their expectation of income mobility in 1954; while they are the most optimistic group on both these aspirations in 1965. It may be that they answer these items more cognitively in 1954 and 1965, and the difference is a learning process. If so, again mobility appears to be a teacher of norms.

Results coordinate with this view are also obtained when we ask about the respondent's aspirations for the children. When asked what level "you eventually expect your children to reach," there is a general tendency, shared across all groups, to elevate expectations from 1954 to 1965. Yet here, too, group 3 shows a notable difference. In 1954, only, 2 of the 11 group 3 members (18%) expected their children to live like those in the highest part of the social ladder, and this was the lowest proportion of all groups. In 1965, 6 of this group (55%) aspire that high for their children and this is topped only by group 4, the high status mobiles (with 75%). Thus, relative to groups 1 and 2 (but especially group 1, the low status, non-mobiles), group 3 shows the most marked change on this item, *i.e.* they start low and end up high. Again we make the interpretation that mobility is the teacher of norms rather than the pupil.

So far we have examined how the respondents evaluate what has happened to them (ambitions) and what they expect in the future (aspirations). In both respects, but especially in aspirations, we find that the traditional-to-modern mobiles often show the most change; that they are more like group 1 in 1954 and more like group 4 in 1965. The one significant partial reversal is in occupational aspirations, where they were the most optimistic group in 1954 and 1965.

The Availability and Value of Education. We can now examine their evaluation of the means of mobility, specifically the availability and value of education. Table 10.5 reports on our respondent's estimates concerning the access to education they think their children will have, and their view of the importance of education. The estimates of availability and value given here are based upon reactions to the statements described in the note to Table 10.5. The major finding is that most of our respondents believe education to be *less* accessible to their children in 1965 than they did in 1954. And the largest shift down is reported for the modernizing mobiles.

They were quite sanguine in 1954 (only 3, or 27.3%, of 11 feeling that less than 6th grade was available). In 1965, 63.6 per cent feel that their children will not be able to go past the 5th grade. And these are people with relatively high aspirations for their children and who have experienced significant occupational mobility.

The results regarding the importance of education are also surprising. Three of the four groups *lower* the importance they feel education has for mobility. In group 3, the change is most marked. In 1954 only 4 of 11 (36.4%) said education was of little importance, whereas in 1965 fully 8 of 11 (72.7%) fall into the low category. So those who have had the greatest mobility, who have made the transition from traditional-to-modern occupations, and who report the highest aspirations for self and children have lowered markedly the estimate of the availability of education and have drastically lowered their evaluation of the importance of education for mobility.

TABLE 10.5

Number and Per cent Estimating Low Availability of Education, and Low Importance, by Occupational Mobility, for 1954 and 1965

Occupational Change Groups	*Year*	*Available*		*Low Importance*	
		Number	*Per cent*	*Number*	*Per cent*
Group 1: Non-mobiles	1954	13	44.8	14	48.0
low status	1965	18	62.0	20	69.0
Group 2: Higher status	1954	8	19.0	8	19.5
non-mobiles	1965	11	26.2	15	35.7
Group 3: Traditional to	1954	3	27.3	4	36.4
modern mobility	1965	7	63.6	8	72.7
Group 4: Mobile within	1954	0	0	1	12.5
modern system	1965	0	0	0	0

Note: N's are as in Table 10.1. For availability, the question reads: "For people of your social class, it is almost impossible to send your children beyond the sixth grade" (high school and college also asked, but not presented here). The "importance" score was trichotomized and is based on three questions (*e.g.*, "Reading and writing are all you need to make your way in life").

The experience of modernization, at least in these regards, does not lead to the kind of consistency of normative orientations one would have expected.

Interpretations and Conclusions

We think that this analysis locates a number of themes that are at least worthwhile hypotheses:

1. For the most part, the kinds of normative changes we have been able to measure, however crudely, are shared throughout the sample. Thus at least with regard to the *direction* of value or normative change, modernization as experienced during the past 11 years in Puerto Rico is not a differentiating process. And the respondents who were peasants in 1954 and remain peasants in 1965 show the same *direction* of normative change as does the peasant in 1954 who became a factory worker in 1965.

   If these data are trustworthy, and if Puerto Rico is sufficiently similar to other modernizing societies, our results argue against modernization as a creator of the "dual society."

2. If modernization does not distinguish modernizing participants from non-participants with regard to the direction of normative change, it certainly does distinguish them with regard to *degree* of normative change. In most of our tables, the traditional-to-modern mobile showed the *greatest degree of change*. And while we would again call attention to the small and variable N's, we feel that we are on firmer ground for arguing the salience of distributive for normative change with regard to all items but one—namely, aspiration for occupational mobility.

   Thus the experience of traditional-to-modern mobility seems to generate large amounts of normative change. These mobiles are not all that modern in value before their mobility. They are much more modern—*i.e.*, they aspire more, think they have achieved more, are more sensitive to instrumental norms—after their mobility.

3. The results on availability and importance of education are particularly interesting. Although the traditional-to-modern mobile attests to the openness of the society in his aspirations for self and children in 1965, he also says in 1965 that education is less available and less important as an avenue of mobility than he did in 1954.

These findings lead us to put forward rhe following hypothesis regarding the experience of modernization. The change that modernizing mobility brings on is largely cognitive. The mobile has his own experience on which to base his optimism of aspiration. Thus his personal history is the basis upon which he feels his children can improve their lives. *But this same history also attests to the relative unimportance of education for experiencing this mobility.*

The case studies frequently report phrases like, "it takes luck and the breaks, not education." In these senses, the mobile is quite realistic with regard to the chances for, and avenues of, mobility for lower stratum children societies undergoing modernization.

We would argue that the responses concerning the importance and availability of education for mobility are expressions of modern and not traditional beliefs. Thus, they are empirically consistent with the mobiles' experience of modernization, even though sociologists might have a tendency to label anti-education responses as anti-modern. This tendency is a cliche, appropriate only to middle-class mobility even in industrial or currently modernized societies. The traditional-to-modern mobile sounds a good deal like the successful blue-collar worker in industrial societies.

Modernization will affect most of the population of

modernizing societies by moving them to modern blue-collar occupations. We feel that the achievement literature, and the industrial man hypothesls, is too much a description of the middle class in both the modern and modernizing society. To this extent many of these hypotheses may not be applicable to the mass of participants in modernization.

REFERENCES

1. The term "modernization" has many difficulties as a social scientific concept. For example, it is, of course, vague and all inclusive. Additionally, the term is quite vulnerable to an ethnocentric interpretation—*e.g.*, modern values often seem descriptions of the presumed values of middle-class Americans; cf. David C. McClelland, "The Impulse to Modernization," in M. Weiner, ed., *Modernization*, New York: Basic Books, Inc., 1966, pp. 28-40, particularly p. 36.
2. Compare the similarity in the definitional lists given in the following: R. Bendix, *Nation Building and Citizenship*, New York, John Wiley and Sons, Inc., 1964, p. 5; A. Feldman, and W. Moore, "Industrialism and Industrialization," in *Transaction of the Fifth World Congress of Sociology*, Washington, D.C., 1962, pp. 151-169; D. Lerner, *The Passing of Traditional Society*, Glencoe, Illinois: Free Press 1958, pp. 43-74; E.E. Hagen, *On the Theory of Social Change* Homewood, Illinois: The Dorsey Press, 1962, pp. 217-237; and B. Hoselitz, and W. Moore, *Industrialization and Society*, New York: UNESCO Press 1963; N. Smelser, *Social Change in the Industrial Revolution*: An *Application of Theory to the British Cotton Industry*, Chicago: The Unversity of Chicago Press, 1959, pp. 1-49.
3. Of course these are only some of the factors emphasized by students of "modernization." We here slight the economists, in part because the concept of modernization most often focuses on the social and political concomitants of economic growth rather than on exclusively economic factors. See Bendix, *op. cit.*, and J.H. Kautsky, *Political Change in Underdeveloped Countries*: *Nationalism and Communism*, New York: John Wiley and Sons, Inc., 1962, pp. 13-29; and T. Parsons and N. Smelser, *Economy and Society*; Glencoe, Illinois: The Free Press, 1956, pp. 306-309.
4. Most of the data falling within what we have labelled institutional data consist of economic, political, or demographic studies. See: Bendix, *op. cit*, particularly his last chapter on India; N. Smelser,

"Mechanisms of Change and Adjustment to Change", in Hoselitz and Moore ,*op. cit.*: Hagen, *op. cit*; and Lerner, *op. cit.*

Also included in this category are numerous community studies of social change. For example, see, P. Foster, *Education and Social Change in Ghana*, Chicago, Illinois: The University of Chicago Press, 1965; C. Geertz, *Peddlers and Princes: Social Change and Economic Modernization in two Indonesian Towns*, Chicago, Illinois: The University of Chicago Press, 1963; M. Nash, *The Golden Gate to Modernity: Village Life in Burma*, New York: John Wiley and Sons, Inc., 1965.

5. See the citations in footnote 4. Even where direct observations of behaviour are made, they are almost never longitudinal data. For example, See Lerner, *op. cit.*,; W. Bell, *Jamacian Leaders: Political Attitudes in a New Nation*, Berkeley: University of California Press, 1964; and Foster, *op. cit.*

5. See B. Hoselitz, "Main Concepts in the Analysis of the Social Implications of Technical Change" in Hoselitz and Moore, *op. cit.*, pp. 11-31; and Smelser, *op. cit.*

7. C. Kerr, *et al.*, *Industrialism and Industrial Man*, New York: Oxford University Press, 1964, pp. 3-29; Particularly p. 29 and pp. 221-139; A. Inkeles, Industrial Man: The Relation of Status to Experience, Perception, and Value, *American Journal of Sociology*, 66 (July, 1960), pp. 1-31 (particularly conclusion of article); T. Parsons, *Structure and Process in Modern Society*, New York: The Free Press, 1965, p. 197; R. Marsh, "Values, Damand and Social Mobility", *American Sociological Review*, 28 (Agu., 1963) p. 575.

8. A Feldman and W. Moore, *Labour Commitment and Social Change in Developing Areas*, New York: Social Science Research Council, 1960, p. 362; A. Feldman and W. Moore, *op. cit.*, particularly pp. 158-159.

9. W. W. Rostow, *The Stages of Economic Growth*, Cambridge, England; Cambridge University Press, 1960, pp. 148-149: N. Smelser, *op. cit.*, pp. 158-179; particularly p. 167; Hoselitz, B., "Main Concepts in the Analysis of the Social Implications of Technical Change" in Hoselitz and Moore, *op. cit.*

10. W. Wertheim, *et al.*, *Indonesian Economics: The Concept of Dualism in Theory and Policy*. The Hague, Netherlands: W. Van Hoeve Publishers, Ltd., 1961, pp. 69-109, particularly p. 89. N. Smelser, "Mechanisms of Change and Adjustment to change," in Hoselitz and Moore, *op. cit.*, p. 47.

11. McClelland, *op. cit.*; Hagen, *op. cit.*; and B. Rosen, "The Achievement Syndrome and Economic Growth in Brazil," *Social Forces*,

42 (March, 1964), pp. 341-354, and B. Rosen, "Socialization and Achievement Motivation in Brazil" *American Sociological Review*, 27 (October, 1962), pp. 612-624.

12. The best compendium of these studies is Hoselitz and Moore, *op. cit.*

13. See particularly the chapter by Hoselitz in Hoselitz and Moore, *op. cit.*

14. M. Tumin, with A.S. Feldman, *Social Class and Social Change in Puerto Rico*, Princeton: Princeton University Press, 1961 .

15. Our classification of respondents into groups was done on an *ad hoc* basis. We examined the occupational history of each respondent and coded him into the appropriate group. The major problem is that of distinguishing lower class jobs in general from traditional lower class jobs. Of course, whether the job was rural or urban helps, but is not definitive. For example. we classified a street singer in a town who moved to construction work as traditional to modern mobile.

16. Job changes were defined as those that did not involve status mobility, *e.g.* change of employer, etc.). Category changes were defined as those that changed the status of the respondent.

Index

INDEX

V

W

Z